BOB DYLAN: A DESCRIPTIVE, CRITICAL DISCOGRAPHY AND FILMOGRAPHY, 1961–2007

SECOND EDITION

D1281974

BOB DYLAN: A DESCRIPTIVE, CRITICAL DISCOGRAPHY AND FILMOGRAPHY, 1961–2007

SECOND EDITION

John Nogowski

McFarland & Company, Inc., Publishers
Jefferson, North Carolina, and London

LIBRARY OF CONGRESS CATALOGUING-IN-PUBLICATION DATA

Nogowski, John, 1953–
    Bob Dylan : a descriptive, critical discography and filmography,
1961–2007 / John Nogowski. — 2nd ed.
        p.   cm.
    Includes bibliographical references (p.) and index.

    ISBN 978-0-7864-3518-0
    softcover : 50# alkaline paper ∞

    1. Dylan, Bob, 1941– — Discography.   2. Dylan, Bob,
1941– — Film catalogs.   I. Title.
ML156.7.D97N64   2008
782.42164092 — dc22   2008008616

British Library cataloguing data are available

On the cover: Bob Dylan in the recording studio, 1965 (Photofest);
background ©2008 Shutterstock

Manufactured in the United States of America

McFarland & Company, Inc., Publishers
    Box 611, Jefferson, North Carolina 28640
    www.mcfarlandpub.com

To Liz,
whose unselfish, boundless love and encouragement
inspired me more than she'll ever know

and to John Jr.,
who did finally get to see
"The Real Live Bob" on Valentine's Day

Contents

Introduction

*Derrick Morgan, the unrivalled king of ska. Well, actually, he did
have some rivals. The biggest one was Prince Buster. The two of them
became embroiled in a fierce musical feud which quickly spilled over
among their fans. In 1963, battles between the two sets of fans became
so intense, the leaders of the Jamaican government had no choice but to
step in. They called a cease-fire and brought the two performers
together and had them pose for publicity pictures, burying the hatchet.
I had a very similar thing with Gordon Lightfoot.*

Bob Dylan,
Theme Time Radio, 2006

Wry, unpredictable, ruthlessly hilarious and deadly serious —
sometimes all in the same sentence — there's never been an American
voice quite like Bob Dylan's.

Not just his audible voice, though that is certainly distinctive
enough. The voice Bob Dylan brings to his songs is by turns, bold and
bitter, wise and wary, mournful and majestic. It's a voice that does
seem, as Don McLean once suggested in "American Pie," to come from
you and me.

In an article that appeared in *Wanted Man,* the late great Harry
Smith, compiler of the fabled "Anthology of American Folk Music"
noted exactly the same thing, overhearing a Dylan visit with Allen
Ginsberg late one night. Smith noted "how human" Dylan had
sounded.

Perhaps it is this unexpected intimacy with our own heart — or is
it ours with his? — that can explain why, after all the ducks and dodges

1

and intended and unintended mystery that has always surrounded his private life, so many regard him with such genuine affection.

Few performers have done less to achieve popularity. Whether in releasing albums or giving unpredictable concerts featuring quasi-familiar versions of his greatest hits, or even reluctantly or awkwardly interacting with his own fans, Bob Dylan has always gone his own quirky way. Many of us have simply loved him for it.

When "Time Out of Mind" came out in 1997, the album's effect on Dylan Nation was sweeping and astonishing. Hearing it, hearing HIM — really him — was like discovering a presumably long-lost favorite Uncle was actually OK. Not only that, he was coming over to dinner tonight. And he was bringing a great dessert and those just-what-you-always-wanted presents, as always.

Shortly after the album's release, one long-time fan was discussing the record with the editor of a Dylan fan magazine, an unusually gentle, considerate lady, not the kind of single-minded, hyper-obsessed madwoman you might think would do a Dylan fanzine. Yet as the conversation continued and as each spoke about their initial shock and awe at the record — truly, a bolt from the blue — there came a stunning and simultaneous realization that *Bob had been paying attention all along.* Their conversation stopped for a moment, choked by profound emotion. Here were two reasonable, intelligent, fully grown adults and Bob's comeback left them speechless.

When on the "Weld" tour, Neil Young and Crazy Horse unexpectedly lurched into the first notes of "Blowin' in the Wind," the arena was filled with a rush of emotion, many older fans nearly bursting into tears. Why? Bob Dylan.

As *New Yorker* writer Alex Ross explained in his exemplary May 10, 1999, article called "The Wanderer" — "The highest emotion hits late, in the wordless windups of his greatest songs — from 'Sad-Eyed Lady' to 'Not Dark Yet' — when the band plays through the verse one more time and language sinks into silence."

How does he do this to us? Perhaps "Time Out of Mind" gives us a key. The record was profound and razor-sharp, like a camera lens suddenly coming into focus. The longer you listened, the album became more than just a late-night phone call from an almost forgotten old friend; it was a clarion's call — "Hey, I'm still here. I see what's going on. What's gone on. And yeah, I'm going to sing about it. *All* of it." Thrilling stuff.

As events turned out, that album marked the start of the Great Bob Dylan Renaissance, a flood of long-sought after, never-dreamed-of treasures ("No Direction Home," "Live 1964," "Live 1975," etc.) and a slew of surprises, one right after the other.

He's going to do what, a weekly radio show? He's going to do a memoir that will actually make sense? (Unlike the extraordinarily weird — even by his standards — *Tarantula*.) He's going to release two more well-thought-out and superbly performed albums over the next few years? He's going to write (?) and star in and help direct a strangely captivating and equally inexplicable movie? And, oh yes, while all this is happening, he'll stay on the road, offering some simply wonderful — if unpredictable — concerts all over the world?

All these years later, Bob Dylan's dramatic and wholly unexpected surge of mastery — what else to call it? — prompts a thoughtful reconsideration of a formidable, some would even say staggering, body of work. It is certainly the main reason for this volume, the second edition of my 1995 book, *Bob Dylan: A Descriptive, Critical Discography and Filmography, 1961–1993*. Having seen, heard and read so much extraordinary material in the years since that book, it seemed important and wholly appropriate — to me, at least — to bring the Book of Bob up to date and into context. Particularly since, unlike so many of his predecessors and peers, he has found his way all the way back. His 2006 album "Modern Times" reached No. 1 on the Billboard charts. Amazing.

He's made a huge resurgence with the Grammys, too. After winning Best Traditional Folk Album for "World Gone Wrong" in 1993, the album "Time Out of Mind" won Best Album and Best Contemporary Folk Album, and Dylan himself won Best Male Rock Vocal Performance (for "Cold Irons Bound") in 1997. And he's kept the momentum going. In 2002, he won another Best Contemporary Folk Album award from "Love and Theft," and in 2006, he won the Grammy's Contemporary Folk/Americana Album for "Modern Times" and even won a Grammy for Solo Rock Vocal Performance for "Someday Baby." If that wasn't enough hardware, in 2001, his soundtrack song "Things Have Changed," included in the film "Wonder Boys," won him an Academy Award for Best Song. It also won a Golden Globe for Best Original Song. Even "No Direction Home" — the stellar Martin Scorcese compilation that covers Dylan's career through 1966 — won a Peabody Award in 2006.

When you add in Dylan's recent Kennedy Center Award, Sweden's Polar Music Prize, an honorary degree from St. Andrews in Scotland, Spain's Prince of Asturias honor, a nomination for the Nobel Prize in literature and the impressive achievement of having his memoir, *Chronicles, Vol. 1,* nominated for a National Book Award *and* the National Book Critics Circle Award in 2005, we're talking about a major career resurgence.

Imagine this: *Chronicles, Vol. 1* climbed all the way to No. 2 on the New York Times Hardcover Non-Fiction best seller list in 2004. And in 2008, a Pulitzer Prize! Who would have predicted that in 1962?

THE BIG COMEBACK: HOW?

Bob Dylan getting it all back again all seems to come down to him finding precisely the right voice — for him. Instead of having Arthur Baker trying to update his sound or Don Was attempting to inspire him with a different all-star band every day in the studio or simply resorting to recording old songs in his garage studio, Dylan apparently went into "Time Out of Mind" with "Oh Mercy" producer Daniel Lanois once again, with a particular sound in his head.

Moody, murky, adrift, all you have to do is look at Lanois' intentionally shoddy focus on the album's cover picture and you sense what's inside — dark, reflective, penetrating music, composed and performed late into many a steamy Florida night.

As Dylan himself explained in a *Guitar World* interview two years later, he knew what he wanted. The sound of records from years ago. "Truthfully, records that were made in that day and age all were good," he said. "They all had some magic to them because the technology didn't go beyond what the artist was doing.... The guys that helped me make it went out of their way to make a record that sounds like a record played on a record player. There wasn't any wasted effort on *Time Out of Mind.*"

Dylan has ridden that creative momentum through the two studio albums that followed. "Love and Theft" and "Modern Times" were equally adept, flat-out romps through a couple dozen Dylan songs that sound as if they were as much fun to play as to write. For the first time in many years, you got a sense that Dylan was the master of the studio instead of vice versa.

What's more, instead of writing songs and doing albums because he felt obligated (by contract, guilt or whatever else) you now have a guy who clearly *wants* to do this. He's talked in interviews about an epiphany at a show in Switzerland, and he wrote about the revelations that came from seeing a jazz singer in *Chronicles, Vol. 1,* both possible key factors in the revival of his art.

But it may also be simply Dylan reminding himself that there are a lot of people who love hearing him. It may be him finally acknowledging that yes, he indeed is good at what he does. And, yes, as he's suggested in some interviews, maybe it was time for him to write some new songs for his new audience, some songs that are theirs. It sure seems as if these relentless "Never-Ending Tours" have helped Dylan rediscover his writing voice, find a way to refuel his art and live out his life.

There doesn't seem to be any logical reason a man in his 60s should spend nearly half his year (or so it seems) on tour, but Dylan apparently loves it. It may be that after all this time, he needs the applause, the recognition, the excitement of creating, which is what he does every night on stage. It may also be that there isn't much else in life that truly interests him. Like he says in "Handy Dandy"—"something in the moonlight still haunts him."

From a fan's perspective, all this touring and late-in-life recognition seems to have reawakened Dylan's often impish sense of humor, a particular delight on his early albums. Consider his playful commentary about "the unrivalled king of ska." The very idea of Gordon Lightfoot, an earnest, competent Canadian folk singer, as Dylan's real "rival" shows how ludicrous it is to compare anyone to Dylan's continuing achievement in American song. And the very idea of Dylan posing for "bury the hatchet" pictures is well, hilarious.

This wry sense of humor is something that people who have known him for a long time have always said. The late George Harrison, for example, talked about that when they were doing the Traveling Wilburys records. "Bob's very funny — I mean, a lot of people take him very seriously, and yet if you know Dylan and his songs, he's such a joker, really."

We're hearing that wonderful sense of humor on *Theme Time Radio.* "George Jones once had to drive down the freeway on his riding lawnmower," Dylan tells his audience. "His wife, Tammy Wynette, was sick of his constant drinking. She emptied the house of liquor, she took away his car keys and made him a virtual prisoner in an attempt to ward off the booze. One afternoon, alone in the house, George wanted a drink. The house was quite a distance from Nashville — too far to walk. So George hopped on the only vehicle he still had the keys to. You could see George heading down the side of the highway, going towards the liquor store on his riding lawnmower. You know, I have over 70 George Jones records. If you look at them all, it gives you a great history of men's haircuts."

These days, Dylan doesn't mind cracking a joke on his stiff, inaccessible self and his "legend." Ask novelist Jonathan Lethem, who interviewed him for *Rolling Stone.* Innocently, Lethem asked Dylan about his inaccessibility. Bob just about jumped out of his chair. "'Well, isn't that funny,' he says. 'I've just seen that Wenner Books published a book of interviews with me that's *that* big.' He stretches out his hands to show me. 'What happened to this inaccessibility? Isn't there a *dichotomy* there?'"

Later in the same interview, he boldly — some would say, baldly — declares the Sixties his. His alone. "You know, everybody makes a big deal about the Sixties," Dylan tells Lethem. "The Sixties, it's like the Civil War days. But, I mean, you're talking to a person who *owns* the Sixties. Did I want to acquire the Sixties? *No.* But I own the Sixties — who's going to argue with me? I'll give 'em to you if you want 'em. You can have 'em."

Note that these phrases aren't being funneled through a spokesperson, a focus group or a publicist. It's him. That unmistakable, unsullied and unrelenting voice in yet another "pure transmission." Who else could have come out with that one?

In *Rolling Stone's* fortieth anniversary edition, editor Jann Wenner sits down with Bob and Dylan promptly corrects him on misquoting his lyrics — "It's *mystic* garden [Wenner had called it mystical]" — cracks wise on global warming — "Where's the global warming? It's freezing here" — and is blunt when Wenner asks him why people reacted so strongly to him in the 1960s.

"Because I had — and perhaps still do have — that originality that others don't have," Dylan says. "Because I come from a time when you had to be original, and you had to have some kind of God-given talent just to begin with. You couldn't manufacture that. Just about everybody who was around in the Fifties and Sixties had a degree of originality. That was the only way you could get in the door."

Delightfully, he is still displaying that originality. Whether on his radio show, laced with simply wonderful, surprising asides and wry observations, or on his three recent, first-class albums or in delightful, sassy interviews or even his superbly drawn *Chronicles, Vol. 1*, we're getting witty, vintage Bob.

Finally, he has felt free — wholly free — to speak his mind, write his songs and sing them as though nothing came before. It's not that he was silent before, of course. He's consistently released some sort of album just about every year since he made the big return in 1973-74.

But there seems to be a focus, a unity and a confidence in his current work that isn't as evident in much of his post–"Blood on the Tracks" work. Some of that may due to the fits and starts of inspiration, a wide assortment of bands and the vagaries of unusual recording circumstances. Some of it may be he just wasn't that interested any more.

Somehow though, everything changed with "Time Out of Mind" and the overwhelming critical acceptance of the record. Though naturally, some Dylanologists who know better claim the album is overrated and all atmosphere and no substance and so on, the overwhelming success of the disc seemed to convince Dylan that, as an artist, he still had something to say. Something he hadn't said before. And yes, America was still listening. Tell us more, Bob.

It was as if that achievement meant he was finally over not having to write another "Like a Rolling Stone" or "Tangled Up in Blue."

Hearing him now, it's hard to remember that in 1987, Dylan seemed completely stuck. In talking with Clinton Heylin for "Behind the Shades," U2's Bono felt sorry for the guy.

"He's very hung up on actually being Bob Dylan," he said. "He feels he's trapped in his past and, in a way, he is. I mean, no one asks Smokey Robinson to write a new "Tracks of My Tears" every album, you know.

"But, like, we were trading lines and verses off the top of our heads and Dylan comes out with this absolute classic: 'I was listening to the Neville Brothers, it was a quarter of eight/ I had an appointment with destiny, but I knew she'd come late/ She tricked me, she addicted me, she turned me on the head/ Now I can't sleep with these secrets that leave me cold and alone in my bed.'

"Then he goes, 'Nah, cancel that.' Can you believe it? He thought it was too close to what people expect of Bob Dylan."

We don't get a sense of that hesitancy now. He's playful, bold, outrageous (a 17-minute song?) and delighting in his work again and understandably proud. It's an unexpected joy to hear all this new work. It may be that 10 years from now, when *Bob Dylan: The Bootleg Series, Vol. 48* comes out, we'll realize all these terrific new songs were only half as good as the ones he sat on, but for now, they're plenty.

These late Dylan renaissance releases — never-before-heard outtakes from *Blonde on Blonde* to the live *Bootleg Series* recordings from 1966, 1964 and 1975 not only reveal Dylan's insistence — or maybe it's a compulsion — to always try to do something different, they also point somewhere else — considered in their totality. They are, collectively, the biggest "I Told You So" in recorded popular music history.

They say that yes, Bob Dylan was right all along. Whether it was in changing from protest music to personal songs or changing to rock 'n' roll or to country. Changing all the time is how he kept himself alive. Remarkably, as Dylan found himself getting ripped by the press and by some in his own audiences, he never seemed to waver in what he was doing. Maybe he was just too stubborn or looking too far ahead.

You truly get a sense of where he was in relation to the rest of the world in Martin Scorcese's film *No Direction Home*. It does an excellent job of taking us back to that time when Dylan changed from folk to electric music and shows how defiantly Dylan went about his work.

It could not have been easy on anybody, yet Bob never backed down. You have to admire an artist that determined.

As the Band's Robbie Robertson noted in previous interviews, "the only reason tapes of those [1966] shows exist today is because we wanted to know, 'Are we crazy?' We'd go back to the hotel room, listen to a tape of the show and think 'Shit, that's not bad. Why is everybody so upset?'"

And maybe it took the stunning raw footage of Dylan and the Hawks combating his fans in England in 1966 to show us all how completely committed to his music he was and also how fearless he was. Would the Beatles or the Rolling Stones have played on facing that kind of booing? Maybe, after all this time, Dylan felt he should share what his life truly has been like.

That may be why, all these years later, we find out that Dylan agreed to tape interviews on his life, the work that led to *No Direction Home*. Not only that, Dylan would also decide to write a memoir and finally release these albums and songs that his fans have clamored about for years. And what the heck, he'll also do a weekly radio show, as long as he doesn't have to play his own songs. The man is full of surprises.

Once upon a time he used to be willing to have his lawyers go to any extent to protect his songs, his privacy. Now he is opening the doors, windows, shutters and everything else. Only on his own terms, of course. Why?

Some of it may be he likes to make money — and so does Columbia/Sony Records — and both may have decided to clean out the vaults while he's still around. By asking fans to submit their choices for songs, obscurities, etc. and sharing their own Dylan stories for 2007's three-disc *Dylan*, it's a canny move to legitimize yet another opportunity to repackage old material. And sure enough, the material included — excepting the Mark Ronson remix of "Most Likely You Go Your Way, I'll Go Mine" — is the 50 songs that generally have already come out on *Greatest Hits, Vol. 1, 2, 3, Biograph, The Essential Bob Dylan, The Best of Bob Dylan* and many other retrospectives.

One surprise is the DVD of his appearances at the Newport Folk Festival, a collection of 80 unreleased minutes of performances, several of which were excerpted in *No Direction Home*.

This is standard record company practice. Repackage, repackage, add a few obscurities for the completists out there and get it in the stores. When Dylan made the move to iTunes around the time *Modern Times* came out, making all of his recorded work instantly available on the Internet-only *Bob Dylan Collection*, the principal selling point was the collector-driven oddities. You could find songs that appeared on tribute albums ("Pretty Boy Floyd," "Blue-Eyed Jane") or the B-side of an import single ("Dead Man, Dead Man") or on obscure soundtracks ("Cross the Green Mountain").

Even the rerelease of the two lively Traveling Wilburys albums on Rhino Records in the summer of 2007 was treated with great celebration. All this for a pair of unreleased tunes (you could hear them on a BBC Special) and a brief DVD of some home movies of the fabulous Wilburys just getting their start in Bob Dylan's kitchen.

The feature film *I'm Not There* is based on a famously unreleased Basement Tapes song (which is included on the accompanying soundtrack) was released in November 2007. The songs on the soundtrack are all written by Dylan but performed by others, with that one notable exception. The film uses different actors or actresses to portray Dylan at varying points of his life.

If that isn't enough diversity for you, go on YouTube on any particular day and you can see Bob Dylan performances from all over the years, all over the world. You can find everything from his stirring performance of "A Hard Rain's a Gonna Fall" with The Great Musical Experience (and a symphony orchestra) in Japan in 1994 to rarely seen footage of Bob on "The Johnny Cash Show" singing "Girl from the North Country" in 1969.

And there's more. Or will be tomorrow. Or the day after. Whether it's rehearsals for the *David Letterman Show* or live performances all over the world, it's almost comical that the guy whose passion for privacy led to the bootleg era now is a regular YouTube star.

When Columbia started the website Bobdylan.com, one of its big selling points in the early days was offering current live versions of various songs Bob was playing on tour, sort of heading bootleggers off at the pass, so to speak. Now Bobdylan.com doesn't even bother. Sort of makes you wonder what would have happened to The Basement Tapes had the Internet been around back then.

THE HOME STRETCH

As Bob Dylan heads for 70, we getting to see and hear a heck of a lot more from him. The guy who ain't gonna work on Maggie's Farm has signed on to do another full year of his delightful satellite radio show. There may be two volumes of *Chronicles* on the way. Maybe even a sequel to *No Direction Home.*

Heck, he even exhibited 170 of his paintings at Germany's Chemnitz Museum in fall-winter 2007-2008. Who knows what else he has up his sleeve?

Amazingly, with all this extra access over the past dozen years, the man himself— subject of quite a few more tell-all biographies since the first edition of this book — remains as inscrutable as ever.

We can hear him more often, see him in concert, even read more interviews than at any time since his heyday in the 1960s. Yet we are no closer to grasping the true essence of the man.

In a strange way, it seems Dylan not only understands this, but wants to do something about it. Hence the film, the book, the radio show, the releases of long-sought after film and recordings, items that he recognizes his devout fans will devour.

This may be a particularly innocent way to look at the Dylan industry. It's much easier to take the cynical view, one shared by experts like Clinton Heylin, who suggest uncovering all these old tunes is the record company's idea of making a few bucks in lieu of new product. Maybe.

But when these cynics suggest that *No Direction Home* is strictly propaganda, a collage of old film that tries to make sure that the Dylan myth gets the most positive spin available, this seems a hollow criticism.

Heylin and others say that the film doesn't address Dylan's drug use. Well, watch him on stage in England. What else does he need to add? Doesn't that say enough? Would it be better to cut to a remorseful Bob Dylan, hat in hand, saying "Yeah, folks, I did take some speed back then, to keep going. But I don't recommend it." Come on.

Frankly, regarding the interviews, it seems silly to criticize him or his management for not sitting him down in front of some fabled get-to-the-truth journalist instead of somebody who works for him. Sure, the guy who works for him isn't likely to ask him ball-busting questions. But even if he did, folks, this is Bob Dylan. Do you think he would give you a straight answer if you asked him what time it was? Isn't that something about him that we've always loved?

If you try to take a deeper, more open-hearted look at this recent flood of material, it's not that hard to believe that, in his own inscrutable way, he's trying to show "his affection for all those that sailed with me."

No, we may never see the official rerelease of *Renaldo and Clara* or *Eat the Document*. But look what we *do* have. And if we had projected this kind of output back in 1974 or even 1985, nobody would have believed it.

A passage from Anthony Scaduto's biography of Dylan comes to mind. The two are talking about Dylan's unusual *John Wesley Harding* album and Scaduto makes an observation. Dylan responds, then goes into quite a lengthy explanation of the record and his intentions, astonishing Scaduto.

Scaduto says, "Let me ask you something. Why are you telling me things I don't know about you? Why are you doing this for me?"

And Dylan replied, "Because you wrote a good book and I want to help you make it better."

It may be that this Dylan renaissance is his inscrutable way of saying thanks for sticking with me. Whether we should thank Jeff Rosen's (Dylan's longtime manager) idea or somebody else for filming the interviews that compose much of *No Direction Home*, we will never likely know. Same goes for the release of all this long sought-after material.

If you are interested in Bob Dylan, you have to agree that it's our great fortune that someone was able to keep after him all these years and that he finally agreed to actually do these interviews, write this book, do this film, record three more terrific albums, you know, keep his hand in. He didn't have to.

Finally, it's exciting that somebody somewhere was able to convince Dylan that yes, he *was* right before any of us recognized it. That yes, he had a remarkable story to tell. And that yes, we wanted to hear it from him. As only he could tell it.

ONE

Albums

Bob Dylan

Produced by John Hammond for Columbia Records
Recorded in New York City (November 20, 22, 1961)
Released: February 1962

Chart Position *Bob Dylan* was one of three Dylan studio albums that did not make the Billboard charts. The other two are the 1986 album *Knocked Out Loaded* and the 1988 album *Down in the Groove.* It took 11 years, but *Bob Dylan* finally went gold on December 21, 1973.

Outtakes "He Was a Friend of Mine," "Man on the Street," "House Carpenter" (all were later released on *The Bootleg Series, Vols. 1–3,* 1991).

Singles No singles were released from this album.

The Cover A very young Bob Dylan, aged 20, poses with his hands wrapped around the neck of his acoustic guitar. With his bunny fur suede jacket, brown corduroy cap, and yellow sweatshirt, it is hard to imagine that just four years later, this unknown hick would become the definition of cool.

The Liner Notes Gushy but prophetic ("Bob Dylan is the most unusual new talent in American folk music"), the liner notes by Stacey Williams (a pseudonym for *New York Times* reviewer Robert Shelton) promised more for Dylan's first album than the record delivered, especially since the record featured only two Dylan compositions — the humorous "Talkin' New York" and the devotional "Song to Woody."

The notes also include the famous *New York Times* review by Shelton of Dylan's performance at Gerde's Folk City in which Shelton says that Dylan is "bursting at the seams with talent" and explains that Dylan's "highly personalized approach toward folk song is still evolving." He didn't know the half of it.

Reading his closing sentence, it is not difficult to imagine the thrill these words must have given a young, ambitious Bob Dylan: "Mr. Dylan is vague about his antecedents and birthplace, but it matters less where he has been than where he is going, and that would seem to be straight up."

The Record   Recorded at a cost of $402, Bob Dylan's debut record featured the exuberant 20-year-old on guitar and harmonica. There were only two original songs, "Song to Woody" and "Talkin' New York," but they clearly were the best songs on the album.

Listening to it again in the 1990s, one is struck by Dylan's joy of performing. He sounds fresh and alive, as if he would keep singing all day if you left the microphone on and the tape running.

SIDE ONE   1. "You're No Good": An energetic performance of an old Jesse Fuller song, it is addressed to a woman Dylan says he loves but cannot quite figure out why. (C+)   2. "Talkin' New York": The first of his own songs Dylan ever recorded is a delight. His wry comments on life in New York, the deft needle in his "hillbilly" pronunciation of "GreenRICH Village" and dry wit mark him as a distinctive songwriting talent. (A)   3. "In My Time of Dying": A song later adapted (and songwriting credit borrowed) on Led Zeppelin's *Physical Graffiti*. Dylan strains to sound like an old man. (C+)   4. "Man of Constant Sorrow": A song later covered and songwriting credit borrowed by Rod Stewart on his first album. A cursory run-through. (C) 5. "Fixin' to Die": The 20-year-old Dylan strumming fast, singing hard. It's OK. (C+)   6. "Pretty Peggy-O": A fun strum-and-holler number, it includes nice hillbillyish "eeeeohhh"s in midsong. (B+)   7. "Highway 51": Another fast blues with a melody Dylan would later reprise for his classic "It's All Right, Ma" off his first venture into rock and roll music, *Bringing It All Back Home*. A few years later, Dylan added 10 to the title of this song to come up with the title of perhaps his greatest album, *Highway 61 Revisited*. (C+)

SIDE TWO   **8.** "Gospel Plow": A frenetic old blues number with some fierce harmonica playing. (C)   **9.** "Baby, Let Me Follow You Down": A cute song with a spoken introduction crediting Cambridge, Massachusetts, guitarist Eric Von Schmidt with teaching Dylan the song. Later reprised with The Band on his 1966 tour of Europe, you would not recognize it as the same song. (C+)   **10.** "House of the Risin' Sun": A folk song that the Animals made a smash hit helped lure Dylan into rock and roll music. Dylan, who recorded it first, has fun with it, taking on the persona of a woman. (B)   **11.** "Freight Train Blues": This old Roy Acuff number is one of the funniest early Dylan songs. Not only is the song taken at a breakneck tempo, it also features Dylan's longest recorded note — over 25 seconds! Whooping and hollering, hitting notes that you would never expect, Dylan makes the song a surprise from start to finish. (B+)   **12.** "Song to Woody": It is interesting to note that even at 20, Dylan is cautious enough not to open or close his debut album with one of his own compositions. This song is a touching tribute to his mentor; the respectful Dylan is not about to put himself in the category of a Guthrie — not yet anyway. In the closing lines, he admits that he has much to learn and many places to travel as yet. (A)   **13.** "See That My Grave Is Kept Clean": An old Blind Lemon Jefferson song, it closes the album on a dark note. Dylan's guitar strumming is ominous, his singing tortured — a very bleak rendition for someone so young. (C+)

Some saw the serious tone of so many of these songs as evidence that smooth-faced Bob Dylan wanted to be known as a serious artist. He would get his wish soon enough. (Album Grade: B-)

The Freewheelin' Bob Dylan

Produced by John Hammond
Recorded in New York City (April 25; July 9; October 26, 27; November 13–15; December 6, 1962; April 24, 1963)
Released: May 27, 1963

Chart Position   *Freewheelin' Bob Dylan* was Dylan's first album to reach the Billboard charts. It rose to No. 22 and was on the charts for 14 weeks. Seven years later (December 18, 1970), Dylan was awarded a gold album for it.

Outtakes   "Baby, I'm in the Mood for You"; "Mixed Up Confusion" (later released on *Biograph,* 1985); "House Carpenter"; "Talkin' Bear Mountain Picnic Massacre Blues"; "Let Me Die in My Footsteps"; "Rambling, Gambling Willie"; "Talkin' Hava Negeilah Blues"; "Quit Your Low Down Ways"; "Worried Blues"; "Kingsport Town"; "Walls of Red Wing"; "Paths of Victory"; "Talkin' John Birch Paranoid Blues"; "Who Killed Davey Moore"? (all later released on *The Bootleg Series,* 1991) and "Rocks and Gravel." "Sally Gal" was included with the *No Direction Home Soundtrack, The Bootleg Series, Vol. 7.*

Singles   Bob Dylan's first single was "Mixed Up Confusion," backed with "Corrina, Corrina." It was released on December 14, 1962, several months before *Freewheelin'* appeared. Neither song was included on the album, which was released in May.

"Confusion" was one of Bob's first tracks working with a band, which consisted of Bruce Langhorne on guitar, George Barnes on bass, Dick Wellstood on piano, Gene Ramey also on bass, and Herb Lovell on drums. This same lineup recorded "Don't Think Twice, It's All Right" which was included on *Freewheelin'.*

"Confusion" was later released on *Biograph,* 1985. The B side of the single, "Corrina, Corrina," has not been re-released. A later version of the same song was included on *Another Side of Bob Dylan.*

A single from *Freewheelin',* "Blowin' in the Wind," backed with "Don't Think Twice," was released in August 1963.

The Cover   Arm in arm with his girlfriend at the time, Suze Rotolo, Dylan strolls down the middle of West Fourth Street, showing perhaps, that he is not a native New Yorker, for what New Yorker would dare walk down the middle of a busy New York City street in the middle of the day?

His hair is tousled and his top two coat buttons are buttoned, but his bottom two aren't — just the opposite of the way most people unbutton their coats. With his hands hitched in the pockets of his blue jeans, there's a folksy, yet hip aura about him.

Suze, resting her right cheek against Bob's left shoulder, is clutching his left arm tightly with both of hers. She's looking at photographer Don Hunstein and seems as if she'll never let go.

Bob, of course, seems cool and noncommittal, with other things on his mind. He looks like a man in a hurry to be somewhere else.

The Liner Notes   Written by the distinguished journalist Nat Hentoff, they are a little overwrought, considering that Dylan's first album didn't even hit the charts. Maybe Hentoff was trying to generate some sales for an ambitious young man.

The information included in these notes has been the subject of much debate among Dylan devotees in later years. Most don't believe a whit of what Dylan told Hentoff.

For example, according to Hentoff: "During his first 19 years, he lived in Gallup, New Mexico; Cheyenne, South Dakota; Sioux Falls, South Dakota; Phillipsburg, Kansas; Hibbing, Minnesota (where he graduated from high school), and Minneapolis (where he spent a restless six months at the University of Minnesota)."

He got the bits about Hibbing and Minneapolis right. The rest seems to come from Dylan's imagination.

Later, Dylan tells Hentoff that "anything I can sing, I call a song. Anything I can't sing or anything that's too long to be a poem, I call a novel. But my novels don't have the usual storylines. They're about my feelings at a certain place at a certain time."

Dylan tells Hentoff he is working on three "novels" in addition to songs and poems.

"One," Hentoff dutifully reports, "is about the week before he first came to New York and his initial week in that city. Another is about the South Dakota people he knew. And the third is about New York and a trip from New York to New Orleans."

In 1994, we only know of one Dylan novel — *Tarantula*, which, as near as anyone can figure, does not have much to do with any of the three topics Dylan told Hentoff about.

Hentoff's liner notes also hint where Dylan's music is headed.

"I still say that some of the biggest criminals are those that turn heads away when they see wrong and know it's wrong," Dylan told Hentoff. "I'm only 21 years old and I know that there's been too many wars.... You people over 21 should know better."

It is interesting that 28 years later, as the United States was congratulating itself for its successful invasion of Iraq, Dylan was honored

17

by the Academy of Recording Artists and Performers for lifetime achievement. He replied by performing in the angriest, most raucous rock and roll style he could muster, his strongest antiwar message — "Masters of War."

The Record A landmark album for Bob Dylan and his listeners. Try and think of a contemporary album that includes songs as good as "Blowin in the Wind," "Girl from the North Country," "A Hard Rain's a-Gonna Fall," and "Don't Think Twice."

Bob Dylan came of age as a songwriter on this record, not only with the four classics already mentioned, but with the hilarious "I Shall Be Free" and the satiric "Talking World War III Blues." Dylan's sense of humor stole the show. Dylan himself said he "felt real good about doing an album with my own material" and with songs like these, it was no wonder.

An interesting sidelight to this album is that a promotional copy of the record was released to radio stations in April and about 300 albums were released to the general public with four songs not on the record before Columbia recalled it.

On May 12, after the promo record had been released, Dylan had been booked to appear on "The Ed Sullivan Show." The song Dylan decided to do was "John Birch Society Paranoid Blues," a wry number that poked fun at the remnants of McCarthyism in 1963 America.

The song had passed through numerous rehearsals and Dylan was all set to perform it when, moments before air time, the CBS censors feared a libel problem and refused to let Dylan do so.

"They wanted me to sing a Clancy Brothers song," Dylan said in a radio interview years later. "And it didn't make any sense for me to sing a Clancy Brothers song. So I left."

Compare Dylan's decision with that of the Rolling Stones, who agreed to change the lyrics of "Let's Spend the Night Together" to "Let's Spend Some Time Together" so Sullivan's censors would let them appear, and you can measure the weight of Dylan's decision. A national television audience would have meant thousands, maybe millions, in record sales. But Dylan stuck to his guns.

He did lose the battle with Columbia, though. It refused to release the song on *Freewheelin'*, and two weeks later, Dylan remade the record, adding four new songs, "Bob Dylan's Dream," "Masters of War," "Girl from the North Country," and "Talking World War III Blues." He bumped "John Birch Society Paranoid Blues"; "Rambling, Gambling Willie"; "Rocks and Gravel"; and "Let Me Die in My Footsteps."

Three of those songs were eventually released on *The Bootleg Series, Vols. 1–3* 28 years later, but collectors who held on to the promo still had something quite rare.

"Rocks and Gravel" has never been released, and the version of "Talking John Birch Paranoid Blues" that was released on *The Bootleg Series* is a live version from Dylan's October 26 show at Carnegie Hall, not the studio version released on the promotional record.

On *The Bootleg Series* cut, Dylan shared his frustration with the censorship the song received with the Carnegie Hall audience. "This is called 'Talking John Birch Blues,'" he says, starting to play, "and there ain't nothing wrong with this song." His audience cheers wildly.

The album, without "John Birch" was finally released on May 27.

SIDE ONE   **1.** "Blowin' in the Wind": A hit for Peter, Paul and Mary, it was covered by Harry Belafonte, Stevie Wonder, and just about every other notable singer around. Dylan said years later that when he is singing some of his old songs, it never occurs to him that he wrote them. "Blowin in the Wind" is that kind of song. It doesn't really have the trademark Dylan stamp on it; it just seems to have always been around. (A)   **2.** "Girl from the North Country": Bob's first recorded love song. Supposedly written for his first girlfriend, Echo Halstrom, it is a wistful number, interesting because of Dylan's vulnerability on the song's bridge, where he wonders if his girlfriend remembers him. (B+)   **3.** "Masters of War": Bob's first "finger-pointing song" is a minor-chord diatribe against the war industry. It includes a nice little verse that again addressed those parents who held their age over their children, telling them well, you're just too young to understand. No wonder he became a hero to the young. (B)   **4.** "Down the Highway": A love song to his then-flame, Suze Rotolo (then off in Italy). It's a simple blues song and forgettable except for Dylan's nasty little fifth verse where he says his baby took his heart in her suitcase all the way to Italy. (C)   **5.** "Bob Dylan's Blues": A whimsical song with a barbed introduction, taking a shot at Tin Pan Alley's "folk songs," which Dylan says are quite unlike his. "Unlike most of the songs nowadays that are being written uptown in Tin Pan Alley," Dylan says, "that's where most of the folk songs come from nowadays, this one, this isn't written up there, this one is written somewhere down in the United States." (C) **6.** "A Hard Rain's a-Gonna Fall": Unlike anything Dylan had written to that point, "Hard Rain" is one of those songs Dylan described as "flashing chains of images." Dylan told an interviewer once that every single line of this song could have been a song in itself, and since he didn't know if he'd have enough time on Earth to write them all, he combined them into this song. On *Freewheelin'* Dylan's performance is somber, sincere, but a little sterile. A much better, more moving version of the song is available on *The Concert for Bangladesh* album of the 1971 benefit concert in New York City, where Dylan was a surprise guest of former Beatle George Harrison. Dylan never sang better than he did that night. (A)

SIDE TWO　　7. "Don't Think Twice, It's All Right": Side Two opens with Dylan's classic kiss-off (in more ways than one) song. Dylan gets nasty with Suze and her parents (who reportedly urged their breakup) in a nicely understated way. This song was one of Bob's first recorded tracks working with a band. Dylan also cut a single with this outfit, "Mixed Up Confusion," which was more of a rock number than anyone might have expected back then. The single, released the day before Christmas, 1962, was backed with "Corrina, Corrina" and has long been a prime collector's item. Never included on any album, "Mixed Up Confusion" was included in Columbia's stellar Dylan sampler, *Biograph,* released in December 1985. (A+)　　**8.** "Bob Dylan's Dream": This ode to idealism and days gone by is more than a little corny, and Bob gets a D for grammar on verse four, a rotten-tooth tense obviously thrown in for authenticity, too obviously. (C)　　**9.** "Oxford Town": A Dylan broadside against the racism shown James Meredith when he tried to enroll at the University of Mississippi in Oxford. The song presents an interesting musical experiment, later swiped by John Lennon, as Dylan juxtaposes a jaunty, happy melody to bitter lyrics about a very sad incident. Lennon did the same thing on his solo album *Imagine* with the song "Crippled Inside." (B)　　**10.** "Talking World War III Blues": One of Bob's great talking blues, it assesses the country the morning after World War III struck. Dylan says he's having a dream that he's the only one left after the war. He then runs into a man who runs away, a woman who tells him he's crazy for wanting to play Adam and Eve, and a doctor who comforts him by informing him that these dreams "are only in your head." Dylan has rarely been more charming than he was in this song. (A) **11.** "Corrina, Corrina": A rare Dylan cover of an old song of mixed origin. Dylan sings it sweetly and tenderly as if he is resigned to the loss of his Corrina. (B) **12.** "Honey, Just Allow Me One More Chance": A fast and funny little ditty with a side-splitting Dylan war whoop in the middle. Clocked at a little over a minute, it is a great little song to toss in at the end of a cassette. (B-) **13.** "I Shall Be Free": A talking blues that really rambles. On it, Dylan talks about, in order, women, getting drunk, racism, talking to President Kennedy, women, women working, women, politicians, commercials, women, and making love to Elizabeth Taylor. (A)

A record that still stands as one of his best. (Album Grade: A)

The Times They Are a-Changin'

Produced by Tom Wilson
Recorded in New York City (August 6, 7, 12; October 23, 24, 31, 1963)
Released: January 1964

Chart Position This album went to No. 20 on the Billboard charts and stayed there for only five weeks. As of 1991, it was one of only a handful of Dylan studio albums that had not gone gold.

Outtakes "Percy's Song," "Lay Down Your Weary Tune" (later released on *Biograph*, 1985), "Suze," "Moonshiner," "Only a Hobo," "Seven Curses," "Eternal Circle," "Walls of Red Wing," "Paths of Victory" (later released on *The Bootleg Series, Vols. 1–3*, 1991).

Singles Surprisingly, "The Times They Are a-Changin'," one of Dylan's signature songs, was never released as a single in the United States. The song did make the pop charts in England, as is mentioned in D. A. Pennebaker's *Don't Look Back*, a film of Dylan's tour of the

British Isles in the summer of 1965. No singles from this album were released in the United States.

The Cover　A stark, sepia-toned shot of a young, almost gaunt Bob Dylan trying to look serious — and like Woody Guthrie — at the same time. He succeeds.

The Liner Notes　One of Dylan's more noted attempts at free verse, "11 Outlined Epitaphs" serves as the liner notes on the back of the record and on both sides of an insert with the record.

This was probably the first time an American recording artist included a lengthy prose-poem with his recorded work.

With the success of *Freewheelin'*, Dylan began to see himself as more than just a singer-songwriter. And he offers plenty of evidence that he is more than that in "11 Outlined Epitaphs."

The Record　There is not much to laugh about on this album. *Freewheelin'* has a nice mixture of whimsy and serious comment, this one is all business. It is not a fun album.

A lot had happened to the country since Dylan's last record. President John Kennedy had been assassinated, and his reputed assassin, Lee Harvey Oswald, had also been killed. With the Vietnam War splitting the country down the middle, the entire mood of the nation was somber, frightened, and withdrawn. The country seemed to have lost its innocence and so, this record said, had 23-year-old Bob Dylan.

SIDE ONE　1. "The Times They Are a-Changin'": One of six Dylan albums named for a song on the record, the title song warns us of a world in flux. One of the last songs recorded, it was the peg on which to hang the rest of the songs. Even if you do not notice the Old Testament tone of the lyrics, the song sounds like something special, just from its opening notes. Nearly thirty years later, the song still sounds like an alarm, exactly what it was, from a young man who was beginning to feel as though his generation expected him to speak for it. (A+)　2. "Ballad of Hollis Brown": One of Dylan's bleakest songs, a harrowing portrait of an unemployed farmer who cannot get a break and finally kills himself, his wife, and their five children. Dylan opened his three-song set at Live Aid in 1985 with this number. (A)　3. "With God on Our Side": A somewhat lesser effort. Dylan takes a sarcastic look at imperialism in American history and how, he notes somewhat dryly, whatever war we were in, we've always had "God on our side." Or at least, that's how we explained it. (B+)   **4.** "One Too Many Mornings": A wistful footnote to a lover who left, and Dylan knows she is not going to return. Judging from concert performances, this song seems to be one of Dylan's personal favorites. He has performed it on every tour he has done in recent years, dating way back to a stunning electric version of it with The Band at the Royal Albert Hall in May 1966. He also did a nice version of it on his TV special "Hard Rain" in 1976, releasing it on the soundtrack LP. (A)   **5.** "North Country Blues": Another song Dylan sings in the persona of a woman, this is a sad tale of a lonely woman left to care for three children. It is notable now because Gordon Lightfoot borrowed the tune, made it more sprightly, and wrote "The Wreck of the Edmund Fitzgerald"—a big hit in the late 1970s. (C)

SIDE TWO   **6.** "Only a Pawn in Their Game": A sincere, politically correct yet musically dull account of the killing of Medgar Evers. (C+)   **7.** "Boots of Spanish Leather": A lonesome love ballad, possibly to his girlfriend at the time, Suze, who had broken up with Dylan and headed for Italy. The melody and even the longing of the lyrics are somewhat reminiscent of another Dylan song from this period "Tomorrow Is a Long Time," which was not released until Bob Dylan's Greatest Hits, Vol. II in 1972. (C+)   **8.** "When the Ship Comes In": An uplifting, up-tempo number of a day when justice will finally prevail, a day, you might say, when the meek will inherit the earth, as promised in the Sermon on the Mount. Though *Times* is far from Dylan's most popular album, "When the Ship Comes In" was the second song from it played by Dylan at the 1985 Live Aid concert. Dylan stared into the cameras and gave particular emphasis to the line that says that everyone, everywhere will be watching this event. (B)   **9.** "The Lonesome Death of Hattie Carroll": This is perhaps the album's most enduring protest song. Dylan's impassioned performance on guitar and harmonica is memorable. A nice film version of part of this song is included in D. A. Pennebaker's outstanding film of Dylan's 1965 tour of England, *Don't Look Back*. (A)   **10.** "Restless Farewell": Its tangled syntax and listless melody make it the least distinguished Dylan album closer ever. Dylan has always put a lot of emphasis on the sequence of songs. He once criticized Columbia for putting out *Bob Dylan's Greatest Hits* not so much for its song selection, but for the way the songs were arranged on the record. And when you consider that his next four albums would conclude with "It Ain't Me, Babe"; "It's All Over Now, Baby Blue"; "Desolation Row"; and "Sad-Eyed Lady of the Lowlands," it points out how weak this finisher is. With outtakes like "Moonshiner," "Lay Down Your Weary Tune," Percy's Song," or even "Paths of Victory" available, you wonder if Bob might not have made the wrong choice. He did do a fine version of this for Frank Sinatra in a TV tribute. But this version of this song didn't cut it.(C-)

If you are just starting a Bob Dylan collection, this is one album you can do without. Even if you love the song "The Times They Are a-Changin'," you can find it on *Greatest Hits* and *Biograph*. (Album Grade: C+)

Another Side of Bob Dylan

Produced by Tom Wilson
Recorded: June 9, 1964
Released: August 8, 1964

Chart Position   Dylan's second album to make the Billboard charts, it was on the charts for five weeks and rose to No. 43 — not long enough for a gold album.

Outtakes   "Mama, You've Been on My Mind," later released on *The Bootleg Series, Vols. 1–3,* 1991.

Singles   No American singles were released from this album.

The Cover   A plain black-and-white picture of a much more mature-looking Bob Dylan, left elbow resting on his left thigh, right hand perched on his hip. He looks very serious.

The Liner Notes   As on the previous album's "11 Outlined Epitaphs," Dylan again chose to fill up the back of his record jacket with words, in this case, clever little vignettes called "Some Other Kind of Songs."

The Record   All 11 songs were recorded on June 9, 1964, with a small audience of friends on hand. It is the only Dylan album so far to come out of a single recording session.

The album was a marked departure from the heavy-handed social consciousness that overloaded *The Times They Are a-Changin'*.

There was humor ("I Shall Be Free — No. 10"), and there was honesty ("All I Really Want to Do"), signs of artistic growth ("It Ain't Me, Babe") and personal growth ("My Back Pages").

With Dylan's relaxed manner (he almost laughs during the last verse of "All I Really Want to Do"), you can imagine him in the studio, hammering this out in a single night.

SIDE ONE   **1.** "All I Really Want to Do": Dylan matches his outrageous rhyme scheme with a wild, daring delivery that is guaranteed to have you laughing by the second verse. It almost seems that Dylan was tired of people telling him he couldn't sing, so he went out and recorded a song to prove he *really* couldn't sing. (A-)   **2.** "Black Crow Blues": Dylan's first recorded number on the piano. Nothing to brag about. (C)   **3.** "Spanish Harlem Incident": A passionate Dylan sermonette about a Gypsy woman with "pearly eyes" and "flashing diamond teeth." (C)   **4.** "Chimes of Freedom": An unprecedented, alliterative explosion of words, attempting to describe a lightning storm. Nowadays, much of it seems overwritten and forced. Yet somehow, the song retains an innocent integrity in that it seems to be the first song in which Dylan tried to get to the outer reaches of his artistic vocabulary. Try reading it out loud sometime. It's hard to imagine that Dylan managed to find a melody — even if it was an old one — to go with such intricate verses. (A-)   **5.** "I Shall Be Free — No. 10": A welcome bit of Guthriesque comic relief after the verbal maelstrom of "Chimes." Dylan's delivery is effortless. As the last "talking blues" he has recorded so far, it remains a classic. (A-)   **6.** "To Ramona": An interesting bit of writing, in a standard love song. (B)

SIDE TWO   **7.** "Motorpsycho Nitemare": A tall tale that combines a little bit of Alfred Hitchcock's *Psycho* with the myths of the traveling salesman. It is a funny song, even 20-plus years later. (B)   **8.** "My Back Pages": Of the five songs on Side Two — "My Back Pages"; "I Don't Believe You"; "Ballad in Plain D"; and "It Ain't Me Babe" — four probably deserve the rating of "classic." The one miss — "Ballad in Plain D" — is such a miss that even years later, Dylan admitted that it's the one song he wishes he had never recorded. But the five-song sequence remains one of the more interesting Dylan has put together on a recording. Dylan once read an insightful review that explained why he had sequenced the songs the way he did on *Greatest Hits, Vol. II,* and he was amazed that the reviewer had gotten it right. In "My Back Pages," Dylan looks back at his life, his art, particularly his "protest-song" days, and recognizes how he and everyone else in the movement failed by trying to depict things simply. In one of his most quoted lines, Dylan says that now he is changed. Then, perhaps, he gets down to the reasons why. (B+)   **9.** "I Don't Believe You": Here Dylan chides a former lover who behaves as if she did not know him. It is wonderfully written and performed. (B+)   **10.** "Ballad in Plain D": An apparent diatribe-in-verse against Suze Rotolo's family for their interference in Dylan and Suze's relationship. In an interview with Bill Flanagan in his wonderful book on rock songwriting, *Written in My Soul,* Dylan referred to that song: "That one I look back at and say 'I must have been a real schmuck to write that.' I look back at that particular one and say, of all the songs I've written, maybe I could have left that alone." (C-)   **11.** "It Ain't Me, Babe": The album concludes with one of Dylan's most famous statements of personal and artistic independence, a statement that says he doesn't need Suze, he doesn't need anyone. And Dylan hasn't stopped believing that. In the acoustic portion of a 1986 show with Tom Petty and the Heartbreakers in Hartford, Connecticut, Dylan heard a request for "Mr. Tambourine Man." "Naw, I'm not going to play 'Mr. Tambourine Man,'" he said, a snarl in his voice. "So sorry." What he did play, with a little extra gusto, was the extraordinary "It Ain't Me, Babe." (A+)

Though Side One is not as interesting as Side Two, we still see Bob Dylan developing as a singer-songwriter and as a public personality. You can almost trace the development from song to song. And to think he recorded all these in a single night. (Album Grade: B)

Bringing It All Back Home

Produced by Tom Wilson
Recorded: January 14, 15, 1965
Released: March 22, 1965

Chart Position   This album was Dylan's most successful record to date, climbing to No. **6.** It earned him a gold album (August 25, 1967) and was on the charts for 32 weeks.

Outtakes   "If You've Gotta Go, Go Now"; "Subterranean Home-sick Blues No. 10" (acoustic); "Farewell Angelina" (all later released on *The Bootleg Series, Vols. 1–3,* 1991); "I'll Keep It with Mine" (later released on *Biograph,* 1985). Outtakes of "Mr. Tambourine Man" "She Belongs to Me" and "It's All Over Now, Baby Blue" were included in the *No Direction Home Soundtrack, The Bootleg Series, Vol. 7*

Singles   "Subterranean Homesick Blues" backed with "She Belongs to Me" was released as a single in March 1965. It spent eight weeks on the charts, climbing to No. 39.

The Cover   One of the first rock and roll album covers that tried to do a little more than advertise the record, it depicts a serious Bob Dylan seated in front of a fireplace with a dark-haired, exotic woman seated behind him to his right.

The woman is Sally Grossman, wife of Dylan's manager at the time. She wears a stylish, red pantsuit and holds a cigarette poised just so.

Dylan wears a pinstriped shirt with cufflinks and sport coat. He holds a gray cat, who stares at the camera, and a movie magazine is spread over his knee.

Carefully arranged on the couch beside Dylan are records (by The Impressions, Robert Johnson, Lotte Lenya, and Eric von Schmidt).

On a table next to Grossman is an issue of *Time* magazine, with Lyndon Johnson on the cover. On one side of the table is a black-and-yellow fallout shelter sign. Way in the background, behind Grossman, is the jacket to *Another Side of Bob Dylan.*

The photo seems to dare: "Go ahead, call me a folksinger now."

The Liner Notes   Funny, sassy, Dylan is just bursting with play-

27

ful creativity at this point. He describes a recording engineer coming by to pick up his latest "works of art."

Notice he doesn't refer to himself as just a singer or a rock and roller, but as an artist. That was a foreign concept to contemporary performers in 1965.

In his notes, Dylan talks about the influences on his life and the craziness he is going through. The notes are interesting — and the songs are even better.

The Record   It is hard to imagine what record buyers thought when they heard "Subterranean Homesick Blues" on the radio for the first time in the spring of 1965. It is part rap, part blues, part hilarity, part social comment — pure Bob Dylan.

And as the song that kicks off *Bringing It All Back Home* — Dylan's first rock and roll album — it was an appropriate departure musically and lyrically from *Another Side*.

Taking the leap — and it was a leap, not just a step — into rock and roll music was a daring move for Bob Dylan. Already accepted and revered in folk music circles, he could have been tempted to milk that vein for years. But Dylan, of course, had other ideas — lots of them, in fact — and he uses them in the songs on *Bringing It All Back Home*.

SIDE ONE   **1.** "Subterranean Homesick Blues": One of Dylan's more riotous songs. You can imagine the fun he had writing it. What is surprising is that the thumping drums and bass that seem to propel that electric version really aren't missed that much in the exciting acoustic version of the tune, released in *The Bootleg Series* in 1991. Both are great, perhaps because of Dylan's snarling, hip, sarcastic vocal. He sounds like he had a flip answer for everything. And he did. (A+)   **2.** "She Belongs to Me": An oft-quoted Dylan love ballad to a mysterious woman. The title is ironic because Dylan spends the whole song convincing the listener she doesn't belong to him. His performance is almost as delicate as the song. (B+)   **3.** "Maggie's Farm": Another breakthrough song for Dylan. It is a wonderfully wry expression of personal independence and a slam at socialism at the same time. Every verse is funny. (A)   **4.** "Love Minus Zero/No Limit": Another "soft" song that seems to be a sister song to "She Belongs to Me." It contains some interesting lines that stand alone better than they fit into the song.

(B+) **5.** "Outlaw Blues": This is one of Dylan's most raucous rock and roll tracks with some whacky lyrics. What it all means, who knows? (C) **6.** "On the Road Again": A standard blues song in which Dylan humorously explicates the horrors of his girlfriend's family. (B) **7.** "Bob Dylan's 115th Dream": One of Dylan's funniest songs. The song get laughs before it even starts because Dylan's band fails to come in on cue, sending the boss into hysterics. Once it begins, Dylan playfully recounts a wild trip on the *Mayflower* in which he arrives in America, has a crazy series of adventures, and leaves — just in time to pass another ship and another captain who just happens to be Christopher Columbus. (A)

SIDE TWO **8.** "Mr. Tambourine Man": One of Dylan's most enduring songs. Though it has often been cited as a "drug song," which angered Dylan, in another reading the song seems to be a plea to his muse for inspiration and the freedom that it brings. Dylan once said that there was only one of his songs that he ever tried to imitate and implied that it was this one. (A+) **9.** "Gates of Eden": The weakest of the four songs on Side Two. Dylan is really reaching here and doesn't quite make it. But there are some fine verses, particularly the last one. (B+) **10.** "It's Alright, Ma (I'm Only Bleeding)": One of Dylan's more remarkable lyrical achievements, he was reaching here and succeeded. From the fast, drone like guitar line to Dylan's no-nonsense delivery, he has never sounded more angry, more omniscient, or more prophetic. On his 1974 tour, when Dylan reached the line about the president having "to stand naked," audiences stood and cheered wildly. President Nixon was then going through the Watergate saga. It was a moment that reaffirmed the sure hand that penned that line nearly a decade earlier. (A+) **11.** "It's All Over Now, Baby Blue": A beautiful song. It seems to depict a world in which all seeming certainties are certain no longer. Everything you know is wrong. You may even conclude that a certain protest singer may not be targeting the same old foes and issues anymore. (A)

As a singer, songwriter, performer, and all-around creative artist, Dylan seemed miles ahead of everyone — critics, fellow musicians, and even his audience. And there was yet more to come. (Album Grade: A)

Highway 61 Revisited

Produced by Bob Johnston (except for "Like a Rolling Stone," which
was produced by Tom Wilson) for Columbia Records
Recorded in New York City (June 15–16; July 29–30; August 2–4, 1965)
Released: August 30, 1965

Chart Position   *Highway 61 Revisited* bettered Dylan's previous
release *Bringing It All Back Home*, rising to No. 3 and earning Dylan
his second straight gold album in two years. But the record stayed on
the charts for only 24 weeks, two months less than its predecessor. The
shorter time on the charts is surprising, in light of the success of "Like
a Rolling Stone" as a single (No. 2).

Outtakes   "Jet Pilot," a snippet of an outtake that later became
"Tombstone Blues," and "I Wanna Be Your Lover" were released on
1985's *Biograph*. "Sitting on a Barbed Wire Fence"; "It Takes a Lot to
Laugh, It Takes a Train to Cry"; and a rehearsal version of "Like a
Rolling Stone" were released on *The Bootleg Series, Vols. 1–3*, in 1991.
Alternate versions of "Desolation Row," "Highway 61 Revisited," "Just
Like Tom Thumb's Blues," "Tombstone Blues" and "It Takes a Lot to
Laugh, It Takes a Train to Cry" were included on the *No Direction
Home, The Bootleg Series, Vol. 7*.

Singles   "Like a Rolling Stone" was backed with "Gates of Eden"
from *Bringing It All Back Home* and was released on July 20. It was the
most successful of all Dylan singles, spending 12 weeks on the charts,
including two weeks at No. 2. No other singles were released from this
album.

Dylan's next two singles, "Positively Fourth Street" (released Sep-
tember 7, 1965) and "Can You Please Crawl Out Your Window?"
(released November 30, 1965) went to No. 7 and No. 58, respectively.
Although neither appeared on the album, both featured tracks from
Highway 61 on the B side. "Fourth Street" was backed with "From a
Buick 6," and "Crawl Out" had "Highway 61 Revisited" on the B Side.

"Fourth Street" was later included in 1967's *Bob Dylan's Greatest
Hits*. "Crawl Out Your Window" was not included on any American-
released Dylan album until 1985's *Biograph*.

The Liner Notes   Similar to the notes Dylan offered for *Bringing It All Back Home,* but a little more obscure, these notes reveal a prose style that is not all that different from Dylan's songwriting technique — allusive and funny, with little bursts of insight gleaming through. Most telling is the closing paragraph, in which Dylan is by turns sarcastic (to *Sing Out* magazine writer John Cohen): "You are right, John Cohen — quazimodo was right — mozart was right...."; funny: "when I speak this word eye it is as if I am speaking of someone's eye I faintly remember...."; and revealing: "You are lucky — you don't have to have to think about such things as eyes & rooftops & quazimodo."

The Record   If you had to pick one Bob Dylan album to send to the Library of Congress as his shining achievement, it probably would be *Highway 61 Revisited.* The album contains at least six Dylan classics, probably his greatest song ("Like a Rolling Stone"), and a wildly diverse cast of characters drawn from history and imagination to flesh out the nine remarkable songs.

As folksinger Phil Ochs told Dylan biographer Anthony Scaduto in *Bob Dylan: An Intimate Biography*:

"From the moment I met him I thought he was great, a genius, Shakespearean. Every succeeding album up to Highway 61, I had an increasing lot of secret fear: 'Oh my God, what can he do next? He can't possibly top that one.' And then I put on Highway 61, and I laughed and said it's so ridiculous. It's impossibly good, it just can't be that good. The writing was so rich I couldn't believe it.... He's done something that's left the whole field ridiculously in back of him."

Dylan agreed. "I'm not going to be able to make a record better than that one," he said. "Highway 61 is just too good. There's a lot of stuff on that record I would listen to."

SIDE ONE   **1.** "Like a Rolling Stone": This is his greatest song. Powerful, brilliantly sung, and dynamically performed, it has all the earmarks of greatness and carries a sense of majesty. The song's rising melody builds in intensity before the chorus resolves things. Best of all, it still sounds good on the radio decades later. The lyrics seem to be about someone who has fallen from grace, someone once in a high position who now has to beg for meals, for help, for understanding, for compassion.

Though some critics have said that Dylan wrote this song, in part, about himself, it seems more likely that after two years of the most intense stardom a 24-year-old could stand, he was striking out at those in a position of privilege — those who went to the right schools, wore the right clothes, and read the right books only to be cast adrift once they had to live in the real world. (A+)   **2.** "Tombstone Blues": Comprises an incredible cast of characters. Ma Rainey, Beethoven, Paul Revere's horse, Galileo, Belle Starr, Jack the Ripper, strung together to a thumping beat, Dylan paints a hilarious portrait of a world gone mad. Rife with all kinds of memorable lines, it is the kind of song only Bob Dylan could have written. (A)   **3.** "It Takes a Lot to Laugh, It Takes a Train to Cry": One of George Harrison's favorite Bob Dylan songs, which Harrison coerced Bob to play at his 1971 benefit concert for Bangladesh. It's a sweet, understated blues song to a lover. (B+)   **4.** "From a Buick 6": A simple, low-key rock blues, with a couple of great lines, it was later covered by Gary "U.S." Bonds on a comeback album in the 80s. (B)   **5.** "Ballad of a Thin Man": One of Dylan's most terrifying songs, it is a haunting blues number, played by Dylan on the piano, about a mysterious "Mr. Jones," who just does not seem to understand the world around him. In later years, this became one of Dylan's more potent songs in concert because he could talk the lyrics to dramatic effect. A classic. (A+)

SIDE TWO   **6.** "Queen Jane Approximately": Taking Dylan at his word, this seems to be a song of compassion and understanding concerning a drag "queen." Dylan tells the character that if he (or she) needs someone whom he does not have to talk to, to see him. Some have said that the song could be about Joan Baez, the "queen" to Dylan's "king," who had recently fallen out of favor. Others have implied it is about homosexuality. Whatever the song's "meaning," a beautifully ragged version appears on the live album *Dylan and the [Grateful] Dead.* (B+)   **7.** "Highway 61 Revisited": Like its sister song "Tombstone Blues," it is a raucous, irreverent look at the world, playing off the old theme of the traveling minstrel. The title comes from a song on Dylan's first album called "Highway 51." It invokes God, Abraham, Billy the Kid, Mack the Finger, and all sorts of American heroes. A great example of Dylan's imagination at its best. (A)   **8.** "Just Like Tom Thumb's Blues": A song seldom mentioned as one of Dylan's greatest, yet it paints an extraordinary picture of a sad, empty night in a border town and a man whose life and career are in ruins. Studded with great lines like most of the songs on this album, it really came alive on stage. Dylan's performance of it with The Band in Liverpool on the hard-to-find single is definitive. An interesting anecdote: When singer Joe Strummer took a brief hiatus from his group the Clash in the 1980s, he said he spent most of his time in a Paris hotel, playing this song on the piano over and over. (A)   **9.** "Desolation Row": Whenever anyone suggests that John Lennon/Paul McCartney or Bruce Springsteen or Paul Simon were greater songwriters than Bob Dylan, "Desolation Row" ought to be the first argument on Dylan's behalf. Has any rock and roll songwriter ever attempted as much in a single song? Romeo, Einstein, Robin Hood, Cinderella, the Good Samaritan — they are all in this song, all important societal myths that Dylan plays with and makes inescapably his own in his extraordinary depiction of the world as "Desolation Row." It is one of Dylan's great moments on vinyl. (A+)

Beginning the album with his greatest song and closing it with one of his most ambitious undertakings, perhaps as ambitious a song as any rock songwriter ever attempted, Bob Dylan stepped into uncharted territory with this record. He has never attempted another record as ambitious as this one. Neither has anyone else. (Album Grade: A)

Blonde on Blonde

Produced by Bob Johnston for Columbia Records
Recorded: October 20; November 30; December 1, 1965; January 21, 24, 25; February 14–17; March 8–9, 1966
Released: May 16, 1966

Chart Position   *Blonde on Blonde*, likely the first double album released by a major rock and roll performer, peaked on the charts at No. 6. It remained on the charts for 15 weeks and earned Dylan his third straight gold album, on August 25, 1967.

Singles   While the record was being recorded, Dylan released "Please Crawl Out Your Window" in November.

In February, before the record was finished, he released one of its tracks, "One of Us Must Know," which was probably recorded in January with members of The Band. It was backed with a *Highway 61* track, "Queen Jane Approximately" and did not make the charts.

In April, a month before the record was released, he put out two album tracks, "Rainy Day Women #12 and 35," backed with "Pledging My Time" as a second single. Then, as he headed off to England for a wild tour with The Band, "Rainy Day Women" went all the way to No. 2, as high as "Like a Rolling Stone" a year earlier.

In June, he followed that single with the release of "I Want You," backed with a rarity, a live recording of Dylan and The Band performing "Just Like Tom Thumb's Blues" barely a month earlier in Liverpool, England. That recording is still not available on an American-release Dylan album. But even with that tantalizing song tucked on the B side, "I Want You" got no higher than No. 20.

In August, he released his third single from the album "Just Like a Woman," backed with "Obviously Five Believers"; it reached No. 33.

The following March, to coincide with the release of *Bob Dylan's Greatest Hits,* Columbia released "Leopard-skin Pillbox Hat," the final single from the album "Blonde on Blonde," though it was not included on *Greatest Hits.*

The single "Leopard-skin Pillbox Hat," backed with "Most Likely You Go Your Way, I'll Go Mine," went only to No. 81.

Outtakes   According to the inside jacket of the record, this four-sided disc was "recorded at Columbia Recording Studios, Nashville, Tennessee." But of the ten studio dates listed, only the last four took place in Nashville.

Dylan apparently was having a fierce case of writer's block. It is revealing that out of all that studio time, only the "Please Crawl Out Your Window" single (released November 30) and two outtakes have emerged. They include the epic "She's Your Lover Now" (recorded January 21 in Los Angeles) and a version of an older Dylan song "I'll Keep It with Mine" (recorded January 27, no location given, though Los Angeles seems likely).

Apparently Bob Johnston, Dylan's producer, recommended going to Nashville to complete the record and that proved to be the tonic.

Once in Nashville, Dylan came up with more first-rate material at one time than ever before or since and found musicians capable of enhancing his songs. The record stands as a landmark achievement.

Finally, some 40 years after the fact, three outtakes from the *Blonde on Blonde* sessions were included in the *No Direction Home Soundtrack, the Bootleg Series, Vol. 1.* They were "Leopard-Skin Pillbox Hat" "Stuck Inside of Mobile with the Memphis Blues Again" and "Visions of Johanna."

The Cover   A somewhat out-of-focus Bob Dylan, wearing a brown jacket and a checked scarf, left hand in pocket, leans against a wall and stares at the camera. When he returned to the concert stage in 1974 after a lengthy absence, he wore a similar scarf. The name of the album is nowhere to be found on the front or back; it is only along the spine of the double-record set.

Liner Notes   For the first time in his career, Dylan offered no liner notes to go with his record. Instead, the inside jacket features seven photographs, six of Dylan, seemingly demonstrating the five senses. He is depicted lighting a cigarette (taste), apparently rolling a joint (smell), playing the guitar on stage (sound), riding in a car (sight), and holding an ornamental frame and a pair of pliers (touch). He is also shown staring at the camera. In the far-right corner, there is a photo of an unidentified man.

The recording information has one interesting tidbit. It notes that the electric guitar solo on "Leopard-skin Pillbox Hat" was played by Bob Dylan. It is his only official recorded guitar solo.

The Record   If *Highway 61 Revisited* was Bob Dylan's most brilliant work, a scathing, crystalline-clear depiction of the horrors and joys of the modern world, then *Blonde on Blonde* was a look at life from the inside out.

It was backed by a slew of gifted musicians from Nashville, where the bulk of the double-album set was recorded, and their musical versatility lent a richness to the sound of the album that Dylan has never again achieved.

As he himself told Ron Rosenbaum, of *Playboy* magazine, in 1978: "The closest I ever got to the sound I hear in my mind was on individual bands in the 'Blonde on Blonde' album. It's that thin, that wild mercury sound. It's metallic and bright gold, with whatever that conjures up. That's my particular sound."

In many ways, *Blonde on Blonde* is an easier album to listen to than *Highway 61 Revisited*. Though there isn't an individual song as dynamic as "Like a Rolling Stone," cuts like "I Want You," "Stuck Inside of Mobile with the Memphis Blues Again," and "One of Us Must Know" have a warmth and a compassion that you don't sense on *Highway 61 Revisited*.

The album goes from broad farce ("Rainy Day Women #12 and 35" and "Leopard-skin Pillbox Hat") to deep introspection ("Visions of Johanna") to delightful parody ("4th Time Around") to wild rock and roll ("Obviously Five Believers").

One of the great rock and roll albums of all time. A tour de force.

SIDE ONE   1. "Rainy Day Women #12 and 35": Not only is this one of Dylan's craziest songs, it is also one of his most commercially successful singles, which went to No. 2 on the charts, as did "Like a Rolling Stone." For the most accomplished lyricist of his generation to come up with such a delightful stroke of lunacy was not only refreshing, it was great fun for Dylan and the musicians in the background. (A)   2. "Pledging My Time": Dylan has included a blues song on almost every album he has ever released. This one is well performed with some exciting harmonica work. (B)   3. "Visions of Johanna": One of Dylan's most enigmatic love songs, it was reputedly inspired by Dylan's relationship with Joan Baez, the woman who took him on tour and introduced him to her audience. Of course, the song is about more than repaying a debt; it has an overpowering sense of regret and loss. This is a fine version of the song, but the solo version included on 1985's *Biograph* may be even more poignant. Perhaps the best one is on a bootleg recording of Dylan's 1966 Australia tour. He is exhausted, his voice is barely a croak, and his guitar keeps going out of tune. He kiddingly explains that the guitar is only for folk music. Once he gets down to the song that he retitled "Mother Revisited," there is a bittersweet vulnerability in the performance that is almost without parallel in Dylan's live work. (A+)   4. "One of Us Must Know": A grand, stately number, propelled by some wonderful piano-organ interplay, this was the first single released from the double-record set. Though it was not a success commercially, the song captures Dylan's *Blonde on Blonde* sound perfectly. His voice, a tinny howl in "Like a Rolling Stone," is fuller and warmer here. In "She's Your Lover Now," a song recorded then but not released until 1991 (*The Bootleg Series*), Dylan compares his voice to the final gunshot of a dying man. That's just about it. (A)

SIDE TWO   5. "I Want You": This song has a lilting melody, a wonderful harmonica solo, and a great guitar figure by Wayne Moss. The notes to *Biograph* tell us this was the last song cut for *Blonde on Blonde*. Something about the song captures the irrepressible feeling of new love. There is a great off-hand moment when Dylan stumbles on a line that someone like Paul Simon might have edited out. Yet with Dylan, the little goof only serves to enhance the performance. (A)   6. "Stuck Inside of Mobile with the Memphis Blues Again": A brilliantly funny portrait in black velvet of a world gone mad. Dylan wrote several songs in this vein, but none are as richly descriptive as this one. The music is delightfully upbeat, a perfect counterpoint to the chaos of the lyrics. This song also includes a little mistake, when, in the fourth verse, Dylan starts to say the wrong words before he quickly shifts to the right ones. Certainly, Dylan could have recut the song, but evidently he liked the feeling of it and stayed with this version. It remains one of his most perfectly realized songs. (A+)   7. "Leopard-skin Pillbox Hat": A good joke, it's another standard blues with some funny lyrics. But it's also a good trivia question, for it contains Dylan's only credited electric guitar solo. He's no Eric Clapton, but it's fun, nevertheless. (B+)   8. "Just Like a Woman": It's hard to know what to think about this song. Written well before the women's liberation movement, many of its critics have branded it as "a catalog of sexist slurs." Yet it was included on *Bob Dylan's Greatest Hits* and was Dylan's closing song at the 1971 Concert for Bangladesh, drawing a tremendous response from the audience. Over 20 years later, the song remains a concert favorite, particularly among female fans — the very people Dylan is supposedly offending. (A)

SIDE THREE   9. "Most Likely You Go Your Way and I'll Go Mine": Dylan's personal Declaration of Independence, set to a martial beat, this song was either Dylan's opening or closing song on his triumphant comeback tour in 1974. Sometimes it was both. (B+)   **10.** "Temporary Like Achilles": A puzzling song. The kind of song you'd expect to hear at two in the morning in an empty Bourbon Street bar, the refrain never seems to be resolved. Maybe we need "Queen Jane." (B)   **11.** "Absolutely Sweet Marie": Those who found Dylan's music too depressing had no complaints about this uptempo cut, one of the most exuberant songs Dylan had recorded since "Honey, Just Allow Me One More Chance" years earlier. And as a bonus, it includes a wild harmonica solo in the middle. (A)   **12.** "4th Time Around": Reportedly inspired by the Beatles' "Norwegian Wood" (an elliptical tale of an affair John Lennon had), Dylan's saga of sexual infidelity is more sharply drawn and easier to follow. His biting wit carries the song. Later on, Dylan claimed to have written his song first. (A)   **13.** "Obviously Five Believers": It is doubtful if Dylan has ever recorded a better pure rock and roll song. It comes complete with great drum breaks; rousing harmonica work by Charlie McCoy; stinging guitar work by Robbie Robertson; and one of Dylan's most assured, commanding vocals. This might have made a far better single than "One of Us Must Know." I wonder why nobody ever picked it. (A)

SIDE FOUR   **14.** "Sad-Eyed Lady of the Lowlands": The only song to which Dylan ever devoted a whole album side, it remains an ambitious, mysterious, puzzling song-poem. Presumably written to and about his new wife, Sara, it is filled with haunting images of a woman who seems to have taken over Dylan's world. And just in time, it seems. There are some strange images and lines that would challenge even the most expert analysts. But none of those mysteries is as intriguing as Dylan's motive for writing such a song. Why is he sharing this private, extremely personal song with us? Is it his only way of really expressing himself to Sara? For someone known as a privacy freak, it seems an unusually public gesture. The song asks a lot of questions, in verse and in performance. And once you hear the mournful harmonica solo that closes the album, you sense how much Bob Dylan, at this point in his life, depended on his new wife. It also remains one of the few songs Dylan has ever referred to in his later work. Eleven years later, in the closing song on the 1976 album, *Desire,* Dylan tells of staying up for days in the Chelsea Hotel writing "Sad-Eyed Lady" for her. Was his public confession a desperate attempt to lure her back? Or was it the sad, resigned recollection of a man who "threw it all away" and knew it? We don't know, and "Sad-Eyed Lady" doesn't offer any easy answers. (B+)

If any rock album deserves the term *monumental*, it has to be *Blonde on Blonde*. The first double album in rock history, it is also the finest. Dylan's backing bands are superb, his singing is expressive, and there's a musical diversity unmatched on any Dylan record before or since. A rock critic once said that he would buy a record of Dylan breathing heavily. An album like *Blonde on Blonde* is the reason why. (Album Grade: A)

Bob Dylan's Greatest Hits

Compiled by Columbia Records
Released: March 27, 1967

Chart Position   While Dylan was reportedly recuperating from a motorcycle accident he had suffered in the summer of 1966, Columbia decided to release Bob Dylan's Greatest Hits in March.

Though the only song on the record that was not on a previously released Dylan album was his 1965 hit single "Positively Fourth Street," the record went to No. 10, was on the charts for 21 weeks, and earned Dylan his first platinum album. No doubt it helped to whet the public's appetite for the next album, *John Wesley Harding,* which appeared in late December.

The Record   SIDE ONE   **1.** "Rainy Day Women #12 & 35": From *Blonde on Blonde,* 1966.   **2.** Blowin' in the Wind": From *Freewheelin' Bob Dylan,* 1963.   **3.** "The Times They Are a-Changin'": From *The Times They Are a-Changin',* 1963.   **4.** "It Ain't Me, Babe": From *Another Side of Bob Dylan,* 1964.   **5.** "Like a Rolling Stone": From *Highway 61 Revisited,* 1965.

SIDE TWO   **6.** "Mr. Tambourine Man": From *Freewheelin' Bob Dylan,* 1963.   **7.** "Subterranean Homesick Blues": From *Bringing It*

All Back Home, 1965.   **8.** "I Want You": From *Blonde on Blonde,* 1966.
9. "Positively Fourth Street": Recorded at CBS Studios just four days
after Dylan appeared at the Newport Folk Festival in July 1965, it wasn't
released until September as a follow-up to "Like a Rolling Stone." It
was a hit, despite the angriest, meanest lyrics ever heard on AM radio
to date. (B+)   **10.** "Just Like a Woman": From *Blonde on Blonde,* 1966.
(Album Grade: A)

John Wesley Harding

Produced by Bob Johnston for Columbia Records
Recorded: October 17; November 6 and 29, 1967
Released: December 27, 1967

Chart Position   This was Dylan's first official album release in
a year and a half—an inordinate period of silence for someone who
had released three majestic records in a 14-month period from March
1965 to May 1966.

It rose to No. 2 on the charts and stayed there for four weeks. It
was on the charts for 21 weeks and earned Dylan his fifth straight gold
album.

Singles   No singles were released from this album.

Outtakes   There have been no outtakes from the three session
dates for this album.

The Cover   One of the strangest of all Bob Dylan album covers. Standing in the middle of two of the Bengali Bauls, wandering
minstrels who happened to be staying at manager Albert Grossman's
home in Woodstock, New York, Dylan wears what looks like the
same jacket he wore on *Blonde on Blonde.* He seems slimmer, wears a
hat and has a faint beard. There is no mention of who the other men
are nor any reference to the straw cowboy hat in the foreground, apparently on the head of someone who has been cropped out of the photograph.

Liner Notes   Dylan recounts a strange tale that is a parody of the
Three Wise Men visiting the baby Jesus in the manger in Bethlehem.

Three "jolly" kings visit Frank, Vera, and Terry Shute, hoping for the "key" to open up Mr. Dylan's new record. Frank asks them how far they want to go in.

"Just far enough so's we can say we've been there," one says.

Frank then goes through an absurdist routine, climaxed by putting his fist through a plate-glass window, a feat that should shatter their illusions. Instead, it seems to satisfy the three kings, who leave as new men. Dylan's work is a lot easier to understand if you reduce it to a clever epigram.

The Record   One of the most curious albums in the Bob Dylan canon. After the wild, impressionist watercolor sound of *Blonde on Blonde,* the last thing Dylan fans expected to hear was a stark, simple album of acoustic guitar, drums, and bass. But that's what they got on *John Wesley Harding.*

And the lyrics! What a changeover! It was as if William Faulkner decided to be Ernest Hemingway. Undoubtedly, Dylan is one of the few rock lyricists capable of changing his writing style so abruptly and so effectively.

However, if we had been able to hear "The Basement Tapes" Dylan was making with The Band that summer (they weren't released until 1975), the change in Dylan's writing might not have seemed as abrupt.

But fused with Dylan's newfound belief in Christianity on this album — Dylan's first "religious album" — the stripped-down lyrics worked.

Coming on the heels of the glorious excess of the Beatles' *Sergeant Pepper* album and the Rolling Stones' *Satanic Majesties Request, John Wesley Harding* was widely seen as a conscious back-to-the-roots statement by Dylan.

It may not have been quite that deliberate.

"I didn't intentionally come out with some kind of mellow sound," biographer Anthony Scaduto quoted Dylan as saying in *Bob Dylan: An Intimate Biography:*

> I would have liked a good sound, more musical, more steel guitar, more piano. More *music.* At that time, so many people were into electronics, and I didn't know anything about that. I didn't even know

41

anybody who knew it. I didn't sit down and plan that sound. It wasn't a question of this is what I'm doing and come over here.

Whether that was Dylan's intention or not, that is exactly the impact the album had on the rock music scene. It made everyone take stock of where the music was headed and seemed to be bring everyone back to the starting point.

SIDE ONE   1. "John Wesley Harding": Three verses and no chorus about a traveling man who opened many doors, never hurt an honest man, and carried a gun in every hand. Could it be the author? (B+) 2. "As I Went Out One Morning": In 1963, Dylan was the recipient of the Tom Paine Award from the Emergency Civil Liberties Committee. At the awards ceremony, he made an unpopular speech which is quoted at length on Martin Scorsese's "No Direction Home" (it's Scorsese who reads Dylan's speech!) and Dylan was supposedly booed and hustled off the stage. Four years later, Tom Paine appears at the end of this song about a man who is tempted to try to rescue a woman in chains — a symbol of oppressed people everywhere. He offers a helping hand, she takes his arm, and the rescuer immediately sees that he may be the one being exploited. Finally, Tom Paine appears on the scene, apologizing for her behavior. A protest song about the people who protested when Dylan stopped writing protest songs. (A)   3. "I Dreamed I Saw St. Augustine": Dylan has a revelation about his own career as a messiah through St. Augustine, a would-be prophet who recognized he had been sending a hollow message in an uncontrolled voice — a subtle wink at the critics who claimed that Dylan couldn't sing. When St. Augustine warns there is no martyr extant that the people can truly call their own, Dylan realizes his own hypocrisy. (A)   4. "All Along the Watchtower": In 12 vivid, concise lines written to a relentless melody, Dylan captures the mood shortly before the apocalypse. His own life, like that of the joker in the song, was filled with confusion and excess. He needed to get it straightened out before it was too late. And at least for a while, he did. The proof is *John Wesley Harding*. (A+)   5. "The Ballad of Frankie Lee and Judas Priest": A delightful tale of temptation and its consequences, Dylan's singing and harmonica playing carry the day. (A)   6. "Drifter's Escape": As Side

One closes, Dylan casts himself as a drifter who appears in court and is found guilty of something, perhaps also casting himself as a false prophet. The judge tells him that he, Dylan, doesn't understand. And as the crowd and jury cry for more, lightning strikes the courthouse. Dylan escapes. (B+)

SIDE TWO   7. "Dear Landlord": This song, Dylan's first at the piano since "Ballad of a Thin Man" two albums before, doesn't seem to fit thematically with the well-drawn songs on the first side, unless it is pointed at his audience. In the closing lines, he asks them not to underestimate him. He promises to do the same. (B)   8. "I Am a Lonesome Hobo": Dylan depicts himself as a man who once was wealthy but failed to trust his fellow man. This lack of trust led to his demise. (B)   9. "I Pity the Poor Immigrant": Similar to the song that preceded it, Dylan describes a man who simultaneously detests life and is afraid of death. Musically, he is running out of steam here. A much better and more lively version of this song was performed with Joan Baez on the Rolling Thunder Revue TV special "Hard Rain." (C+)   10. "The Wicked Messenger": The last "religious" song to be heard from Bob Dylan for a while, it is a scathing portrait of a con man. The closing line is a signpost for what lay ahead. This song was later covered by the Small Faces (and Rod Stewart) on their 1970 debut album *First Step*. (B+)   11. "Down Along the Cove": It's hard to imagine that this jaunty little tune at the piano came from the same man who had written "Sad-Eyed Lady of the Lowlands" or "Stuck Inside of Mobile with the Memphis Blues Again" a year earlier. (B+)   12. "I'll Be Your Baby Tonight": After hearing this country classic, it's hard to understand why Dylan's move into country music on his next album *Nashville Skyline* came as such a shock. This song would fit on that album nicely. (A)

Though the record falters on Side Two, *John Wesley Harding* remains a groundbreaking record for Bob Dylan. Certainly it marked an enormous change in his writing style, but it also revealed a man who no longer seemed to care about changing the world, as long as it left him alone. The Bob Dylan who wrote the songs for *Bringing It All Back Home* and *Highway 61 Revisited* did care. (Album Grade: B+)

Nashville Skyline

Produced by Bob Johnston for Columbia Records
Recorded: February 13, 14, 17, 1969
Released: April 9, 1969

Chart Position   One of Bob Dylan's shortest albums (just 27 minutes and 20 seconds), it was also one of his most commercially successful. Buoyed by the success of the single "Lay Lady Lay," *Nashville Skyline* rose to No. 3 and was on the charts for 31 weeks, earning Dylan his first platinum album for a regular release. *Greatest Hits* and *Greatest Hits, Vol. II* both became platinum albums for Dylan later on.

Singles   "I Threw It All Away," backed with "Drifter's Escape" from *John Wesley Harding*, was the first single released when the record came out in April; it rose to No. 85 on the charts. But "Lay Lady Lay," backed with "Peggy Day," came out in July and was a smash, going all the way to No. 7, spending 14 weeks on the charts, longer than any previous Dylan hit.

The third single from the record, "Tonight, I'll Be Staying Here with You," backed with "Country Pie," didn't do much on the charts, getting only to No. 50, but the song has remained one of Dylan's enduring favorites.

Outtakes   There are a wealth of outtakes from these sessions, most of them recorded on February 18 with Johnny Cash, including loose versions of Cash standards "Ring of Fire," "I Walk the Line" and "I Still Miss Someone." They have never officially been released either on *Biograph* or on *The Bootleg Series, Vols. 1–3*.

The Cover   A writer once described this cover as a photo of "Ragtime Country Bob," and that's a good description of the cover shot. Dylan is about to tip his hat, a brown fedora, as he holds his guitar in his left hand and smiles into the camera that looks up at him. He sports a wispy beard and looks much older than on previous albums, the lines around his eyes having deepened.

Liner Notes   Dylan turns the back of the album jacket over to his new friend, Johnny Cash, and Cash comes up with a pretty strange poem that concludes: "Here-in is a hell of a poet. And lots of other things. And lots of other things." Cash won a Grammy for these liner notes. Dylan has never won one for any of his. Go figure.

The Record   When this album hit in the spring of 1969, it was another shock. If *John Wesley Harding* was seen as a return to the basics, what about this Bob Dylan record with a steel guitar?

The record was extremely successful commercially, giving Dylan his first platinum album and a smash single: "Lay Lady Lay." And as so often is the case with Dylan, the whole is greater than the sum of its parts.

Still, it is hard to imagine Dylan doing a less consequential record. It's fun, like a sweet, cream-filled pastry, hardly the work of the doom-saying rock prophet of 1965.

Dylan was apparently having trouble with material. A record that is under 30 minutes to begin with hardly needs fillers. Yet how else would you classify the instrumental "Nashville Skyline Rag" and the cheery throwaways, "Peggy Day" and "Country Pie?"

When Dylan's next record was an awful two-album set of mostly cover versions, it appeared his muse had left him.

But you'll never hear Dylan's voice any sweeter or clearer than it is on this record. As he explained to *Rolling Stone*'s Jann Wenner, he had quit smoking: "When I stopped smoking, my voice changed.... That's true, I tell you, you stop smoking those cigarettes ... and you'll be able to sing like Caruso."

SIDE ONE   1. "Girl from the North Country" (with Johnny Cash): Since Dylan is so unpredictable, he's a hard guy to duet with. This sounds as if Cash wandered in off the street and Dylan handed him a set of lyrics and turned the tape on. But their voices sound good together. And it's fun. Wait until you hear Bob's voice. (B+)   2. "Nashville Skyline Rag": A lively instrumental. Dylan would revive a similar tune for his *Pat Garrett and Billy the Kid* soundtrack three years later and call it "Turkey Chase." (B)   3. "To Be Alone with You": A pleasant, country-flavored love song, later appropriated by Dylan — in a somewhat unrecognizable fashion — as his opening song on 1991 and 1992 tours. (B+)   4. "I Threw It All Away": An interesting song, written in the middle of what was a supposedly blissful time in Dylan's life. There is a sly sense of humor and a sadness at the loss of something he never knew he had. It was a strange time for a song like this. (A)   5. "Peggy Day": Though not exactly "It's

All Right, Ma," it is a pleasant, country-tinged ditty that's notable for Dylan's Elvis Presley–style finish. (B+)

SIDE TWO   **6.** "Lay Lady Lay": The song was written for the film *Midnight Cowboy*, but Dylan didn't have it finished in time so Fred Neil's "Everybody's Talkin'" was chosen. When Dylan recorded it, Columbia Records president Clive Davis heard it and wanted to release it as a single. "I begged and pleaded with him not to," Dylan said in the notes to *Biograph*. "I never felt too close to the song or felt it was representative of anything I do." But Davis released the song. "He thought it was a hit single," Dylan admitted. "And he was right." According to Patrick Humphries, in *Absolutely Dylan: An Illustrated Biography* (Patrick Humphries and John Bauldie, 1991), Dylan even offered the song to the Everly Brothers. They misunderstood one of the lyrics, which they thought said "across my big breasts," and thus declined it. (A)   **7.** "One More Night": Another song about love lost, only this time, it seems to be with a twinge of infidelity. Dylan sings he was so mistaken when he "thought that she'd be true." (B+)   **8.** "Tell Me That It Isn't True": Another song dealing with infidelity and insecurity — standard country music material, granted. But in back-to-back songs? Trouble in the Dylan kingdom or merely fantasy? (B)   **9.** "Country Pie": A crazy song, it's a good one to remember when you're trying to fill up a cassette and need one minute and 35 seconds of music. Dylan's having fun. (B)   **10.** "Tonight I'll Be Staying Here with You": A nice Nashville ballad to close Dylan's first step into country music. (A)

It certainly isn't indicative of the music Bob Dylan did before or after, but for its place and time, *Nashville Skyline* was a bright, pleasant statement that Dylan had found contentment in his life. At least for a while. (Album Grade: B+)

Self-Portrait

Produced by Bob Johnston for Columbia Records
Recorded: May and August 31, 1969; February–March, 1970
Released: June 8, 1970

Chart Position   Though the record deservedly drew slams from practically every major rock and roll critic, it rose to No. 4 and stayed on the charts for 12 weeks. It earned Dylan a gold album.

Singles   The only single released from this album was the instrumental "Wigwam," backed with "Copper Kettle." It went to No. 41 on the charts, higher than two of Dylan's previous three singles. Maybe some disc jockeys needed some background music.

Outtakes   Some of the outtakes from this record ended up being used for Columbia's 1973's release *Dylan*. One song, purportedly about Dylan meeting Elvis — "Went to See the Gypsy" — was released on *New Morning*. The rest of the them stayed in the can.

The Cover   Dylan had been interested in painting for a while. You wouldn't necessarily know it from the cover, a garish painting of a short-haired man with a large, blue-shaded nose and big ears.

Liner Notes   There are no liner notes for this album. Perhaps Dylan had nothing to say, a view that is not disputed by the record.

The Record   If someone had never heard of Bob Dylan and you played this record and told the person that Dylan was the finest songwriter of the rock and roll era, he or she would think you were crazy.

Ironically, Dylan went to Princeton University to receive an honorary doctorate in music the month this record was being released. Had the good folk there heard it, they might have withdrawn their offer.

In retrospect, *Self-Portrait* sounds like it was intended to be a mass-market record, something that Perry Como or Johnny Mathis might pick a song from. With the exception of a few songs, it is terrible. And the first blatantly wrong step Dylan had taken in a seven-year recording career.

Because of who he was, the record sold well — better than *The Basement Tapes* or *Oh Mercy* or even *Another Side of Bob Dylan* — earning Dylan a gold album that he must have wanted to give back.

Of course, Dylan has since dissociated himself from the record. "I didn't live with those songs too long," he told *Rolling Stone*'s Ben Fong-Torres in 1974. "They were just kind of scraped together."

The curious thing is that Dylan began recording it the month after *Nashville Skyline* came out. Why? Was he unsatisfied with that record — which seems unlikely — or did he think he had found a successful commercial formula and was anxious to do a follow-up record? Dylan has so repudiated what he did on this record that it's impossible to know the truth.

But we know these were difficult times in Bob Dylan's professional life. He continued to record, but since his motorcycle accident in 1966, his live performances were rare.

In June 1969, he appeared on "The Johnny Cash Show," performing "I Threw It All Away," "Living the Blues," and a duet with Cash, "Girl from the North Country."

The only two notable in-concert appearances were his participation at a Carnegie Hall concert honoring Woody Guthrie in January 1968, at which he did three sassy Guthrie numbers ("Dear Mrs. Roosevelt," "I Ain't Got No Home," and "Grand Coulee Dam"), backed by The Band (later released on Columbia) and a headline appearance, again backed by The Band, at the Isle of Wight Festival in August of that year.

Four songs from the Isle of Wight show ("Like a Rolling Stone," "The Mighty Quinn," "Minstrel Boy," and "She Belongs to Me") appear on *Self-Portrait.*

It was around this time that the first "bootleg" albums started to appear. The most famous of these albums was *Great White Wonder,* which combined early rare Dylan material with some cuts from *The Basement Tapes,* the demo Dylan made with The Band the summer he was recuperating from his motorcycle accident. The unreleased material, which was better than what Dylan was officially releasing, caused a sensation. Actually, it started a million-dollar black market industry, much to Dylan's distress.

As he explains at some length in the wonderful memoir *Chronicles, Vol. I,* it was a difficult time in his life. He told *Rolling Stone's* Kurt Loder in 1984,

> I was in Woodstock and I was getting a great degree of notoriety for doing nothing.
>
> I'd also seen that I was representing all these things that I didn't know anything about.... It was all storm-the-embassy kind of stuff—
> ... and they sort of figured me as the kingpin of all that. I said, "Wait a minute, I'm just a musician. So my songs are about this and that. So what?"

And when the Woodstock "nation" brought a generation of people to Dylan's town, he didn't know how to get rid of them.

> You'd come in the house and find people there, people comin' through the woods, at all hours of the day and night, knockin' on your door. It was really dark and depressing. And there was no way to respond to all this, you know? It was as if they were suckin' your very blood out. I said, "Now, wait, these people can't be my fans. They just can't be." And they kept comin.' We had to get out of there.

So, as Dylan explained to Loder, he decided to make a record that would convince those devotees that he wasn't the person to follow.

> But the whole idea backfired. Because the album went out there and people said "This ain't what we want" and they got more resentful.
> It wouldn't have held up as a single album — then it really would have been bad, you know. I mean, if you're going to put a lot of crap on it, you might as well load it up.

He did that, all right. But if he really wanted people just to leave him alone, why did *New Morning* follow just four months later? Dylan sort of explains that in *Chronicles, Vol. 1.* Sort of.

SIDE ONE   1. "All the Tired Horses": Dylan doesn't sing on this string-ridden, cocktail-hour soundtrack. Grim. (D)   2. "Alberta #1": Low-key blues with forgettable lyrics. (C)   3. "I Forgot More Than You'll Ever Know": This is a decent song that Dylan revived on his tours with Tom Petty and the Heartbreakers in the mid–80s. A whole album of songs like this would have been tolerable. (B)   4. "Days of 49": A fun, folky song, invoking the days of the old West. Memorable for Dylan's aside. (B)   5. "Early Mornin' Rain": A fair cover version of the Gordon Lightfoot hit. Dylan seems to have been a fan. (C+)   6. "In Search of Little Sadie": It's awful — no tune and terrible, wild singing. What could he have been thinking? (D)

SIDE TWO   7. "Let It Be Me": This is a nice, respectful cover of the old hit. Dylan later rerecorded this song as the B side of a European-released single "Heart of Mine." (B)   8. "Little Sadie": A catchy reworking of the song that ended Side One, its musicianship is lively, and so is Dylan's singing. (B+)   9. "Woogie Boogie": Uncle Bob leads the band through an instrumental romp. Fun. (B)   **10.** "Belle Isle": The strings are lame, and Dylan's singing is forced and out of tune. Otherwise, it's fine. (C)   **11.** "Living the Blues": This is a clever reworking of an old theme — the kind of song you would have thought someone would have written by then. Performed on Johnny Cash's TV show. (B+)   **12.** "Like a Rolling Stone" (live): You don't even have to hear the entire song. All you have to do is hear the chorus. Bob sounds like he's whining. Awful. (D)

SIDE THREE   **13.** "Copper Kettle": Strings again, and Bob is whining (out of tune) once more. Don't these producers listen? (C+) **14.** "Gotta Travel on": With conga drums and a halfhearted vocal, the urgency of the original is gone. (C)   **15.** "Blue Moon": If Dylan just played the crooner, it would be a lot easier to take. But the female chorus of "ooohs" makes it hard to take. The wild fiddle at the end helps. (C+)   **16.** "The Boxer": Dylan duets with himself without a clue about how to do it. It sounds like one voice is trying to catch up with the other one, and listening to it, you're so intent on the race that you don't notice what Paul Simon's lyrics say. (C)   **17.** "The Mighty Quinn (Quinn the Eskimo)" (live): A great, roaring version of a song from *The Basement Tapes* from the Isle of Wight concert. Dylan's voice is wild and all over the place, but the great chorus pulls it all together. (B+)   **18.** "Take Me as I Am": It's pure country, and not bad. Dylan's calm, honey-sweet voice sounds natural. (B)

SIDE FOUR   **19.** "Take a Message to Mary": The female chorus that opens the song is awful and trite. After that, the song is OK. (C+)   **20.** "It Hurts Me Too": A bluesy number with erratic singing that, in light of the rest of this record, is not bad. And the good news: There's no female chorus or strings. (B)   **21.** "Minstrel Boy" (live): A somewhat unusual song from the Isle of Wight concert, but not a good one. The Band and Dylan seem to be shouting about something instead of singing. (C)   **22.** "She Belongs to Me": Live from the Isle of Wight and sung in a nasal, hillbilly style *Nashville Skyline* voice that won't make anyone remember the gentility and honesty of the initial sentiment. It gets a good hand from the crowd. Not sure why. (C)   **23.** "Wigwam": Dylan wrote the "duh, duh, duh" lyrics to this otherwise instrumental his "ownself." And Columbia released it as a single! Talk about insulting your audience. (D)   **24.** "Alberta #2": Better than Alberta #1, but not by much. But we get the chorus again. (D)

If nothing else, *Self-Portrait* is a historic album, being the biggest miss by a star in rock and roll history. There are plenty of rock albums that are far worse than this, but none of them was recorded by an artist of Dylan's stature. Even John Lennon and the Elephant's Memory band were better than this. (Album Grade: C-)

New Morning

Produced by Bob Johnston for Columbia Records
Recorded: May 1; June–August, 1970
Released: October 21, 1970

Chart Position   Following the bust of *Self-Portrait,* Dylan appeared to have pangs of regret and rushed out *New Morning* just four months later, the fastest follow-up record in his career. His listeners were forgiving. It rose to No. 7 and was on the charts for 12 weeks, long enough to get Dylan his seventh gold album two months later.

Singles   There were no singles released from this album.

Outtakes   Four songs from these sessions made it onto 1973's *Dylan.* An alternate version of "If Not for You" with George Harrison on slide guitar came out on *The Bootleg Series, Vol. 1–3* in 1991.

The Cover   A famous portrait of Dylan, sporting a wispy beard, peering into Len Siegler's camera. He looks mature, serious and introspective.

Liner Notes   There are no liner notes to this album. The back cover features a photo of a young Dylan with the old blues singer Victoria Spivey from 1961.

The Record   After releasing the awful *Self-Portrait* on an unsuspecting, devoted audience, Dylan apparently felt ashamed — as well he should — and rushed out *New Morning* four months later, as close to an apology as Dylan fans were ever to get.

The critics were exultant but listening to the record in a more objective light, it's hard to understand their enthusiasm. It is merely a decent record, one that Dylan pulls off with the spirit of his performance more than with the quality of his writing.

One unusual feature of the record — Dylan plays piano on seven songs, more than he had ever done on any previous album. As he explains in *Chronicles, Vol. 1* some of these songs were written for a play written by Archibald MacLeish. Apparently, Bob was composing at the piano in those days.

On some numbers ("Time Passes Slowly") his singing is almost painful. It seems as if he's reaching for something with his voice he couldn't get with his pen.

SIDE ONE   **1.** "If Not for You": Bright and catchy love song with lusty harmonica breaks. George Harrison recorded his own version of this song on his first solo post–Beatles album *All Things Must Pass*. (A)   **2.** "Day of the Locusts": Reportedly written about his trip to Princeton to get his honorary degree; Dylan does a good job portraying how uneasy he felt around the halls of academia. And just to show these stuffed shirts he could play in their league, he borrowed the title of Nathaniel West's horrific 1939 novel for this song. (B+)   **3.** "Time Passes Slowly": The sounds of silence apparently drive Dylan nuts. Beneath the apparent contentment resides a disconcerting uneasiness in the lyric, music and Dylan's delivery. Strange. (C+)   **4.** "Went to See the Gypsy": Supposedly about meeting Elvis Presley, Dylan again seems uneasy in the presence of the King. But in the closing line, as he evokes dawn in a small Minnesota town (like Hibbing, Dylan's hometown), you can imagine Dylan, approaching 30, pondering his future. Not long after that, Elvis wound up in Las Vegas. Would Dylan? (B)   **5.** "Winterlude": A humorous little waltz that showed Dylan does not always have to be such a serious lyricist. (B)   **6.** "If Dogs Run Free": Dylan scats this jazzy tune while a cocktail piano and Maeretha Stewart wail away. A great song to play to stump your friends. Dig it, man. (A-)

SIDE TWO   **7.** "New Morning": A bright, lively cut, it was surprising this song never made it on Bob Dylan's Greatest Hits, Vol. II which appeared the following year. Nice organ by old friend Al Kooper (who played on Like a Rolling Stone). (A)   **8.** "Sign on the Window": Back at the piano again, Dylan's gentle singing comes as a surprise. It has a gospel quality to it. When Dylan gets to the last verse, where he describes the joys of being married and fatherhood you wonder if he really believes it. (C+)   **9.** "One More Weekend": An updated version of the same kind of blues vamp he did on "Leopard-Skin Pillbox Hat," it is good to hear him stomp again. (B+)   **10.** "The Man in Me": A concise, personal song to his wife; Dylan makes up in conviction what he lacks in melody. (B)   **11.** "Three Angels": Bob's first real hymn. To a prayer-like accompaniment, he talks the lyrics, which are corny but sincere. He seems to be trying so hard to be a believer. (C+)   **12.** "Father of Night": Back at the piano with a little more gospel. Not the kind of tune you would play at a party but... (C)

Though you may be convinced of Dylan's sincerity and his good intentions, the record fades badly after "One More Weekend." Would anyone play "Three Angels" or "Father of Night" or even "The Man in Me" for enjoyment?

It seems Dylan meant to heal things with this record and the religious finish to Side Two is appropriate.

But not very listenable. (Album Grade: B)

Bob Dylan's Greatest Hits, Vol. II

Compiled by Bob Dylan (uncredited) for Columbia Records Released: November 17, 1971

Chart Position   Unlike his other *Greatest Hits* collection, this one was released with Dylan's approval and assistance. But like his other *Greatest Hits* album, it brought Dylan a platinum album, his third. It went to No. 14 and stayed on the charts for 17 weeks.

Singles   "Watching the River Flow," a single recorded with Leon Russell, backed with a *Self-Portrait* outtake, "Spanish Is the Loving Tongue," was released in June, four months before the album came out, and rose to No. 41. In December, Dylan released what many called his first protest song in many years, "George Jackson," as a single. The song got as high as No. 33 and is somewhat of a collector's item. It has never been included on an American issue Dylan album.

The Cover   This album cover follows the same blue-background motif of *Bob Dylan's Greatest Hits*. The photos inside and on the back are from Dylan's surprise appearance at George Harrison's benefit concert for Bangladesh in August 1971.

Liner Notes   There are no liner notes to this album, only recording information that points out that the last three songs, "I Shall Be Released," "You Ain't Going Nowhere," and "Down in the Flood," were recorded in October 1971, which made the record appealing to Dylan devotees who had all his records. However, except for "Watching the River Flow," all the other "new" material was at least four years old.

The Record   It was more than a little ironic that at a time when Dylan's muse seemed to be drying up, he cut a single "Watching the River Flow," which included such a revealing opening line. Recorded with Leon Russell on piano, the single was released four months before *Greatest Hits, Vol. II,* shortly before Dylan's five-song performance at George Harrison's benefit Concert for Bangladesh, his first concert appearance in nearly two years.

In October, Dylan went into the studio with old friend Happy Traum and recut some old material. The two did "I Shall Be Released," which was included on The Band's *Music from Big Pink* and released in 1968. They also did "When I Paint My Masterpiece," which was included on The Band's *Cahoots* album, released earlier in 1971, and "You Ain't Going Nowhere" and "Down in the Flood," two songs from *The Basement Tapes.*

The only other previously unavailable song on the album was "Tomorrow Is a Long Time," a live recording from a 1963 concert at Carnegie Hall.

Oddly, Dylan included almost all the "new" material as the last five songs on the record following his farewell to the protest movement — "It's All Over Now, Baby Blue." What could that mean? What's all over, Bob?

In December, Dylan released "George Jackson," his first protest song in many years. Written about a black author and activist killed by guards in a California prison, it went to No. 33 on the single charts and quickly disappeared.

And so did Bob Dylan.

SIDE ONE   **1.** "Watching the River Flow": This is a jaunty little number with Leon Russell at the piano. Dylan, sounding as if he has a cold, zips through the song in fine form. (B+)   **2.** "Don't Think Twice, It's All Right": From *Freewheelin' Bob Dylan,* 1963.   **3.** "Lay Lady Lay": From *Nashville Skyline,* 1969.   **4.** "Stuck Inside of Mobile with the Memphis Blues Again": From *Blonde on Blonde,* 1966.

SIDE TWO   **5.** "I'll Be Your Baby Tonight": From *John Wesley Harding,* 1968.   **6.** "All I Really Want to Do": From *Another Side of Bob Dylan,* 1964.   **7.** "My Back Pages": From *Another Side of Bob Dylan,* 1964.   **8.** "Maggie's Farm": From *Bringing It All Back Home,* 1965.   **9.** "Tonight I'll Be Staying Here with You": From *Nashville Skyline,* 1969.

SIDE THREE   **10.** "She Belongs to Me": From *Bringing It All Back Home,* 1965.   **11.** "All Along the Watchtower": From *John Wesley Harding,* 1968.   **12.** "The Mighty Quinn (Quinn, the Eskimo)": From *Self-Portrait,* 1970.   **13.** "Just Like Tom Thumb's Blues": From *Highway 61 Revisited,* 1965.   **14.** "A Hard Rain's a-Gonna Fall": From *Freewheelin' Bob Dylan,* 1963.

SIDE FOUR   **15.** "If Not for You": From *New Morning,* 1970.   **16.** "It's All Over Now, Baby Blue": From *Bringing It All Back Home,* 1965.   **17.** "Tomorrow Is a Long Time": A delicate (how often can you say that about a Bob Dylan song?) concert performance, it makes you wonder why it took so long to release the Carnegie Hall Show of 1963. Two songs, "Who Killed Davey Moore?" and "John Birch Society Paranoid Blues," eventually were included on the 1991 *The Bootleg Series.* (A-)   **18.** "When I Paint My Masterpiece": More of Bob's "with a cold" voice. It is a funny, imaginative song, and the backing here, slide guitar and Leon Russell on piano, are superlative, though the singing is a bit out of tune, and somehow the song just misses. (B+)   **19.** "I Shall Be Released": Compare this pleasant, off-the-cuff version to Dylan's beautiful, aching rendition on *The Bootleg Series* and you hear the difference between an inspired performance and one to fill out a record. (B)   **20.** "You Ain't Going Nowhere": From the happy plunking banjo, a first on a Dylan record, to Dylan's joyous delivery, this song sounds like the kind of fun we imagined Dylan was having in his self-imposed exile in Woodstock. (B+)   **21.** "Down in the Flood": A strange song to conclude a greatest hits album, about missing your best friend. His muse, perhaps? (C) (Album Grade: A)

Pat Garrett and Billy the Kid Soundtrack

Produced by Gordon Carroll for Columbia Records
Recorded: January 20 and February 1973
Released: July 13, 1973

Chart Position   Propped up by the success of "Knockin' on Heaven's Door" as a single, the *Pat Garrett and Billy the Kid Soundtrack* went to No. 16 and stayed on the charts for 14 weeks. The album, however, did not go gold, Dylan's first miss out of the last 10 releases.

Singles   One of Dylan's simplest and most perfect songs, "Knockin' on Heaven's Door" was his highest charting single (No. 12) since "Lay Lady Lay" four years earlier. On the charts longer than any other Dylan single, 15 weeks, it was backed with the lively instrumental "Turkey Chase."

Outtakes   No outtakes from these sessions have been officially released.

The Cover   The cover has simple block lettering. Dylan is not shown, even on the back cover, which depicts Billy the Kid (Kris Kristofferson) being threatened with a shotgun.

Liner Notes   There are no liner notes with this album.

The Record   Since Dylan hadn't stepped into a recording studio with the idea of cutting a whole album in almost three years, the release of this record, a soundtrack really, was given more attention than usual — and far more than it deserved. Jon Landau, who later became Bruce Springsteen's manager, wrote a particularly scathing review in *Rolling Stone,* which had always been pro–Dylan. Outside of the shocked reviews of *Self-Portrait,* this was the first sign that Dylan was no longer a favorite of the critics.

SIDE ONE   **1.** "Main Title Theme": A soft Western-style instrumental with acoustic guitars, maracas, and Spanish guitar flourishes, this song is much more listenable than "Wigwam." (C+)   **2.** "Cantina Theme": This song has bongos, more acoustic guitars, and another instrumental. The feeling of the song is similar to that of "Knockin' on Heaven's Door" without the haunting minor chords. (C)   **3.** "Billy 1": First, Bob plays the harmonica and, finally, he sings a mournful ballad about Billy the Kid. His voice sounds like it did on *New Morning,* but maybe a little clearer. This is the best version of the three on the record. Not exactly a wealth of material, is it? (B+)   **4.** "Bunkhouse Theme": Another soft instrumental with acoustic guitars. Nice enough, but nothing outstanding. (C)   **5.** "River Theme": Bob and chorus do a few "duh-duh-duh-duhs" as the acoustic guitars play on for one minute, 32 seconds. (C)

SIDE TWO   **6.** "Turkey Chase": Byron Berline's fiddle and Jolly Roger McGuinn's banjo make this a fun instrumental. (C+)   **7.** "Knockin' on Heaven's Door": An extraordinary song that was Dylan's most successful single in years, it manages to evoke the Old West, sunrise, sunset, life, and death, all in barely more than two minutes. It has been covered by everyone from Eric Clapton to heavy metal bands. Nobody did it better than Dylan did here. (A+)   **8.** "Final Theme": This is an instrumental replaying of "Knockin' on Heaven's Door" with harmonium, cellos, recorder, and flute. It's nice and relaxing. A critic once called this album Dylan's mantra. This song is why. (B)   **9.** "Billy 4": Different lyrics, pretty much the same delivery as "Billy 1," which isn't bad. But three versions of the same song on the same record sort of hints at Bob's musical desperation at this point. (C)   **10.** "Billy 7": A third version of the same song, something Dylan never even tried on *Self-Portrait.* Pitched lower than the previous two, his voice is deep and sounds peculiar. (C+)

For a soundtrack album featuring four new Bob Dylan songs (actually two new songs — one song is played three different ways) in 1973, it's OK. Dylan was lying low at that point and many people were encouraged to pick up the record, just happy to hear from him at all. Still, it's not worth much in the Dylan canon. (Album Grade: C+)

Dylan

Sessions produced by Bob Johnston for Columbia Records
Recorded: May 1969 and February–March, May 1, and June–August 1970
Released: November 16, 1973

Chart Position   For a collection of three- and four-year-old outtakes that were never meant to see the light of day *Dylan* did surprisingly well. It went to No. 17, was on the charts for seven weeks, and earned Dylan his eighth gold album.

Singles   "A Fool Such as I," backed with "Lily of the West," was released in November; it went to No. 55.

Outtakes   Since the record itself consisted of outtakes, there are none from this album.

The Cover   A silver serigraph of Bob Dylan done in profile by Richard Kenerson off an original photograph by Al Clayton, it is as bad as the record.

Liner Notes   Since the record was put together by the Columbia Records staff without Dylan's approval, naturally, there are no liner notes.

The Record   Released by Columbia Records when Dylan decided to pack up and record for David Geffen's Asylum Records, it is a collection of outtakes from previous Dylan albums — make that previous "bad" Dylan albums.

Unless you're an absolute, diehard fan who wants to collect all Dylan's work, pass this one up. It's silly and hardly representative of his work, though it is probably better than *Self-Portrait*.

SIDE ONE   **1.** "Lily of the West": A fast-strumming, predictable tune of life in the Old West. The insipid chorus knocks it down a grade. (C+)   **2.** "Can't Help Falling in Love": Featuring slow, quiet organ music and Bob's harmonica playing and out-of-tune singing, it's pretty grim stuff. (D)   **3.** "Sarah Jane": This is another fast-strumming, funny song, but hearing the finest lyric poet of his generation singing along with a god-awful chorus of "La-la-la-la" is distressing. (C-)   **4.** "The Ballad of Ira Hayes": With Bob sitting in at the piano, the verses of the song are talked. At least Bob can say he didn't write it. Awful. (D)

SIDE TWO   **5.** "Mr. Bojangles": This is not a bad version of this song, even though Dylan's singing is a little out of pitch and you do have to suffer through another chorus. But Bob has a funny moment when, near the end of the song, he calls out to dance. (B)   **6.** "Mary Ann": Some old song that would have been better left forgotten, with another awful chorus that seems determined to drown Bob out. In the end, however, you end up rooting for them. (D)   **7.** "Big Yellow Taxi": Not only does this cover version of Joni Mitchell's song sound as though

Dylan has no idea what the song is about, the organ is spooky and, of course, there's the chorus. It's possibly the dumbest cover version he ever recorded. (F)   **8.** "A Fool Such as I": With his *Nashville Skyline* voice, Bob sounds like a hip combination of Don Knotts, Elvis Presley, and Wayne Newton. Again, the chorus is grim, but the guitar work is snappy and Dylan's singing is surprisingly confident. (B)   **9.** "Spanish Is the Loving Tongue": His heart is certainly in it, and the song is more intricately arranged than any other Dylan song. Though not worth buying the album for, it is a great one to play for people and ask them who is singing. (B)

If Bob Dylan had his way, this record would never have been released. He had the right idea. (Album Grade: C-)

Planet Waves

Produced by Rob Fraboni for Asylum Records
Recorded: November 2, 5, 6, 9, 10, 1973
Released: January 17, 1974

Chart Position   Dylan's first album of all-new material in five years, *Planet Waves* went right to the top of the charts, his first No. 1 record, 13 years after his recording career began. It stayed at No. 1 for four weeks and was on the charts for 12 weeks in all, earning Dylan his ninth gold album.

Singles   "On a Night Like This," backed with "You Angel You," was released as a single in February to coincide with Dylan and The Band's national tour. Neither it nor the follow-up, "Something There Is About You," backed with "Going, Going, Gone," did much on the charts. "On a Night Like This" got to No. 44 in a six-week stint. "Something" didn't even make the Top 100.

Outtakes   "Nobody 'Cept You," recorded the first day of the five-day stint was left off *Planet Waves*. It was finally released on *The Bootleg Series, Vols. 1–3* in 1991.

The Cover   Bob's artwork had not improved much since *Self-Portrait*. The cover, done in black and gray on a white background, seems to depict a guy with an anchor on his forehead, an arrow through his heart, and faces lurking on either side of him.

The word "Moonglow" is along the lower left-hand side of the painting. "Cast-Iron Songs and Torch Ballads" is on the other side, with "Planet Waves" painted on the top.

Liner Notes   For the first time since *John Wesley Harding,* Dylan included liner notes with the early versions of this record, replete with some misspellings ("Richard Manual," "Ann Arbour," and "serpant") and some crudity ("space guys off duty with big dicks and duck tails" and "Furious gals with garters & smeared lips on bar stools that stank from sweating pussy"). It's not one of Bob's better efforts, but it conveys the excitement he felt at recording and touring again after an eight-year absence.

The Record   Recorded in five days in early November before Bob Dylan and The Band set out on a nationwide tour that was Dylan's first in eight years, *Planet Waves* was thrown together quickly, and it sounds it. Which isn't necessarily a bad thing.

The lyrics are basic and surprisingly straightforward. It is hard to think of another album on which Dylan has sounded so open and easy to understand.

Oddly, though they had toured together several times and had been together since the mid–60s, this was the first officially released collaboration between The Band and Dylan.

Some of the critics were overjoyed at the record. Writing in *Rolling Stone*, Ralph J. Gleason called it "an instant classic," which it is not. Others were more perceptive. When "You Angel You" was included on *Biograph* in 1985, Greil Marcus was moved to write:

> That the fact that the 1964 "It Ain't Me Babe" can be placed on an album next to the 1974 "You Angel You" is a denial of everyone's best hopes.... "You Angel You" is a bouncy piece of junk; an affirmation of nothing.
>
> "It Ain't Me Babe" was always a fine song, but on *Biograph,* remastered, the voice brought forward, allowed to change its shape with every word — it is overwhelming. Here Dylan moves from certainty to an ambiguity that frightens him back toward a certainty the falsity of which he has just revealed.

In the liner notes to *Biograph,* Dylan pretty much disavowed *Planet Waves.* About the opening song, "On a Night Like This," he told Cameron Crowe, "Sometimes you're affected by people thinking you're too heavy. You know? — I think this comes off as sort of like a drunk man who's temporarily sober. This is not my type of song. I think I just did it to do it."

About "You Angel You," the B side of the album's first single, "On a Night Like This," Dylan was even more blunt: "I might have written this at one of the sessions, probably, you know, on the spot, standing in front of the mike — it sounds like dummy lyrics."

Or the best a scared Bob Dylan could come up with after eight years off the road.

SIDE ONE   **1.** "On a Night Like This": Propelled by a lively harmonica solo that somehow evokes good times, sea chanteys, and backroom card games, it's a fine introduction to Dylan's first step back to the world of recording. A fun song. (A-)   **2.** "Going, Going, Gone": This is a song of torment, lifted by Robbie Robertson's spooky guitar and Garth Hudson's eerie organ. But for Dylan, the lyrics are pedestrian. (B-) **3.** "Tough Mama": The best song on the record. Dylan's rockin' voice blends perfectly with Hudson's soaring lines on the organ, and the funky, doughty tune the two stomp out has more life than anything he had recorded in years. (A)   **4.** "Hazel": A song performed by Dylan and The Band at the Winterland concert filmed by Martin Scorsese for *The Last Waltz,* but left out of the film, it is a softly sung ballad with lyrics, again, that you would have a hard time believing were written by Bob Dylan. (B-)   **5.** "Something There Is About You": A nice, new love song in which Dylan sings about his past, the hills of Duluth and the "phantoms" of his youth. But with a curious twist, Dylan tells this mystery woman he could say he'd be faithful but to her, it would be "cruelty" and to him, it would be "death." A strange marriage. (B)   **6.** "Forever Young": A song that Dylan said he wrote in Tucson for his sons, it has since become a standard. Bob and The Band do this up proudly. This one made the movie, *The Last Waltz.* (A)

SIDE TWO   **7.** "Forever Young": A jaunty little romp with a playful harmonica solo, it's almost as if Bob thought the previous version might be too corny, so he offered this one as an antidote. The

61

lively accompaniment kind of trashes the lyrics, but what the heck. (A)
8. "Dirge": A scary song with Dylan at the piano, spitting out lyrics
more like his listeners were used to hearing from him. It's a haunted
look at a relationship (Albert Grossman? Joan Baez?) that Dylan can't
quite figure out. Neither can we. (B+)   **9.** "You Angel You": A bouncy
piece of "junk"— that's what critic Greil Marcus called it. Actually, the
song lightens the mood considerably after "Dirge." It loses something
taken out of context. Who said Bob Dylan had to write "A Hard Rain's
Gonna Fall" every time out? (B)   **10.** "Never Say Goodbye": This song
has an unusual melody and lyrics that seem quite simple and direct —
and sort of boring. (C)   **11.** "Wedding Song": An impassioned love
song to his wife (we assume), performed by Bob alone on guitar and
harmonica. It is stark, sharply written, and may be telling us why Dylan
stayed out of the public arena as long as he did. At the end of the fourth
verse, Dylan sings of sacrificing the world for his wife. (A-)

Displaying some lyrics that seem tame, cautious, and even fearful, *Planet Waves* emerges as not quite the portrait of domestic bliss
that some critics have claimed. It depicts an artist in conflict with his
personal life and his calling. (Album Grade: A-)

Before the Flood

Recorded live in January and February 1974 at the close of the Bob
  Dylan/The Band American Tour 1974
Released on Asylum Records (June 20, 1974)

Chart Position   Dylan and The Band's first official live album,
coming on the heels of his first national tour in eight years, climbed to
No. 3 and was on the charts for ten weeks, earning Dylan and The
Band a gold album. It was Dylan's 10th.

Singles   Dylan's "Most Likely You Go Your Way (I'll Go Mine),"
backed with The Band performing "Stage Fright," was released in June
and got as high as No. 55 on the charts.

Outtakes   To date, there have been no officially released outtakes
from the tour.

The Cover   To steal a phrase from former President George Bush, you can spot "a thousand points of light" on this cover as fans hold matches aloft, asking for an encore at one live date.

Liner Notes   There are no liner notes to this album. The inside jacket features color shots of Dylan and the five members of The Band.

The Record   With a wry title, *Before the Flood* (of bootlegs), Dylan's first entirely live recording has held up pretty well since its release in 1974. Though the most recent song on it is 1972's "Knockin' on Heaven's Door," Dylan and The Band play with ferocious energy.

On stage for the first time since 1966, Dylan sounds nervous and frightened much of the time. So instead of trying to sing these old songs differently each night, he decided to holler them. Like Robbie Robertson said to Barney Hoskyns in his book on the band, Across the Great Divide, it was as if he could "drill these songs into people."

There are no introductions, and except for a "Thank You" here and there, Dylan spoke no words to an audience who hadn't heard from him in eight years.

SIDE ONE   **1.** "Most Likely You Go Your Way (and I'll Go Mine)": This is a hard-charging rendition of one of the most straight-forward tracks on *Blonde on Blonde.* Dylan's voice sounds strong and clear. His singing is aggressive, filled with exclamation points, and it's faster and harsher than the record. The Band sounds great. (A-)   **2.** "Lay Lady Lay": This bears no resemblance to the countrified croon Bob turned into a hit single. It sounds more like a dare, which is probably the idea. Different. (B)   **3.** "Rainy Day Women #12 and 35": The Band lends a much more stolid foundation to this tune, which had a Salvation Army band cast to it on *Blonde on Blonde.* There's a nice organ solo by Garth Hudson, and a fine Robbie Robertson guitar solo ends the song. (A-)   **4.** "Knockin' on Heaven's Door": Backed by The Band, replete with harmonies from Rick Danko and Richard Manuel, this version becomes much more of an anthem than the single was. (A)   **5.** "It Ain't Me Babe": Like "Lay Lady Lay," this version bears no resemblance to the bold statement of personal independence on *Another Side of Bob Dylan.* Critics often spoke of Dylan reinterpreting his work on this tour. That is exactly what he did on songs like this. (A-)   **6.** "Ballad of a Thin Man": This version is similar to the

Highway 61 version except faster, and Garth Hudson's spooky organ fills add something unusual to it. This version is not as scary as the first version, but it's funnier and more lively. (A)

SIDE TWO   7. "Up on Cripple Creek": With Dylan off for a short break, Levon Helm's fine singing and some nice ensemble playing make this song an in-concert delight for The Band. It wasn't until the second or third song of their set that the audience started hollering for Dylan. (A)   8. "I Shall Be Released": The late Richard Manuel's falsetto on a Dylan track circa the *Basement Tapes* is nice if a little raspy. A song as intimate as this is hard to put across in concert, but The Band gives it a good treatment. (B+)   9. "Endless Highway": The only song of this double-album set not previously released, it's one of those old songs of the road. Rick Danko's vocal is pleasant, as is Robertson's guitar solo. But on a night of classics, it sounds like a filler. (B)   10. "The Night They Drove Old Dixie Down": One of The Band's trademark songs, it is performed here with passion and delicacy. Garth Hudson's synthesizer is everywhere. (A)   11. "Stage Fright": Some have speculated that this song is about Dylan, particularly since on this tour, The Band would often play it as the opening number of their set — following Bob Dylan. One of The Band's classics, Rick Danko has sung it better than he does here. (A-)

SIDE THREE   12. "Don't Think Twice, It's All Right": Dylan returned to the stage for a three- or four-song solo set. He did a lot of fooling around with his voice, playing the songs faster than he had recorded them. To some people, it was unsettling. This song survives the up tempo treatment pretty well. And the harmonica solo helps. (A) 13. "Just Like a Woman": Whereas the original was gentle, here Dylan's vocal mannerisms, running words together and twisting them all over the place, make the listener uneasy. There is nothing sensitive about this version of the song. There should be. (B-)   14. "It's Alright, Ma (I'm Only Bleeding)": With his speeded-up, angry delivery, the song never sounded better than when Dylan played it on the 1974 tour. With audiences all over the country standing and screaming when he reached the line about the president standing naked — this, in the midst of Watergate — it was Dylan at his most prophetic. (A+)   15. "The Shape I'm In": After the show-stopping Dylan solo sets, The Band came back for three or four numbers before the big finish. This rocker was a good way to get the crowd back on their side. (A-)   **16.** "When You Awake": Never a particularly great song by The Band, Danko's singing is halting. It is the weakest song on the record. (C+)   **17.** "The Weight": The one song by The Band that Bob Dylan probably wishes he had written, Robbie Robertson's tale of moral responsibility is sung and played wonderfully. (A)

SIDE FOUR   **18.** "All Along the Watchtower": Once Dylan returned to the stage, he and The Band closed out their show. With a nod to Jimi Hendrix, this rendition was faster and tougher than the calm, eerie version on *John Wesley Harding*. Robertson's guitar work propels the song. The ending, where it sounds like The Band just decided to stop playing, could have been a little more thought out. (A)   **19.** "Highway 61 Revisited": There may be a melody here somewhere, but it's hard to find it. This version bears little resemblance to the raucous one on the album of the same name. Despite the great lyrics, between Dylan yelling and Robertson's string bending, it's the weakest Dylan-Band song on the record. (B)   **20.** "Like a Rolling Stone": With the house lights on and everyone standing and screaming, Dylan chose his most popular song to climax every show on his triumphant comeback tour. The Band plays with fury, and Dylan sings it surprisingly straight. But as good as this version is, it pales next to the live version from his 1966 tour. But then, so does every other Dylan live recording. (A)   **21.** "Blowin' in the Wind": A little ragged perhaps, but Bob and The Band sent everyone home with this benediction. In some locations, Dylan closed the show with the same song he opened with: "Most Likely You Go Your Way, I'll Go Mine." "It completes a circle in some way," he told *Rolling Stone*'s Ben Fong-Torres. (A-)

For being off the road for so long, Dylan and The Band's return to the stage was a huge success. The shows were sell-outs, and this record sold well enough to earn Dylan and The Band gold albums. In most cases, the renditions of these Dylan classics were not the respectful, familiar ones fans expected. I guess that was the idea. (Album Grade: A-)

Blood on the Tracks

Engineered by Phil Ramone for Columbia Records
Recorded: September 16–17, 23–25 and December 27–30, 1974
Released: January 17, 1975

Chart Position   Dylan's second No. 1 record in two years, it stayed at the top for two straight weeks and was on the charts for 14 in all. It earned Dylan a platinum album award, his fifth, on August 8, 1989.

Singles   "Tangled Up in Blue," one of Dylan's best-liked songs in recent years, wasn't successful as a single, getting only to No. 31. Backed with "If You See Her, Say Hello," it was on the charts for seven weeks.

Outtakes   Dylan first recorded most of the songs for the album in September in New York. Then over Christmas, he apparently decided to recut several of them in Minneapolis. Most of the original versions have since been released.

"You're a Big Girl Now" and "Up to Me" were released on 1985's *Biograph*. The original "Tangled Up in Blue"; "Idiot Wind"; "If You See Her, Say Hello"; and "Call Letter Blues" (an early version of "Meet Me in the Morning") were released on 1991's *The Bootleg Series, Vols. 1–3*.

The Cover   This out-of-focus, impressionistic shot of Dylan in profile, wearing sunglasses, has a wine-red flavor to it. Though it looks like a drawing, on the back Paul Till is credited with doing the cover photo.

Liner Notes   Some introspective liner notes by novelist-journalist Pete Hamill, which were included on the early editions, won Hamill a Grammy. This was the second time that liner notes for a Dylan album won the award; Johnny Cash's was the other. Dylan, however, had the essay removed and replaced by an abstract drawing in later editions.

The Record   The finest record Bob Dylan had released since *Blonde on Blonde, Blood on the Tracks* caused enough of an uproar for *Rolling Stone* magazine to devote its entire review section to a single release — unprecedented for the magazine.

The record is worth it. Dylan's writing has rarely been better; his singing is relaxed and confident, and the melodies are clean and clear. Essentially an acoustic record, it has an edge that *John Wesley Harding* did not, particularly with "Tangled Up in Blue," its finest song.

At the time, it was widely seen as Dylan's desperate plea to his wife, who, rumor had it, had thrown him out. One record critic even went so far as to conclude that the album was Dylan's way of begging Sara for forgiveness. "I find myself hoping she takes him back," he wrote.

Not used to having record reviewers cut so near to his personal life, Dylan has, in the years since the record's release, done everything he could to cloud the circumstances behind the songs on this remarkable record. In *Biograph,* he claimed the record was influenced more by his newfound interest in painting, which it may well have been.

He would have us believe that the painful separation and ultimate divorce had no effect on his music or his songwriting. It obviously did. There is no denying that Dylan has a personal, emotional stake in these songs, more so than any he's done since his return to the music scene in 1974.

Though he only admitted it once, he did own up to what it all meant to him. Speaking on Mary Travers's (of Peter, Paul and Mary) radio show in 1975, he admitted that all the praise for the record threw him: "A lot of people tell me they enjoy that album. It's hard for me to relate to that," he said, "I mean, people enjoying that kind of pain."

Similarly, in recent years, Dylan has dismantled "Tangled Up in Blue"—his best-loved song since "Like a Rolling Stone"—claiming that he didn't get it right on *Blood on the Tracks.* As he told Bill Flanagan in an interview for a book on songwriting, *Written in My Soul* (itself a line from the song):

> I always wanted it to be the way I recorded it on "Real Live." ... But there was no particular reason for it to be that way, because I'd already made the record.
>
> That was another of those songs where you're writing and you've got it, you know what it's about, but half of it you just don't get the way you wanted to. Then I fixed it up and now it's where it should be.

The major change in the song was to take the first person, the "I," out of the first verse. It depersonalizes the song, which is likely what Dylan had in mind.

Instead of a personal, unblinking account of Bob Dylan's life as a modern-day troubadour — which is the way almost everyone heard the original — we get a tangled tale of someone else that only succeeds in confusing us.

When U2 won a Grammy Award for *The Joshua Tree*, one of the people they thanked was Bob Dylan for "Tangled Up in Blue." If they had only heard the version on *Real Live*, they might not have spoken up.

SIDE ONE   1. "Tangled Up in Blue": Rarely has Bob Dylan matched music and words so aptly as he has on this song. The tale of interrupted love is perfectly matched by the melody, built around a two-chord riff. As the riff builds, the song begins to gather momentum as the chorus approaches — like the buildup of the relationship. Then comes a succession of quick chord changes — symbolizing the sudden, abrupt shifts in his life — and he delivers the title line, a perfect metaphor for his situation. He then returns to the opening riff, back to the beginning — the same old problems all over again. And on the song goes. His closing harmonica solo, trying to dance in the face of these heartaches, is almost heroic. (A+)   2. "Simple Twist of Fate": A sad tale of love lost, Dylan has rarely seemed so vulnerable as he does here. His singing, passionate and intense, is superb. (A)   3. "You're a Big Girl Now": Infidelity had seemed a major theme in Dylan's work, since his marriage to Sara in 1965. It ran underneath the happy surface of *Nashville Skyline* and surfaces again here. From this song, the marriage sounds over, and Dylan is filled with regret. (A)   4. "Idiot Wind": In this angry diatribe at someone who has disrupted his life, Dylan sounds like a man trying to, as the lyrics say, "rise above" the circumstances. But he's still too angry, the pain too fresh and too real. The original version included a line about "ladykillers" which was stricken from the record version. What can all that mean? (A-)   5. "You're Going to Make Me Lonesome When You Go": Resigned to her leaving, Dylan tries to make the best of a sad situation. Only when we hear him try to inject the song with humor do we realize how deeply this has all wounded him. (A)

SIDE TWO   6. "Meet Me in the Morning": A country blues

song, developed from the revealing "Call Letter Blues," which was later released on *The Bootleg Series,* it's a song of coping. (A-)   **7.** "Lily, Rosemary and the Jack of Hearts": A strange tall tale with lively backing from Eric Weissberg and Deliverance, the Jack of Hearts appears as a mysterious figure, not unlike "The Man in the Long Black Coat," which would appear on the 1989 album *Oh Mercy.* Some contend that "Up to Me," a powerful declaration of artistic purpose, recorded at these sessions but unreleased until *Biograph,* would have fit better with the songs on this record. That may be true, but this song serves as a fun change of pace. (B+)   **8.** "If You See Her, Say Hello": In this touching, mature song of farewell, Dylan's open-hearted singing and heartfelt delivery are uncharacteristic. (A)   **9.** "Shelter from the Storm": The story of "Tangled Up in Blue" told from a later viewpoint, it is a painful look at a man's life and the shattering of a relationship. Dylan's writing is vivid, poignant, and achingly honest, while the music is gently accepting. A classic. (A+)   **10.** "Buckets of Rain": After the fierce "Shelter from the Storm," this restatement of commitment closes the album on a note of what might have been. (A)

Since his return to the rock and roll scene in 1974, Bob Dylan had never written a better collection of songs and never sung them with as much care or arranged an album with as much devotion as he did this one. Dylan told *Rolling Stone's* Jonathan Cott in 1978 that "everyone agrees [the record] was pretty different, and what's different about it is that there's a code in the lyrics and also there's no sense of time."

What's different about the record is that, for the first and perhaps only time in his professional career, Bob Dylan found himself in a state of such emotional distress that his only method of coping with it was to reach out to his audience through his songs. He never did it any more openly than on *Blood on the Tracks.* (Album Grade: A)

The Basement Tapes

Recorded: Summer 1967 in the basement of Big Pink, West Saugerties, New York
Released: June 26, 1975, on Columbia Records

Chart Position   The long-awaited *Basement Tapes* was officially released in late June and rose to No. 7. But the album was on the charts only for nine weeks, not long enough to earn Dylan a gold album.

Singles   The nonsensical "Million Dollar Bash," backed with "Tears of Rage," was released in July. It did not make the singles charts.

Outtakes   Originally recorded as demo tapes, the album itself contains outtakes. A few not included in the 1975 release have come out since. *Biograph* featured a funny version of "Quinn the Eskimo." *The Bootleg Series, Vols. 1–3* included a delightful "Santa Fe" from the personal archives of Garth Hudson of The Band and another version of "I Shall Be Released," a song Dylan included in a different version on *Greatest Hits, Vol. II.*

The Cover   This is a clever, funny cover, with Dylan and the five members of The Band in circus like getup with a wild cast of characters. The inside photo is even funnier, with Dylan cuddling up to a nun.

Liner Notes   This album gets a scholarly if somewhat perplexing analysis by renowned rock and roll writer Greil Marcus. He does a good job of framing the songs in a historical context, but a somewhat less effective job in explaining how Dylan came up with such imaginative and bizarre lyrics. It was a gallant effort on his part, but largely, the origins and subjects of these songs remain a mystery.

The Record   Certainly one of the more unusual records in Dylan's career, these songs were recorded with members of The Band during the summer Dylan was recuperating from his motorcycle accident.

Since many of the songs were included on *The Great White Wonder* bootleg album, Dylan's audience wondered if he'd ever get around to releasing them officially. Finally, in 1975, Robbie Robertson started compiling the two-record set, and it was released in June. Dylan was not impressed.

"I never really liked *The Basement Tapes*," he told *Rolling Stone* magazine's Kurt Loder. "I mean, they were just songs we had done for the publishing company, as I remember. They were used only for other artists to record those songs. I wouldn't have put them out. But you know, Columbia wanted to put 'em out, so what can you do?"

A fan of the record, Loder persisted, asking Dylan if he thought the record has a great aura. Dylan replied, "I can't even remember it. People have told me they think it's very Americana and all that. I don't know what they're talkin' about."

Of the 24 titles on the record, Dylan wrote 16 with two collaborations, one with the late Richard Manuel ("Tears of Rage"), the other with Rick Danko ("This Wheel's on Fire").

Writing in New York's *Village Voice,* record critic Robert Christgau called *The Basement Tapes* the best record of the year. "We needn't bow our heads in shame because this is the best album of 1975," he wrote. "It would have been the best record of 1967 too. And it's sure to sound great in 1983."

SIDE ONE **1.** "Odds and Ends": The published lyrics have a different first line than what is on the record. A mid-tempo rocker, it seems to be a Dylan brush-off. (B+) **2.** "Orange Juice Blues": A solid Richard Manuel composition, featuring an outstanding tenor sax solo from Garth Hudson. (B) **3.** "Million Dollar Bash": This is one of the craziest of Dylan's songs. His campy delivery of such nonsensical lyrics is a delight, even if no one understands what the song is about. Dylan has said he wrote these songs for other people. Who would record this one: The Carpenters? (A-) **4.** "Yazoo Street Scandal": One of Robbie Robertson's best rockers, it recalls his description of The Band's beginnings. "We had one thing on our minds," Robertson told Greil Marcus in *Mystery Train:* "Stomp." (A) **5.** "Goin' to Acapulco": Dylan's sly, sober delivery of a trip to Mexico is a scream. How he was able to sing it all the way through without The Band cracking up is amazing. (A-)

SIDE TWO **6.** "Lo and Behold": This is another funny song that has some great, ribald lines, with members of The Band joining in with Dylan on the chorus. It seems to have something to do with Molly's mound and Moby Dick's trip to Chicken Town. (A-)

7. "Bessie Smith": There is some good ensemble singing by The Band on this tribute to the late blues singer. (B) **8.** "Clothes Line Saga": This is a scathing parody of Bobbie Gentry's "Ode to Billie Joe." Only Dylan could write a song about hanging clothes and talking to neighbors and make it seem like an act of subversion. (A) **9.** "Apple Suckling Tree": There is no explanation for the lyrics to this song. But Garth

71

Hudson's organ solo is wonderful and Dylan's singing is, well, jubilant. What does it all mean? These guys have a good time playing together. (A) **10.** "Please, Mrs. Henry": More bawdy lyrics about trying to make it to the men's room in time. Reportedly, Neil Young always kept a copy of *The Basement Tapes* around when he was recording. Good-natured, droll humor like this was sure to lighten any recording session. (A) **11.** "Tears of Rage": One of the "serious" songs on the record, it was the first known collaboration between Dylan and another artist. Dylan hinted to *Rolling Stone* magazine interviewer Jonathan Cott that this song and "Too Much of Nothing" were influenced by Shakespeare's *King Lear.* (A)

SIDE THREE **12.** "Too Much of Nothing": In this stately number with an unusual ascending melody, Dylan harmonizes with The Band on the chorus. Quite a change from the levity of "Please Mrs. Henry." (A-) **13.** "Yea, Heavy and a Bottle of Bread": Back to the weirdness, with lyrics that don't quite make sense, sung in Dylan's deadpan style, which must have had every member of The Band ready to break into laughter. (B+) **14.** "Ain't No More Cane": One of The Band's finest songs, evoking gospel, country, and good-time music in three-part harmony, you wonder how this never made it onto a record. You can imagine hearing this song at a 1910 hoedown. And that's a compliment. (A) **15.** "Crash on the Levee (Down in the Flood)": An alternative version of the song Dylan included on *Greatest Hits II,* it seems infinitely preferable to the version Bob cut with Happy Traum. Dylan's voice is more evocative, and The Band's backing, particularly Garth Hudson's organ, is very nice. (B) **16.** "Ruben Remus": This is one of The Band's rare novelty songs. Richard Manuel's vocal is loose and funny, and there's a great chorus. (B) **17.** "Tiny Montgomery": Sounding like Father Time, Dylan sends cryptic greetings to an old friend. The Band pitches in full bore. On songs like this, they sound as if they were meant to record with one another. (A-)

SIDE FOUR **18.** "You Ain't Going Nowhere": Another song reprised on Greatest Hits Vol. II, this version, with Dylan as relaxed and as warm as he's ever been, is terrific. (A) **19.** "Don't Ya Tell Henry": One of the highlights on the record, it was written by Dylan but sung by Levon Helm of The Band. It's a spirited, jumpy tune, and

Levon's vocal is perfect with a great guitar solo from Robbie Robertson and a nice Helm turn on mandolin. It would have been interesting to hear Bob sing it. (A)   **20.** "Nothing Was Delivered": The mood turns serious as Bob steps back in front of the mike. There are pleasant harmonies from The Band on the chorus and curious lyrics again. (B+)   **21.** "Open the Door, Homer": In typical Dylan fashion, he calls the song "Open the Door, Homer" then in the chorus, uses the name Richard. What does it all mean? Who knows? Probably not even Homer. Or Richard. (B)   **22.** "Long Distance Operator": Another song written by Dylan but sung by Richard Manuel of The Band, it's a bluesy tune with some good guitar work by Robbie Robertson. (B) **23.** "This Wheel's on Fire": A brilliant vocal by Bob Dylan closes one of his most interesting and puzzling records. The Band included a fine version of this song on their debut album, but Dylan's version has a ominous, end-of-the-world presence. (A)

It is difficult to say exactly what many of the songs on this album are about. Dylan himself probably didn't even know. But at the time Dylan recorded it, he was making a major transition in his career and his writing. Listening to the rich and colorful verbal landscape of *Blonde on Blonde,* it is hard to imagine that the same man came up with the pen-and-ink sketches of *John Wesley Harding.* Once you hear *The Basement Tapes,* it all comes together. Sort of. (Album Grade: A)

Desire

Produced by Don DeVito for Columbia Records
Recorded: July 28–31; October 24, 1975
Released: January 16, 1976

Chart Position   Dylan's third No. 1 record and fifth straight top ten release, brought him to the peak of his commercial success. *Desire* was No. 1 for five straight weeks and earned Dylan a platinum album, joining *Nashville Skyline* and *Blood on the Tracks* as his only regular releases that became platinum albums. *Desire* remained on the charts for 17 weeks.

Singles   "Hurricane" a two-sided tribute to imprisoned boxer Ruben "Hurricane" Carter hit the singles charts in November of 1975. It was on the charts for 11 weeks, but only got as high as No. 33, ironically, the same as his last protest song "George Jackson."

Another single "Mozambique," backed with "Oh, Sister" was released in March of 1976 but got only as high as No. 54.

Outtakes   Three songs from the sessions for *Desire* have subsequently been released on the two excellent Dylan compilations. *Biograph* of 1985 included the wonderful "Abandoned Love" and stunning live versions of two *Desire* songs, "Isis" and "Romance in Durango."

The Cover   A popular shot of Dylan in profile, wearing a gray cowboy hat, a big fur jacket and scarf. He looks very much the part of the gypsy, which was the idea. On the back of the album, Dylan is seen in a variety of poses with a picture of his wife, Sara, in the bottom right hand corner, the only time she was included on a Dylan album.

Liner Notes   Dylan offered a short capsule on the back of the record with more extensive liner notes by Allen Ginsberg inside.

The Record   History tells us that *Desire* remains Bob Dylan's most commercially successful album ever. Part of the reason for that, one supposes, is the great critical success the two albums that preceded it, *Blood on the Tracks* and *The Basement Tapes,* enjoyed. People didn't want to miss out on a good thing.

Part of it was a matter of timing. With Dylan embarked on his Rolling Thunder Revue, his name was in the air again. And coming out right after Christmas, people had money to spend.

There was also the matter of "Hurricane," Dylan's first protest song that also charted as a single in some time.

Most of all, it had to be the music, which is lilting, sweet and delightful with Scarlet Rivera's haunting violin all over the place.

As for the songs, with the exception of "Sara," Dylan seemed to retreat from the wide-open honesty of *Blood on the Tracks*. Instead, he gave his audience a picaresque look at the world around them.

Collaborating with Dylan on some of the lyrics was Jacques Levy, a sometime director of Broadway plays like *Oh! Calcutta*. In terms of commercial success, the collaboration was a huge hit. But it sure didn't bring Bob Dylan face to face with his demons.

SIDE ONE   1. "Hurricane": With congas, that great Rivera violin and a propulsive tune, Dylan sings as he might have put it "in a voice without restraint." With great rhymes, all kinds of wry Dylan asides, impassioned singing and lyrics that cry out for personal justice, it is a song that contains all of the elements that made Dylan such a cultural force. It also helped get Ruben Carter out of jail. A sign that as of 1976, when Bob Dylan had something to say, people listened. (A) 2. "Isis": Dylan occasionally introduced this on the Rolling Thunder Revue tour as "a song about marriage." It is a curious saga about a trip to the pyramids. Though he plays piano on the record, Dylan performed this live without his guitar, thanks to a tip from Patti Smith. Dylan told her he didn't know what to do with his hands. She said to make a fist. (A-)   3. "Mozambique": A great melody that Rivera's violin really shows off. It was later released as the second single off the record. Lyrically, it's as inconsequential as anything off *New Morning*. (B+)   4. "One More Cup of Coffee": A little melodrama amidst the sounds of the Old West. Dylan seems to love melodies like this that evoke dusty boots, wagon wheels, spurs and squeaky saloon doors. This could have come off the soundtrack of *Pat Garrett and Billy the Kid*. Not exactly praise. Something about this song just sounds fake. Something seldom said about a Bob Dylan song. (C)   5. "Oh Sister": A more encouraging hymn to sisterly love; Dylan and Emmylou Harris harmonize pretty well. It's a little sappy but considering the topic, it could have been worse. (A-)

SIDE TWO   6. "Joey": If the double-album disaster *Self-Portrait* was Dylan's first major career misstep, this puzzling 11-minute ode to thug Joey Gallo might have been No. 2. It certainly angered the New York radical press, normally Dylan's biggest boosters. "Wake up Dylan, Joey Gallo was no hero" trumpeted a headline in the *Village Voice*. Considering its pairing with Side One's opener about another former prisoner, "Joey" cheapens everything. It makes you wonder what Dylan was thinking of. Then again, if an artist wants to record a tribute to Adolf Hitler, do we have a right to tell him he can't? Maybe not. We can refuse to listen. "Joey" isn't all bad and features some great lines.

But if you think the criticism might steer Dylan in another direction, guess again. He reprised this song on his 1989 tour with the Grateful Dead, including it on the live album *Dylan and the Dead*. (D)   **7.** "Romance in Durango": Another song that sounds like an outtake from Pat Garrett and Billy the Kid, it is an uptempo number that was one of the highlights of Dylan's live performances at the time. A fine live version of this song is included on 1985's *Biograph* collection. (B+)   **8.** "Black Diamond Bay": A cross between "Lily, Rosemary and the Jack of Hearts" off *Blood on the Tracks* and "Bob Dylan's 115th Dream" off *Freewheelin' Bob Dylan*, it's a funny tale about true love, a panama hat and an earthquake. Not necessarily in that order. (B+)   **9.** "Sara": Along with "Ballad in Plain D," "Sara" seems a real aberration in Dylan's recording career. For someone who has taken great pains to deceive, derail, deride and destroy anyone who has tried to analyze or interpret his work, to come out and write a plain, sentimental, heart-on-his-sleeve ballad to his wife, from whom he was estranged at the time, it was startlingly out of character. There is an interesting story about the recording of this song in Bob Spitz's 1989 biography *Dylan*. "Bob obviously wanted to surprise her with it," said one unidentified observer. "Bob had the lights dimmed more than usual, but as the music started, he turned and sang the song directly at Sara, who sat through it all with an impervious look on her face. The rest of us were blown away by it, maybe even embarrassed to be listening in front of them. He was really pouring out his heart to her. It seemed as if he was trying to reach her, but it was obvious she was unmoved." When Dylan debuted the song on the Rolling Thunder Revue at Southeastern Massachusetts University two months before *Desire* was released, members of the audience were hushed, looking at each other in amazement. Why was he baring his soul like this? He had never done this before — why now? Following the song with "Just Like a Woman," the tension grew almost unbearable. People in the front rows had tears in their eyes, it was like sitting in Dylan's living room. Amazingly, Dylan picked up on their discomfort. When he reached the bridge of the song and the line about dying of thirst, he rolled his eyes in campy, Al Jolson fashion, breaking up bassist Rob Stoner and everyone in the first seven or eight rows. It was clearly intentional. For an artist who has made a career out of being difficult to understand, it was a rare moment of openness. Perhaps because at that time, and perhaps never again, he needed us. (A)

In some ways, *Desire* ends the Bob Dylan story, capping a remarkable five-year period in his life.

After the disaster of *Self-Portrait* and the middling success of *New Morning,* by 1971, Dylan's recording career appeared pretty much over. He was having trouble coming up with any new material and his days as America's preeminent rock and roll songwriter seemed way behind him.

Returning to the concert stage for the first time in 1974 and finding the inspiration that had eluded him for so long, he came all the way back to the top.

Looking back, *Desire* is a pleasant if relatively harmless reminder of that chapter of Dylan's life. (Album Grade: B+)

Hard Rain

Produced by Don DeVito and Bob Dylan for Columbia Records
Recorded in Fort Worth, Texas (May 14, 1976) and at Fort Collins, Colorado (May 23, 1976)
Released: September 10, 1976

Chart Position   This live album, culled from two stops on the Rolling Thunder Revue tour, was released on September 10 to coincide with NBC's televised special of the same name. It went to No. 17 and earned Dylan his 12th gold album, but remained on the charts only five weeks.

Singles   A live version of "Stuck Inside of Mobile," backed with a studio version of a clever Dylan ditty, "Rita May," was released on November 30. It did not make the charts.

Outtakes   There have been no official outtakes from the "Hard Rain" shows released on record. However, the televised show included several songs not on the live album. Among them were Dylan's duet with Joan Baez on "Deportee" and a raucous, Springsteenish "I Pity the Poor Immigrant."

The Cover   An ominous black-and-white close-up portrait of a long-haired Dylan that looked serious, and considering the turmoil in Dylan's life at the time, it was understandable.

Liner Notes   There are no liner notes to this album.

The Record   It's fairly well documented that Dylan's marriage had all but fallen apart by this time. He looked and acted like a man in turmoil.

With the Rolling Thunder Revue tour winding down as Dylan attempted to film a rather peculiar quasi-documentary of the tour called *Renaldo and Clara,* it was a time of craziness, anger, and confusion.

Hard Rain, a live album culled mostly from the NBC television special of the same name, was, like the TV special, ripped by the critics.

Viewers were led to believe that in the Rolling Thunder Revue, Dylan and Joan Baez, the folkies of the 1960s, were reprising their "Times They Are a-Changin'" days in a glorified oldies show that sent everyone home with a warm feeling. Instead, *Hard Rain* depicted a turbaned, bearded Dylan, looking as if he hadn't slept since the Roosevelt administration, roaring his way through his old and new songs.

Though the material is excellent and, in retrospect, revelatory (if one considers the sequence of songs on Side Two as a farewell message to Sara), it was a little too raw for mass audience approval. Years later, it sounds pretty darn good.

SIDE ONE   **1.** "Maggie's Farm": A somewhat predictable treatment of Dylan's protest rocker from *Bringing It All Back Home,* it is possibly the weakest song on the record. (C+)   **2.** "One Too Many Mornings": Nicely sung, this song seems one of Dylan's personal favorites. He first recorded it on his third album, *The Times They Are a-Changin,* and performed a more stately version with The Band on his 1966 tour of England. With the Rolling Thunder Revue ten years later, he takes it a little slower and throws in some tangy steel guitar work. (B+)   **3.** "Stuck Inside of Mobile with the Memphis Blues Again": One of his wildest songs from *Blonde on Blonde,* it was never performed live until this tour. The revue's version doesn't quite match the effortless precision of Nashville's finest on *Blonde on Blonde,* but it's fun to hear Bob sing it again. (B+)   **4.** "Oh Sister": His voice quavers a bit, somebody's guitar is out of tune, and the overall sound is pretty ragged, but Dylan sings it with directness. (C+)   **5.** "Lay Lady Lay": If Dylan's intention by performing this song live was to erase any memory of the tuneful fluke that was a smash hit for him in 1969, he succeeds. There is almost no melody, everybody seems to be yelling, and Bob even reworked the lyrics to reflect his feelings about matters of the heart. (B+)

SIDE TWO   **6.** "Shelter from the Storm": Bob Spitz's biography, *Dylan,* reports that for this concert date, Dylan's wife, Sara, showed up to celebrate his birthday, only to find that her erstwhile husband had two girlfriends in tow. So what does our hero do? He turns the conflict into great art, taking his gracious *Blood on the Tracks* tribute to Sara and turning it into one of the great nose-thumbings in recorded American rock and roll history. The best song on the record and one of the finest live Dylan recordings extant. Bob even plays a little slide guitar. And we thought it was just good old rock and roll. (A+)   **7.** You're a Big Girl Now": What must it have been like for Dylan, his marriage collapsing, to go out and sing songs like this? Sometimes, he sounds like he's mocking Sara, and sometimes, he sounds like he will genuinely miss her. The one line he muffs is the one where he says he can change. You wonder if his subconscious took over for him. (A-)   **8.** "I Threw It All Away": One of *Nashville Skyline*'s most beautiful love songs is rendered in an almost entirely unrecognizable fashion. The guitars are woefully out of tune, the harmonies on the chorus are best described as ragged, and only Bob's undaunted vocal carries it through. He could retitle this song, "Love Revisited." (A)   **9.** "Idiot Wind": Dylan's most angry song since "Like a Rolling Stone" is a good way to conclude a tumultuous chapter in his life and the "Hard Rain" TV special. This version cuts the one on *Blood on the Tracks* in a big way, thanks to Dylan's haughty, laughing, mocking, heroic, gallant, heartbreaking, and ultimately triumphant vocal. If you weren't sure "Idiot Wind" was intended as an anthem, listen to this version. (A)

It would be nice to call this "The Great Bob Dylan Live Album," but it wouldn't be true. If Side One were as good as Side Two, it might have had a chance.

To most people, *Before the Flood* is preferable. Considering that

79

there were three more live albums in the next 15 years, you have a lot of Bob Dylan live recordings to assemble a great album.

But it's probably safe to say that at few other times in Dylan's performing career was he able to exorcize the chaos and frustration of his personal life in performance the way he did on here.

Not for the meek of spirit or faint of heart, it's a sometimes raw, sometimes bitter look at the artist in turmoil. Never again would Dylan sound as committed to his work on stage as he does on this album. (Album Grade: B+)

Street Legal

Produced by Don DeVito for Columbia Records
Recorded at Rundown Studios (April 1978)
Released: June 15, 1978

Chart Position   Dylan's first studio album since *Desire* in 1976, this one rose to No. 11. It was on the charts for only eight weeks, but earned Dylan his 13th gold album.

Singles   "Baby Stop Crying," backed with "New Pony," was released on July 31, 1978. It did not make the charts, and neither did "Changing of the Guards," backed with "Señor," which was released in September.

Outtakes   No outtakes have emerged from the sessions for this album.

The Cover   A small, slim Dylan is featured, standing in a doorway, coat in hand, looking as if he were waiting for a bus. More unusual is the black-and-white photo on the back cover that shows Dylan, in heavy makeup, wearing a fancy Elvis Presley–like outfit.

Liner Notes   There are no liner notes to this album.

The Record   His first studio record in two years, *Street Legal* seems to be the point where fans and critics jumped off the Dylan bandwagon. There was a lot of negative feeling toward him at that time. His divorce was ugly, his film *Renaldo and Clara* was blasted by the press, and his TV special was roundly slammed. There were stories in some magazines about Dylan attempting to trade interviews for cover stories to get more publicity for his film. People who had always considered Bob Dylan a friend they never met were now starting to wonder about him.

Though Dylan tried to temper that anger on stage, broadening his sound; adding a saxophone, a violin, and a three-woman chorus; and actually introducing his songs and talking with his audience, what worked for Neil Diamond and Elvis Presley didn't work for him.

In retrospect, *Street Legal* sounds a lot better than some Dylan albums of similar vintage (*Empire Burlesque* and *Knocked Out Loaded,* to name two) but it had the worst curse of all—bad timing.

Critics who had been waiting for years to say something nasty about Bob Dylan unloaded here. In *Rolling Stone,* Greil Marcus, a respected rock critic, said "most of the stuff here is dead air ... he's never sounded so utterly fake."

Robert Christgau of the *Village Voice,* who had eloquently sung the praises of *The Basement Tapes,* was bitter about *Street Legal:* "Because [Dylan] is too shrewd to put his heart into genuine corn, and because his idea of a tricky arrangement is to add horns or chicks to simplistic verse—and chorus structures, a joke is what *[Street Legal]* is. But since he still commands remnants of authority, the joke is sour indeed."

Dave Marsh, also writing in *Rolling Stone,* said: "Not only does *Street Legal* reveal that Dylan is Elvis Presley's legitimate successor as Clown Prince of Rock and Roll, it also prevents us from ever taking him seriously again."

The attacks were so vociferous that Jann Wenner, *Rolling Stone's* publisher and a diehard Dylan fan, wrote his own rebuttal of the two critics' attacks in the September 21 issue: "Greil Marcus is saying that *Street Legal* is completely without merit, lacks a single song good enough to redeem the effort, and is nothing but junk. Not only that, but Mr. Dylan is insulting to women! Mother of God!"

It was an odd moment in Dylan's career. He is often seen as a controversial figure in rock music, yet except for his shift from folk music to rock and roll in 1965, he was rarely criticized by anyone in the industry.

Dylan seemed so far ahead of the curve that when he put out a new album, whether it was *John Wesley Harding* or *Nashville Skyline* or *New Morning,* invariably some critic would come out and call it "his best album ever."

Looking back at those three records, I think that only *John Wesley Harding* comes even close to Dylan at his best. But at the time, Dylan was riding the zeitgeist and people trusted him and his decisions.

In 1978, they didn't and let him have it for *Street Legal*—a little unfairly, perhaps. Although it is not the best record he ever made, and the low spots are pretty low, it is far from his worst.

SIDE ONE   **1.** "Changing of the Guards": No, you can't figure out what in the world he's singing about; his female chorus simply repeats the last couple words of each line and it would be nice if the voice was out front a little more. But the saxophone riff is kind of catchy, and if you were locked in a room with a tape playing this song and, say, "I Pity the Poor Immigrant," you could come to love this one. (B+)   **2.** "New Pony": This song contains some provocative sexual imagery from ol' Cowboy Bob and a different, stark rendition of the blues. Compare it with another off-the-cuff blues song like "Leopard-skin Pillbox Hat," and it holds up pretty well. (B+)   **3.** "No Time to Think": Sing-songy and, again, somewhat unfocused lyrically. It is here that one starts to get an inkling of the kinds of problems Dylan will be faced with throughout the rest of his career. You get the impression that he is almost too intelligent and too well read to be a good songwriter. For no matter how smart or clever a person is, unless you can write with the clarity of *John Wesley Harding* or *Blood on the Tracks*, it doesn't matter. What good is it if no one can understand what you're writing about? And another thing: Just because a guy can think up a clever rhyme for a big word doesn't mean that the word should be part of a lyric. Dylan doesn't seem to know that here. Can you name another song that mentions high society, loneliness, memory, ecstasy, tyranny, hypocrisy, alcohol, duality, mortality, liberty, humility, nobility, and — get this — simplicity? (D)   **4.** "Baby Stop Crying": A little melodramatic and predictable, it's far from Bob's best effort lyrically. But he's really reaching, trying to do something different. The saxophone solo helps, but this one doesn't quite get around the bend. (C)

SIDE TWO   **5.** "Is Your Love in Vain?": Musically, it's a clever and catchy rewrite of Elvis Presley's "Can't Help Falling in Love." Lyrically, it's rife with self-pity, pretentiousness, and conceit. Otherwise, it's not bad. (C+)   **6.** "Señor (Tales of Yankee Power)": At last, a sign that the man hasn't lost his touch. Another song that would fit well on that imaginary soundtrack for Mountain's *Theme for an Imaginery Western,* it evokes the Old West, mystery, fear, and confusion — especially confusion. (A)   **7.** "True Love Tends to Forget": The song has a clever bridge, but otherwise isn't anything to brag about. Dylan knows it's a good bridge, too, for he reprises it near the end of the song to try to save things. (C)   **8.** "We Better Talk This Over": An even-handed look at his disintegrating marriage, it sounds like Bob is waving the white flag and hoping Sara will do the same. There's nice piano backing by Alan Pasqua, and the lyrics make sense. (B+)   **9.** "Where Are You Tonight? (Journey Through Dark Heat)": Except for "Restless Farewell" on *The Times They Are a-Changin,* Dylan has always been selective about the closing song on his albums, making it sort of a parting shot. A sharply drawn, dramatic summation of all he was going through at the time, "Where Are You Tonight?" is a song of determination and relentlessness. At times, the music overwhelms Dylan's voice, and it's unfortunate that the lyrics aren't more clearly presented. He was a troubled man, and he sounds like one here. (A-)

In *Dylan,* Jonathan Cott wrote that "Where Are You Tonight (Journey Through Dark Heat)" reminded him of "the last work Van Gogh painted before his suicide — a work unstable and charged with tempestuous excitement.... The artist's will is confused, the world moves toward him, he cannot move toward the world. It is as if he felt himself completely blocked, but also saw an ominous fate approaching."

Cott didn't know the half of it. (Album Grade: B-)

Bob Dylan at Budokan

Produced by Don DeVito for Columbia Records
Recorded at Nippon Budokan (February 28 and March 1, 1978)
Released: April 23, 1979

Chart Position   Dylan's third live album in five years was recorded on a tour of Japan. It was released overseas in November. After there was a demand for its release in the United States, Columbia demurred and released it on April 23. It went to No. 13 and was on the charts for seven weeks, but did not earn Dylan a gold album.

It was the first Dylan album, other than the *Pat Garrett and Billy the Kid Soundtrack,* that did not earn a gold record award since 1964's *Another Side of Bob Dylan.*

Singles   No singles were released from this album.

Outtakes   There have been no outtakes released from this tour.

The Cover   This cover, with a close-up shot of Dylan on stage, has an inside photo that is similar to the one on *Bob Dylan's Greatest Hits, Vol. II.*

Liner Notes   The notes contain a short, sad passage about what Dylan left behind on his trip to Japan: "If the people of Japan wish to know about me, they can hear this record or hear my heart still beating in Kyoto at the Zen Rock Garden," he wrote. "Someday I will be back to reclaim it."

This album, incidentally, Dylan's 23rd official release, was the first to include his song lyrics in the notes.

The Record   This record originally wasn't intended for American release, so taking shots at Dylan for releasing his third live album in five years (and second double-record set) seem unfair. But the critics lambasted Dylan for rearranging many of his greatest songs for the tour.

Of course, Dylan had done the same thing with The Band for his 1974 tour, but The Band was a well-known and respected rock group. His motives weren't questioned there.

The critics complained that on the *Live at Budokan* album, he seemed to be changing the songs just for the sake of changing them, not to amplify their meaning. If the entire record was like his version of "Blowin' in the Wind," nobody would have complained. But doing "Don't Think Twice" as a reggae song is ludicrous.

Overall, the album is pleasant enough. There are no versions that are preferable to the previously recorded ones.

You can look at this record as Dylan cheapening his old war-horses as many critics have noted, but it seems more likely that he was simply trying to find another way of presenting material he knew the public expected him to perform.

The criticism of him rearranging his old songs has not deterred Dylan, by the way. He has continued the practice of toying with his old classics on every concert tour since this one.

SIDE ONE   1. "Mr. Tambourine Man": The musical accompaniment — including flute! — is a little more up-tempo than the original was, and it's pretty good, although it tends to make the song sound more happy than the first version did. Dylan's perfunctory singing slows things down. (B)   2. "Shelter from the Storm": One of the more delicate songs on *Blood on the Tracks*, it stood up to an angry, full-scale overhaul on *Hard Rain*. Here, Dylan gives it a repetitive so-so handling and an annoying chorus and ruins the lyrics. (C)   3. "Love Minus Zero/No Limit": This song, sort of feeble on *Highway 61 Revisited*, is actually improved by picking up the tempo and adding some lively harmonica breaks amid the flute and violin interludes. This version works. (B+)   4. "Ballad of a Thin Man": A song that would become a staple in Dylan's more recent tours, it's given a nice treatment here. Not as starkly accusatory as on *Before the Flood*, it's a decent version. (B)   5. "Don't Think Twice, It's All Right": This version is just plain awful. Some songs, like "Knockin' on Heaven's Door," lend themselves to a reggae treatment, as Eric Clapton's rendition shows — but this is not such a song. Probably the worst song Dylan has put on record. (F)

SIDE TWO   6. "Maggie's Farm": There really isn't a melody here, which may be the idea. A bad idea, that is. (C+)   7. "One More Cup of Coffee (Valley Below)": Performed with a little more camp than on *Desire*, the song improves considerably. And the congas are a hoot. (B)   8. "Like a Rolling Stone": Somehow, Dylan has reconfigured his most famous melody and made it all work, saxophone break and all. The original is far preferable, but compare this version with the mediocre version on *Self-Portrait* from the Isle of Wight concert, and this one is a huge winner. Counting the version on *Before the Flood*, this is the third officially released live version of the song. (B+)   9. "I Shall Be Released": Gone is the delicacy and longing that made the original, recorded around the time of *The Basement Tapes,* so great. Renditions like this, where he can virtually talk the lyrics like a third-rate Las Vegas entertainer, are why some critics called this album Dylan's Las Vegas act. A bad one. (D)　**10.** "Is Your Love in Vain?" Recorded here before he did the *Street Legal* version, the music isn't as good as it was on that record. And the lyrics are still pretty lame. (D) **11.** "Going, Going, Gone": In its original version on *Planet Waves,* it was an interesting if strange protestation of Dylan's quiet life-style and inner turmoil. Here, he reworks the lyrics, making them worse, and there's a god-awful chorus to contend with — not to mention an out-of-place blues vamp near the end. (C)

　　　SIDE THREE　**12.** "Blowin' in the Wind": Taking an ageless melody, Dylan sings the song in front of a respectful piano backing and angelic chorus. If he only didn't say "feeerrreeehhhheee." (A-)　**13.** "Just Like a Woman": The melody is recognizable, and Dylan sings this version very well, backed by piano instead of the usual guitar and drums. The chorus doesn't help, but it doesn't spoil it either. (B+)　**14.** "Oh Sister": The best thing you can say about this version is that it sounds nothing like the version on *Desire.* On that album, Dylan sounded like he was complaining. Here, it sounds like a warning. (B) **15.** "Simple Twist of Fate": He screws up the lyrics, sings the song too fast and generally ruins one of the nicest songs on *Blood on the Tracks.* (C)　**16.** "All Along the Watchtower": Unlike the original, it takes a while for this one to kick in, but once it does, flute tooting and violin soaring all over and around the melody, it's pretty nice. And probably sounded even better later on the tour. (B+)　**17.** "I Want You": A daring performance, just Dylan with Steve Douglas on recorder, it comes off very well except for a couple of minor singing glitches. And it sounds nothing like the original. You wish he'd take more chances like he did here. (B+)

　　　SIDE FOUR　**18.** "All I Really Want to Do": Redone as a sort of big-band rendition of Simon and Garfunkel's "59th Street Bridge Song (Feelin' Groovy)." Dylan has fun with some of his most playful lyrics. It's pretty funny. (B+)　**19.** "Knockin' on Heaven's Door": This reggae version comes off better than the other one on this record, which isn't saying much. The mystery and understatement of the original are

86

replaced by flute and chorus. Some people may go for that kind of thing, but what are they doing listening to a Bob Dylan album? (C) **20.** "It's All Right, Ma (I'm Only Bleeding)": Instead of "Like a Rolling Stone" being the big show closer, Dylan reaches for one of his most challenging songs. He speaks the lyrics a little more slowly, with dramatic pauses, while the band — at full power — waits for him to get to the end of each verse so they can blast for a couple of bars. It's quite a change from the original, but not entirely unsuccessful. (B+) **21.** "Forever Young": The gentle, warm sentiment of the original get tramples in the big-band stampede with chorus, saxophone, and all. In concert, it probably worked pretty well, but it doesn't come across well on record. (B-) **22.** "The Times They Are a-Changin'": A nice gesture, Dylan and his band can't decide at what tempo they want to play this song for the first few lines. By then, the mood is broken, and even a big finish can't quite fix it. (C+)

There is enough good material to have made a decent single album here, and as a document of Dylan's 1979 concert tour, it's OK. *Before the Flood* has much better performances, and *Hard Rain* has much more intensity. But if you like your Dylan a little diluted, which sometimes isn't such a bad idea, this has its uses. (Album Grade: B-)

Slow Train Coming

Produced by Jerry Wexler and Barry Beckett for Columbia Records
Recorded at Muscle Shoals (May 1–11, 1979)
Released: August 18, 1979

Chart Position   The first of Dylan's three consecutive "religious" albums, it was his most commercially successful since the 1976 *Desire*. *Slow Train Coming* went to No. 3 and earned Dylan his sixth platinum album in its 26-week stint on the charts.

Singles   The song "Gotta Serve Somebody," backed with a non album track "Trouble in Mind," was released as the record's first single in August. It went to No. 24 and earned Dylan his first Grammy.

"When You Gonna Wake Up," backed with "Man Gave Names

to All the Animals," was released in November, but did not make the charts. Neither did "Slow Train," backed with "Do Right to Me Baby," which followed in February.

Outtakes   "Ye Shall Be Changed," recorded on the second day of sessions at Muscle Shoals, was included on 1991 *The Bootleg Series, Vols. 1–3.*

The Cover   A pen-and-ink illustration on a brown background by Catherine Kanner depicts a train approaching as track is being laid.

Liner Notes   There are no liner notes to this album.

The Record   As the 1970s came to a close, Bob Dylan seemed a troubled man. After his triumphant comeback in the mid–70s, his marriage had fallen apart, critics began to take shots at his records and concerts, and his first feature film *Renaldo and Clara* was roundly condemned by just about everyone.

In Bob Spitz's book *Dylan: A Biography,* a friend who traveled with the 1978 tour is quoted as saying, "Bob was undoubtedly at the lowest point of his life. He was drinking heavily, just slugging down one brandy after the next. His moods were more inconsistent than usual. It seemed to me like he was trying to blot everything out."

Late in the year, possibly spurred by guitarist T-Bone Burnett or perhaps his then-girlfriend, actress Mary Alice Artes, Dylan became interested enough in religion to become a born-again Christian. In an interview with Karen Hughes in Dayton, Ohio, in 1980, Dylan said: "Jesus put his hand on me. It was a physical thing. I felt it. I felt it all over me. I felt my whole body tremble. The glory of the Lord knocked me down and picked me up."

Talking with Robert Hilburn of the *Los Angeles Times* later that year, he reiterated his experience: "There was a presence in the room that couldn't have been anybody but Jesus.... I truly had a born-again experience if you want to call it that."

It was shocking. Bob Dylan, the ultimate cynic, was converted. Suddenly, he had found something. And *Slow Train Coming,* recorded in ten days at the famed Muscle Shoals Studio, was his testament of faith.

With editor Jann Wenner leading the way (he wasn't taking any chances on his staff disliking this record), *Rolling Stone* trumpeted the news of Dylan's conversion with a review of the record that made it sound like one of the tablets Moses carried down Mount Sinai. Wenner wrote:

> Musically, this is probably Dylan's finest record, a rare coming together of inspiration, desire and talent that completely fuses strength, vision and art. Bob Dylan is the greatest singer of our times. No one is better. No one, in objective fact, is even very close. His versatility and vocal skills are unmatched. His resonance and feeling are beyond those of any of his contemporaries. More than his ability with words, and more than his insight, his voice is God's greatest gift to him.

Even if you agree that Dylan is a great singer, the quality of his voice has always been in question. Or maybe God doesn't like Dylan as much as Wenner suspects He does.

With Dire Straits' guitarist Mark Knopfler helping famed producer Jerry Wexler, *Slow Train Coming* certainly is Dylan's most polished studio recording. They were a couple of real pros. But as quoted in Clinton Heylin's *Bob Dylan, Behind the Shades,* both men were taken aback at Dylan's sudden vault onto the soapbox: "The first night was pretty awful," Knopfler said. "It just didn't happen, but once we got into it, it was good. But all these songs are about God!"

"I had no idea he was on this born-again Christian trip until he started to evangelize me," Wexler said. "I said, 'Bob, you're dealing with a 62-year-old confirmed Jewish atheist. I'm hopeless. Let's just make an album.'"

The three of them did, and the record was a commercial smash. But it also drew a line in the sand that many Dylan fans did not think they'd ever have to cross. On the record, Dylan warns that you either believe or do not believe, concluding that there is no middle ground. The man who had always encouraged his audience to think for themselves had made a major shift in philosophy.

SIDE ONE   **1.** "Gotta Serve Somebody": Bob Dylan's foray into Christianity begins with a declaration of faith and an intentionally diverse list of the people who Dylan suggests need to make that choice. Included is a humorously sly reference to his given name, Zimmerman, and a domed house he was having built in Malibu — one of the rare bits of humor on the record. This song earned Dylan his first Grammy. (B+)   **2.** "Precious Angel": A love song that seems to go astray in mid-course, its closing verses are filled with all sorts of curious biblical references that would be a test for a scholar, never mind a Dylan fan. Mark Knopfler's playing here, as throughout the record, is excellent. (B)   **3.** "I Believe in You": A heartfelt confession of love and devotion to God, Dylan's singing is strained in spots, particularly when he squeals at the beginning of the second verse. But his heart is in it. (B)   **4.** "Slow Train": Using a symbol he first mentioned on the liner notes to *Highway 61 Revisited*, Dylan moves from the personal to the universal with a damning assessment of the state of the Union. Some of his reasoning is unclear, since you get the impression that Dylan sees God as a distinctly American figure, someone who would frown upon sheiks owning "American soil." Upgraded for his artistic ambitions. (A-)

SIDE TWO   **5.** "Gonna Change My Way of Thinking": With the same kind of "Pocohantas" minor-chord progression he used on "Gotta Serve Somebody" and "Slow Train," Dylan opens Side Two with a predictable tract about the "authority on high." (B-)   **6.** "Do Right to Me Baby (Do Unto Others)": The oldest song on the record, it was copyrighted by Special Rider Music in 1978. Therefore, you assume it came first. It is essentially a restatement of one of the Ten Commandments. Only Moses said it better. (C)   **7.** "When You Gonna Wake Up": Dylan gets his anger up one last time on this album with the same kind of variation on the old "Pocohantas" chord progression, and the result is one of the record's standout songs, another angry look at the world around him. Just to show off, Dylan fits Henry Kissinger and Karl Marx into the same line. It's kind of whacky but also kind of fun, as long as you don't take it too seriously. (B+)   **8.** "Man Gave Names to All the Animals": An embarrassment. For a man called "the greatest lyric poet of his generation" to have written a silly, sophomoric song like this is unbelievable. This song makes Paul McCartney's *Ram* look like *Abbey Road*. Bob's excuse, if he ever bothered to give one, would probably be that this was intended as a children's song, which it could easily have been if some eighth grader had a free study period and a keyboard nearby. It's just awful. (F)   **9.** "When He Returns": Dylan's up-close, honest vocal, with all its cracks and warts and occasional tunelessness, carries the day. Originally, Dylan was reluctant to sing this one himself. But eventually, he decided he would, and his impassioned turn at the mike is the most memorable thing on the record. It's not necessarily the best, but he made it clear from this song that he believed in what he was doing. (A-)

It's true that it took a lot of artistic courage for Dylan to take this great leap of faith. It's also true that at the time, he probably didn't have anywhere else to turn.

Slow Train isn't much fun, and if you're someone who has always put a lot of trust in Dylan's honesty, to hear him going on and on about what other people need to do to be saved is simply embarrassing. But it was something he had to do. We know that now.

Since *Slow Train,* the first of a trilogy of "religious" albums, Dylan interviewers have always tiptoed carefully through this period of his career — out of sympathy. (Album Grade: B)

Saved

Produced by Jerry Wexler and Barry Beckett for Columbia Records
Recorded at Muscle Shoals (February 15–19, 1980)
Released: June 20, 1980

Chart Position   Though *Slow Train Coming* was wildly successful, *Saved* clearly was not. The record was on the charts only five weeks and went to No. 24. It is one of only a handful of Dylan albums of new material that failed to earn gold-record status. It was the first in a continuing series of commercial misses.

Singles   The two singles released off *Saved* did not make the singles charts. "Solid Rock," backed with "Covenant Woman," was released in June. August's release was the title track, "Saved," backed with another album track, "Are You Ready."

Outtakes   No outtakes from the *Saved* sessions have been released, fortunately.

The Cover   The initial editions of this record feature a painting of the Lord's hand, index finger pointing downward, touching one of five outstretched hands. Subsequent editions replaced the cover with a similarly colored painting of Dylan on stage. The back features an out-of-focus shot of Dylan and his hand.

Liner Notes   There are no liner notes to this record, only a quote from Jeremiah, Chapter 31: "Behold the days come, saith the Lord, that I will make a new covenant with the house of Israel and the house of Judea."

The Record   As *Village Voice* critic Robert Christgau put it, "the first flush of faith is the deepest." *Saved,* the second of a three-record trilogy tracing Dylan's conversion to born-again Christianity, is pretty lame stuff.

Though recorded at the same location with the same producers as was *Slow Train,* there is no comparison between the two records. What Dylan's music gains in tempo on *Saved,* he gives away lyrically. Any Nashville hack could have written these songs.

With a female chorus backing him, Dylan casually zips through nine tracks that either thank Jesus or warn those who don't. Unless you really like gospel-flavored rock, it is a record most Dylan fans can do without. In fact, it is one of his worst.

SIDE ONE   **1.** "A Satisfied Mind": The first cover version Dylan put on record since *Self-Portrait,* it's a gospel-flavored warm-up tune that leads directly into "Saved." Elvis Presley's gospel warm-ups were never put on record, but are infinitely better. (C-)   **2.** "Saved": An up-tempo testament of faith, "Saved" is the first title song of a Dylan record since "New Morning" in 1970. His voice lacks the authority it had on *Slow Train,* and though the pounding piano is fun, the lyrics are so preachy, they are hard to take. (C+)   **3.** "Covenant Woman": The melody is almost imperceptible, as is the intelligence behind the lyrics. The organ solo is awful, Dylan's singing is flat, and the song is just plain boring. This would have been a good one to leave in the can. (F)   **4.** "What Can I Do for You?": Another slow one. Dylan thanks God for giving him eyes to — can you guess? — see! And a life to — can you guess? — live! If Dylan had been able to pose this question to his audience at that time, their answer would likely have been "shut up before you embarrass yourself further." The harmonica playing is terrible, too. (D)   **5.** "Solid Rock": Dylan goes back to the up-tempo gospel rock to close out the side. His singing is sharper, and the tune is better. An entire album of songs like this would have been a lot easier to take. Fred Tackett's guitar work is, well, uplifting. (B)

SIDE TWO **6.** "Pressing on": A pretty fair gospel number, it sounds like Bob was starting to get the hang of things. The song starts slow with quiet piano backing, then turns on the drums and guitars, to lift your head up. (B-) **7.** "In the Garden": A strange chord progression that Dylan clearly seems to love. One of the few songs from his religious period that he still performs, it's done a bit slower on *Saved* than the way he did it when he toured with Tom Petty and the Heartbreakers. It is nice little tale of what happened in that garden oh so many years ago. (B+) **8.** "Saving Grace": After two hits, Dylan misses big with this predictable, unimaginative tribute to God. There's nothing wrong with saying thanks, but when you've done that on practically every song, it loses some impact by the end of the record — especially when you sing it out of tune. (C-) **9.** "Are You Ready": Can you guess what Bob wonders if we're ready for in this blues vamp? To learn how to skateboard? It's to meet Jesus Christ. Dylan wonders if he's ready to lay down his life. This song makes us wonder, too. (C+)

One hates to be cynical about a man's sincere profession of faith, and there's no question that at this time, Bob Dylan believed in what he was singing. It's just that he sang about his faith in such an insufferably holier-than-thou manner that it was impossible to take him seriously. His on-stage manner on the *Saved* tour was utterly offensive.

In Worcester, Massachusetts, he threatened an unruly audience by telling them they'd "better start thinking about their soul."

If they have record players in Heaven, the members of that Worcester audience won't have to worry about a thing. First, somebody will have to own up for this record. (Album Grade: C)

Shot of Love

Produced by Chuck Plotkin and Bob Dylan for Columbia Records
Recorded: April 7–May 11, 1981
Released: August 12, 1981

Chart Position   Dylan's lowest chart debut since *The Times They Are a-Changin'* in 1963, *Shot of Love* made it only to No. 33 and was on the charts only three weeks. It was Dylan's second straight studio release that did not go gold.

Singles   "Heart of Mine," backed with a raucous non album track, "The Groom's Still Waiting at the Altar," was released September 1. It was not a hit, though "Groom" sparked enough response for Columbia to include it on subsequent reprintings of the record.

Dylan again started playing games with his collectors, releasing "Heart of Mine" as a single in Europe, backed with a track not available anywhere else — a remake of *Self Portrait*'s "Let It Be Me."

Outtakes   A mysterious outtake from these sessions, "Carribbean Wind," was included on the 1985 *Biograph*. Three more outtakes — "You Changed My Life," "Need a Woman," and "Angelina"— appeared on the 1991 *The Bootleg Series, Vols. 1–3.*

The Cover   A brightly colored Lichtenstein-style drawing of an explosion with the words "Shot of Love" in the middle. Dylan is depicted on the back cover contemplating a rose.

Liner Notes   Again, there were no liner notes, but there was a Bible quote, this one from Matthew 11:25: "I thank thee, O Father, Lord of heaven and earth, because thou has hidden these things from the wise and prudent, and revealed them unto babes." Subtle, isn't it?

The Record   By the time *Shot of Love* came out, Dylan was taking shots at record critics, his fans, women, and anyone else who criticized his "born-again" ways. Maybe that wasn't Christian of him, but, then again, neither were the reviews of *Saved*— unquestionably the worst of his career.

More frustrating for Dylan, his audience started to heckle him, prompting the kind of nasty exchanges that Dylan devotees first heard on the live shows on the 1966 tour of England with The Band.

The difference was that in 1966, Dylan was making the greatest music of his life. He knew it, and his audience didn't. In 1981, Dylan was trying to ram religion down his audience's throat, and they weren't buying it.

Shot of Love, released in August, had some religious themes to be sure, but the record seemed a step closer to the kind of record Dylan fans had been hoping for. It was a comeback of sorts, though not quite as accomplished a record as the 1983 release, *Infidels*.

Though *Shot of Love* was not a hit commercially, Dylan has always spoken highly of it. As he told Cameron Crowe in the liner notes for *Biograph:*

> People didn't listen to that album in a realistic way.... Clydie King and I sound pretty close to what's all the best of every traditional style so how could anybody complain about that.
>
> The record had something that, I don't know, could have been made in the '40s or maybe the '50s. There was a cross element of songs on it.... The critics, I hate to keep talking about them, wouldn't let the people make up their minds.

It is certainly true that the rock and roll critical establishment wasn't singing Bob Dylan's praises in 1981. But how much they affected the sales of *Shot of Love* is questionable. Artists like Elvis Costello and Graham Parker have received wonderful reviews, yet sold few records. Others like Madonna, the New Kids on the Block, or even Billy Joel have been roasted pretty well by rock critics, and it certainly hasn't hurt their record sales.

Ultimately, *Shot of Love* was a bust on the Billboard charts, the first Dylan album to miss the Top-30 since 1964's *Another Side of Bob Dylan*.

SIDE ONE   **1.** "Shot of Love": A gospel-flavored rocker, reminiscent of the "Pocohontas" chord progression of "Slow Train" and "When You Gonna Wake Up." Dylan's singing is passionate, as is Clydie King's. The playing is fierce. (A-)   **2.** "Heart of Mine": Dylan's sweetest love song in a while, it's a little ragged, but charming nonetheless. It sounds as if it were recorded live in the studio with Bob having fun on piano and Ron Wood helping out on guitar (though you can't hear him). Sometimes, first takes work. Like here. (B+)   **3.** "Property of Jesus": Thanks to a nifty piano riff played by Carl Pickhardt, this return to religion sounds fine. Dylan's singing is joyful, even exuberant. (A-)   **4.** "Lenny Bruce": It's hard to know what to make of this one. The music is stately, majestic. The lyrics are reverent but with a couple howlers. Saying that Lenny Bruce is a good guy because he never cut off any baby's head falls somewhat short of a compliment. So is saying that he was "really funny." There's a nicely done live version of this song on *Hard to Handle,* Dylan's video of his 1986 tour of Australia with Tom Petty and the Heartbreakers. Is it serious or a grand joke? (B)   **5.** "Watered Down Love": Considering that on the original release of the record, "Groom Still Waiting at the Altar" was kept off, this mediocre cut has no business ruining what would have been the best single side of a Dylan record since, perhaps, *Desire* or *The Basement Tapes.* Another wonderful song, "Caribbean Wind," ultimately released on *Biograph,* was also available. But Dylan chose this pleasant but lightweight filler to close Side One. (C+)

SIDE TWO   **6.** "Groom Still Waiting at the Altar": Originally, the only way you could get this hard-rocking track was to buy the single "Heart of Mine." After Columbia included it on the 1985 collection *Biograph,* subsequent reissues of *Shot of Love* included the song as the first cut on Side Two. Dylan's singing is possessed. If you write the words out, you cannot imagine what this guy can fit in a single line. The song seems to be about Dylan's growing disenchantment with religion. Or maybe not. But it sure rocks the house down. (A)   **7.** "Dead Man, Dead Man": A live version of this song, recorded in New Orleans in 1981, available as the B side of the "Everything Is Broken" single off the 1989 *Oh Mercy* album, is much preferable to this studio cut. It's Dylan's first successful reggae song. (C+)   **8.** "In the Summertime": It wouldn't be a 1980s Bob Dylan album without at least one stiff per side, and this one is it. This also sounds like a first take, and this time, that's not a compliment. And somebody should have shot the harmonica player. (C+)   **9.** "Trouble": Raunchy, ragged, and lovable, Dylan gets down and dirty for the first time since "Hard Rain." The lyrics are a little predictable, but Dylan seems to be having such a good time, you don't mind. (B+)   **10.** "Every Grain of Sand": Where did this come from? Coming at the tail end of six years of fitful inspiration, critical groundfire, and half-hearted records, Dylan writes an absolutely gorgeous, well-thought-out, sharply written, passionately sung number like "Every Grain of Sand." It was easily the finest song he had written since "Tangled Up in Blue" and, more important, seemed to hint that Dylan was closing the chapter of religion, preparing for a return to "secular" music. Dylan has spoken of the significance of the song. As he explained to Cameron Crowe in the *Biograph* liner notes:

"That was an inspired song that came to me. It wasn't really too difficult. I felt like I was putting words down that were coming from someplace else, and I just stuck it out.

"About the song, you have to get past the keeping-up-with-the-times stuff. It's not about being a poet for the eighties, a rock 'n' roller for the nineties, you don't want to get trapped. You learn it all and call it up when you need it." (A+)

After the disaster of *Saved, Shot of Love* was an encouraging step in the right direction. It was evident that Dylan still wasn't about to spend much time in the studio getting things right. By going for a rougher, more roots-rock sound, however, he was able to sound more full of fire than he had in a long time.

"Every Grain of Sand" was an indication that as erratic as his post–1975 albums have been, you never know when that magical Dylan touch will return.

Shot of Love may not be the great album Dylan claims it is, but after the torpor of *Saved,* it sounds heavenly. (Album Grade: B+)

Infidels

Produced by Bob Dylan and Mark Knopfler for Columbia Records
Recorded at Power Station Studios, New York (April 11–May 8, 1983)
Released: November 1, 1983

Chart Position   After the disappointing sales of *Shot of Love,* *Infidels* marked a considerable comeback for Dylan. Billed as his first "nonreligious" album in years, it went to No. 20, was on the charts for 10 weeks, and earned Dylan his 14th gold album.

Singles   More games. "Sweetheart Like You," backed with "Union Sundown," was released as a single in the United States in November and was Dylan's highest-charting single since "Hurricane" seven years earlier. Two days before the American release, "Sweetheart Like You," backed with a song unavailable anywhere else — Dylan doing a Willie Nelson cover, "Angel Flying Too Close to the Ground"—was released in Europe.

On February 20, "Jokerman" was released as a second single, backed with a live version of "Isis" from the movie *Renaldo and Clara.* It did not make the singles charts.

Outtakes   Listening to the five songs released on *The Bootleg Series, Vols. 1–3,* I think that Dylan nearly had enough good-quality material to release a double album. There was "Tell Me," a sweet New Orleans-flavor tune, and an impassioned plea on behalf of his children, "Lord, Protect My Child."

Best of all were two Dylan epics: "Foot of Pride," an angry, remarkable number that stands alongside "Positively Fourth Street" and "Like a Rolling Stone" as one of his most angry songs, and the classic "Blind Willie McTell," easily one of Dylan's most perfectly realized numbers.

Also included was an early version of "Someone's Got a Hold of My Heart," the song that later became Dylan's single off the 1985 album, *Empire Burlesque.* On widely circulated bootleg albums, there were three other interesting songs: a rocker about the Rosenbergs, "Julius and Ethel"; an impressive Stones-like number, "Yonder Comes Sin"; and a strange track, "Death Is Not the End," that later ended up on *Down in the Groove.*

The Cover   In a color shot, Dylan, wearing dark glasses and a wispy beard, stares at the camera, in soft focus. If you look closely enough into the dark glasses, rays seem to be coming from his eyes. It is the first photo of Dylan on the cover of one of his records in five years. The back cover of the album, presumably drawn by Dylan, features a man kissing, or perhaps whispering to, a dark-haired woman.

Liner Notes   There are no liner notes to this album, but for Dylan's first supposedly "nonreligious" record in four years, there's a comment, nonetheless. The inside photo depicts Dylan kneeling on a hill outside downtown Jerusalem.

The Record   Discounting 1977, the year of his divorce, Bob Dylan had released an album and toured every year since his return to the music scene in 1974.

Breaking away from "born-again" Christianity, Dylan took most of 1982 off. He didn't release a record and, as far as is known, he entered a studio only once — in January — to lay down a few tracks that never saw the light of day.

The time off seemed to do Dylan — and his audience — a lot of good, for when he entered New York City's Power Station Studios in April, he had with him the finest batch of songs he had assembled since *Blood on the Tracks*.

Working with Mark Knopler of Dire Straits, who had backed him on *Slow Train Coming*, Dylan seemed intent on making a first-rate record. But as we've come to understand, Dylan's recording habits are not conducive to making great records. As Alan Clark, Knopfler's keyboardist for Dire Straits, told Clinton Heylin in *Bob Dylan: Behind the Shades*:

> He doesn't play anything more than once. If you can get him to play it twice, you're doing well. Three times is really pushing it. We used to just sit at our instruments and Bob would wander in, sit down, put his headphones on and struggle with his guitar strap for a couple of minutes, light a cigarette and then stub the cigarette out, take his guitar off, take his headphones off and walk across to the organ where I was sitting and write down about half a dozen lines of the next tune in tiny meticulous handwriting. It was quite interesting! And he'd sort of wander back over, maybe forget to put the headphones on and start playing the track. Just like that! If you weren't sitting there — if you had to go to the bog or something — he just started, y' know. It was amazing. And that's the way the album went.

Though there were moments of frustration, the record seemed to be going well. With Dire Straits about to go on tour, Dylan and Knopfler put together a rough mix of what was to be on the record.

"I had to go on tour in Germany," Knopfler recalled. "I had a bag at the studio and went to the airport from the studio having just finished recording pretty much the album. But then Bob went on and overdubbed certain things."

And left other songs, like the remarkable "Blind Willie McTell" and the powerful "Foot of Pride" in the outtake bin. The result was a record that Knopfler found an immense disappointment.

"Some of *Infidels* is like listening to roughs [outtakes]," he said.

"Maybe Bob thought I'd rushed things because I was in a hurry to leave, but I offered to finish it after our tour. Instead, he got the engineer to do the final mix, and I must say that listening to it makes me wish I'd done it myself."

Dylan fans weren't so critical. The record hit the stores on November 1. The word was out that Dylan was "back." Imagine what they might have said had they been able to hear "Blind Willie McTell" or "Foot of Pride"?

One of the first songs leaked to radio stations was the hard-rockin' "Neighborhood Bully," a thinly disguised defense of Israel. Politics aside, the song featured a roaring vocal from Dylan to a rock tempo. And he didn't say a word about Jesus!

The record went to No. 20, and for the first time in seven years, Dylan seemed to have his career headed back in the right direction.

SIDE ONE   1. "Jokerman": Using a dazzling sequence of contradictory images, Dylan paints a remarkable, frightening portrait of someone, more likely Someone, who seems intent on remaining above it all. For a revealing three-song tryptych that offers a possible explanation for Dylan turning away from "born-again" religion, listen to "Every Grain of Sand," "Groom Still Waiting at the Altar," and "Jokerman." Knopfler's guitar is crisp and clear, and Dylan matches him at every turn. (A)   2. "Sweetheart Like You": Warning: This song may not be quite what it seems. Dylan as a pickup artist? Or as a social commentator? Or as a sexist pig? Or as a confused song-poet? Or all the above? Is the woman too good for the "dump" of a world we live in? Or is it a trap? One reaction to this song was to call Dylan sexist for the line about the woman belonging at home. Dylan recanted to *Rolling Stone*'s Kurt Loder, saying:

> Actually, that line didn't come out exactly the way I wanted it to. But, uh, I could easily have changed that line to make it not so overly, uh, tender, you know?
>
> But I think the concept still woulda been the same. You see a fine-lookin' woman walking down the street, you start goin' "Well, what are you doin' on the street? You're so fine, what do you need all this for?"

Loder suggested that perhaps these women are going to their jobs. Dylan stiffened. "Well," he said, "I wasn't talking to that type of

woman. I'm not talkin' to Margaret Thatcher or anything." (B+)   **3.**
"Neighborhood Bully": Dylan has consistently denied that this song is
a "political song." He told Kurt Loder that "I'm not a political songwriter. 'Neighborhood Bully' to me, is not a political song, because if
it were, it would fall into a certain political party. If you're talking
about it as an Israeli political song — even if it is an Israeli political
song — in Israel alone, there's maybe twenty political parties. I don't
know where that would fall, what party." We can say this. Turn it up,
listen to that great vocal, and it rocks. (A-)   **4.** "License to Kill": In
this strange song of modern-age foreboding, Dylan sings of corrup-
tion, technology, and other present-day terrors. This version is somewhat more restrained than the wonderfully reckless version he
performed on NBC's "David Letterman Show." A year later, Dylan
included a live rendition of this song on *Real Live*. (B+)

SIDE TWO   **5.** "Man of Peace": The second song on *Infidels*
with religious overtones, Dylan warns of the many disguises of Satan.
Dylan's singing is imaginative and daring; the lyrics, somewhat less so.
(B)   **6.** "Union Sundown": A somewhat simplistic diatribe against
union exploitation, Dylan gets some nice slide guitar work from Mick
Taylor (or is it Mark Knopfler?) and sings the song through an echo
that's kind of interesting. (B+)   **7.** "I and I": You'd be hard-pressed to
find another song like this in the Dylan songbook. In this extraordinarily candid look at the life of a creative person, you get a revealing
glimpse of Dylan's restless, relentless life on the edge. It's extraordinary. (A+)   **8.** "Don't Fall Apart on Me Tonight": The singing gets a
little whiny in spots, but the concept behind it — how sometimes an
artist will rely on someone to be his (or her) touchstone with reality —
seems remarkably candid for someone as willfully contradictory as
Dylan. (A-)

What kind of a musical talent is Bob Dylan? Even 20-odd years
after his first record release? For *Infidels,* he knocked the two best songs
off the record, overdubbed tracks that were intended to stay as they
were, and made somewhat of a hodgepodge of the finished product.
Still, he turned his finest album since *Blood on the Tracks* into a true
"comeback" record.

Some of the songs, like "Neighborhood Bully," "Union Sundown," and "Sweetheart Like You," aren't as well thought out as they might have been, and a couple of the performances on the record are more sterile than they should be. But in the wake of Dylan's creative struggles since 1975, it was an unprecedented outpouring of material.

Unfortunately for Dylan fans, it would be another six years before he would produce another record of this caliber. (Album Grade: A-)

Real Live

Produced by Glyn Johns for Columbia Records
Recorded on Dylan's European Tour (1984)
Released: November 29, 1984

Chart Position   Dylan's fourth live album in ten years was greeted rudely by the critics and his audience. *Real Live* was the first Dylan album since *The Times They Are a-Changin'* in 1963 that failed to make the charts.

Singles   No singles were released from this album.

Outtakes   There have been no outtakes released from this tour.

The Cover   Bob Dylan, with trademark harmonica rack and guitar, is on stage in a color shot.

Liner Notes   There are no liner notes to this record, though there are some up-close color photos of Dylan from the tour, on stage and at a press conference.

The Record   It's hard to know quite what to make of this record, Dylan's fourth live album in a decade. Even an artist as exploitative of his audience as Elvis Presley has never released that much live material in such a short span of time.

At least two of those live albums made sense. *Before the Flood,* following his 1974 tour with The Band, was logical, since a lot of people were unable to get tickets for the sold-out tour. And the live disc from *Hard Rain* was also sensible because Dylan had a TV special and without an official soundtrack, there would have been a tremendous bootlegging problem unless Dylan made it readily available.

You can even make a case for Dylan's next live album. Bob Dylan at Budokan, which was not originally intended for stateside release. If Dylan wanted to release a special memento to his Japanese audience, fine.

But *Real Live* didn't seem to have any real purpose — other than to make a quick buck. Several of the songs, like "Highway 61 Revisited," "Maggie's Farm," and "Ballad of a Thin Man," had already been released in live versions. "Ballad of a Thin Man," for example, was released first on Highway 61 Revisited and then in performance on *Before the Flood, Bob Dylan at Budokan,* and *Real Live.* If you count the version included on *Hard to Handle,* Dylan's in-concert video with Tom Petty and the Heartbreakers, which is unavailable on disc, that's five different versions of the same song.

There were a few rarities on this tour that were included on this record. "Girl from the North Country," "Tombstone Blues," and "Masters of War" (unfortunately) had never been released in live versions, and that was a selling point to Dylan fans.

But he may have had two other important reasons. For one, his European tour was well received. Since Dylan stuck to the original versions of the songs and was backed by a fiery band led by former Rolling Stones guitarist Mick Taylor, he may have felt that the songs sounded alive again. After the poorly received *Budokan* record, Dylan may have wanted to release a live record more indicative of his current show. Or he might have read some of the criticism of the hurried treatment of some songs on *Infidels* and decided to offer alternative versions of "I and I" and "License to Kill," even if it was barely a year later.

The most important change on *Real Live* was Dylan's decision to rewrite one of his most popular songs, "Tangled Up in Blue." Herein may lie the key to understanding the Dylan of the 1980s–90s.

As was mentioned in the section on *Blood on the Tracks,* Dylan told interviewer Bill Flanagan for the book, *Written in My Soul,* that he was never pleased with the original version of the song. "I always wanted it to be the way I recorded it on *Real Live,*" he said. "That was another of those songs where you're writing and you've got it, you know what it's about, but half of it you just don't get the way you wanted to. Then I fixed it up and now it's where it should be."

Or, an artist tired of people picking his songs and his life apart, picks the most popular and apparently most revealing of all those songs and rewrites it, obscuring the theme so completely it hardly sounds like the same song.

Dylan isn't helping us with the answer. We have to make that decision for ourselves.

Real Live is an excellent document of Dylan's 1984 tour. And, as stated, it does offer some rarities. But that it didn't make the charts — something *Saved* and *Pat Garrett and Billy the Kid* managed to do — was a bad sign. And the rewrite of "Tangled Up in Blue" was an even more troubling gesture. The worst was yet to come.

SIDE ONE   **1.** "Highway 61 Revisited": If you ever imagined Bob Dylan fronting the Rolling Stones, this is probably what it would sound like. With snarling guitars, a tinkling piano, and a whip-snake voice, it's much preferable to the herky-jerky rendition Dylan offered with The Band in 1974. (B+)   **2.** "Maggie's Farm": Boogie. The singing is more whiny than usual, but the backing is more hard-edged than the loopy version on *Hard Rain* or the calypso version on *Budokan*. It's a passable version, done faster than on *Bringing It All Back Home*, but nowhere near as well. (C+)   **3.** "I and I": Gone is the ominous calm that made this such a standout on *Infidels*. In concert, it has a reggae feel to it, which — believe it or not — gives the song a more ironic twist. Dylan's performance is impassioned. (B+)   **4.** "License to Kill": Like the tune that precedes it, this song came out just a year before. Perhaps Dylan felt that the rather flat version on *Infidels* didn't do it justice, so he recut it here. Dylan's singing strays in a few spots but he sounds more committed here than in the studio version. You wonder if by recording it here and later playing it live on "Late Night with David Letterman," maybe he was giving this song more attention than it deserves. (B)   **5.** "It Ain't Me, Babe": It's good to hear Bob sing this solo instead of in an ensemble with the boys from the band. One of his most personal songs, Dylan sings it here with enthusiasm and delight. The harmonica solo is fun, too. (B+)

SIDE TWO   **6.** "Tangled Up in Blue": Unless you believe Dylan's rationale, rewriting one of his most popular songs seems mean spirited and perverse. The song doesn't improve, and all it does is illustrate Dylan's ability to find mischievous rhyme scenes. To date, this is the only live version of this song available on record. The version released as a video, taken from *Renaldo and Clara,* features somewhat modified lyrics and is preferable to this one. If you didn't know the original, this one might not matter much. (C+)   7. "Masters of War": The antiwar message is pertinent, but this song sounded dated on *Free-wheelin' Bob Dylan,* and that was in 1963. There's no melody, though Dylan's voice wanders all over the place trying to find one. You wish this would have stayed retired. Of course, guess what song Bob chose to perform in 1991, when the National Recording Academy of Arts and Sciences honored him with a lifetime achievement award? (C+)   8. "Ballad of a Thin Man": Since the mid–1970s, this has been an in-concert staple for Dylan, probably because he doesn't really have to sing the lyrics — just talk them in dramatic fashion. The version with The Band on *Before the Flood* is done with more care, the version on *Budokan* is done with more flash, and this version is more straightforward. The best version was the one he did with Tom Petty and the Heartbreakers in *Hard to Handle.* (B)   9. "Girl from the North Country": A pleasant surprise. Dylan picked another number from *Freewheelin'* and turns in a lovely performance, done solo with acoustic guitar and harmonica. It's not as wistful as the original, but, after all, the guy's 43 (in 1984). (B+)   10. "Tombstone Blues": A sound-alike to the Side One opener "Highway 61 Revisited," this rocker off *Highway 61 Revisited* features Carlos Santana, or so it says. It's hard to pick him out in all the ruckus. (B)

If the intention of *Real Live* was to show Dylan fans that the old guy could still rock ("Highway 61 Revisited") and perform his old acoustic songs ("It Ain't Me, Babe"), then it works fine, even if we could have done without another live version of "Ballad of a Thin Man" and "Maggie's Farm." If the intention was to redefine "Tangled Up in Blue" and show a nation of devoted listeners that they were wrong in liking the original, then it fails. Chances are the truth is where it usually is — somewhere in the middle. (Album Grade: B)

Empire Burlesque

Remix by Arthur Baker for Columbia Records
Recorded in New York (July–August 1984), in Los Angeles (November–January), in New York (February–March 1985)
Released: May 27, 1985

Chart Position   Another commercial bust for Dylan. *Empire Burlesque* made it only as high as *Shot of Love,* No. 33, and stayed on the charts only six weeks. Like the previous post–*Slow Train* studio albums *Saved* and *Shot of Love,* it had not gone gold as of 1992.

Singles   Dylan released two singles with this album: "Tight Connection to My Heart," backed with "We Better Talk This Over," a track off *Street Legal.* "Tight Connection" made it only to No. 103. "Emotionally Yours," backed with "When the Night Comes Falling from the Sky," did not make the charts.

Outtakes   No outtakes have been officially released from these sessions, though a previously recorded version of "Tight Connection," done during the sessions for *Infidels,* was released on *The Bootleg Series.*

The Cover   A tousle-haired Bob Dylan, in a blue shirt and a grey-and-white jacket, cocks his head and puts two fingers to his chin. On the back, Dylan, with eyes closed, is photographed with a dark-eyed beauty.

Liner Notes   There are no liner notes to this album, though the inner sleeve includes all the lyrics, the first Dylan album of new material to include them.

The Record   This album is a major disappointment, and one of the most curious releases in Bob Dylan's 38-record career. Recorded at several studios over a year, it was supposed to be Dylan's first utilization of modern-day recording technology. Instead, the result was a largely unfocused, uninspired effort that is as difficult to listen to these days as is *New Morning.*

Where did Dylan go wrong? First, the instrumentation and backing bands vary so from song to song that there isn't any coherence to the record. Second, for some reason, his lyrics often resemble greeting card sentimentality, particularly on "Emotionally Yours" and "Never

106

Gonna Be the Same Again." Last, his singing wasn't done live, but was often rerecorded. Sometimes it works; sometimes, it doesn't.

It seems that in 1985, Bob Dylan was losing his artistic compass — his sense of what to do, where to go next. Turning to studio technology to help him sort things out was a blunder of monumental proportions.

With the exception of "Tight Connection" and "Clean Cut Kid," this is a forgettable album.

SIDE ONE   1. "Tight Connection to My Heart (Has Anybody Seen My Love)": The original version, released on *The Bootleg Series,* has better lyrics and is sung more tenderly. But Dylan thought he could improve on it, so he worked it around for a year or so before releasing it here. This cry of a man who cannot commit is nicely, professionally, handled. But calling a Bob Dylan album professional isn't necessarily a compliment. (A-)   2. "Seeing the Real You at Last": Having heard an absolutely roaring version of this song on Farm Aid, backed by Tom Petty and the Heartbreakers, this is like "rock lite." You would never know that Dylan had two of the Heartbreakers (guitarist Mike Campbell and pianist Benmont Tench) on this cut. And that's bad. (C+)   3. "I'll Remember You": You can call this song woefully sentimental, or you can see it as confessional. But you find yourself wincing as you read the lyrics and listening to Dylan and Madelyn Quebec trying to sing together. Maybe his heart is really in this one. What's sad is, you always used to be able to tell. (C+)   4. "Clean Cut Kid": Just like that, the old wise-ass, comical Bob Dylan is back with a ruthless song about a Vietnam vet who committed suicide after being unable to adjust to civilian life. And yes, it has Anton Fig, the drummer from Paul Shaffer's "The World's Most Dangerous Band" from the "David Letterman Show." There are some great lines, and Dylan sings the song fine. (A)   5. "Never Gonna Be the Same Again": Yes, it has Syd McGuiness, the guitarist from Paul Shaffer's "The World's Most Dangerous Band" from the "David Letterman Show." And some really soppy lyrics that we haven't seen from Dylan since "Ballad in Plain D." (D)

SIDE TWO   6. "Trust Yourself": Another song Dylan was able to bring to life on the concert stage that hits the dirt here. The televised version with the Heartbreakers at Live Aid rocks. But this is stilted. You can find some perverse humor in listening to Madelyn Quebec trying to guess what the lyrics are as she sings along with Bob. In 1985, when four of his last five albums didn't even go gold, the lyrical message is beside the point. (C+)   7. "Emotionally Yours": Dylan even did a moody black-and-white video for this weeper, sitting alone and playing guitar in a darkened room. The synth horns, by Richard Scher, were a bad idea, as was Dylan's attempt to sing in the higher register of his voice in the closing verse. Sorry, but he sounds like a wounded cow. (C+)   8. "When the Night Comes Falling from the Sky": A rewrite of "All Along the Watchtower," with about half the former version's suspense and a fraction of its lyrical precision, this is a good example of how sometimes, more is less. And vice versa. Dylan says more in the three verses of "Watchtower" than in the ten verses of this monstrosity. A hard-rockin' outtake of this song, with Roy Bittan and Miami Steve Van Zandt of Bruce Springsteen's E Street Band — later released on *The Bootleg Series*— is much preferable. (C)   9. "Something's Burning, Baby": A very peculiar song — another duet of sorts with Madelyn Quebec. What does it all mean? Why she's singing a duet with him on a song to a woman is anyone's guess. Or maybe nobody's. Dismal. (D)   10. "Dark Eyes": Appearing on the syndicated radio show "Rockline," Dylan said this song came to him all at once in a dream. Judging from this song and this record, it seems like Dylan wrote better asleep than awake. A penetrating look at a world he finds disjointed and disinterested. (B+)

Three hits out of ten is a pretty good ratio if you're an outfielder, but for a famous singer-songwriter, that average is just plain lousy. Dylan recorded *Empire Burlesque* at five different studios, had all kinds of different backup bands, and apparently was in no hurry to get the record out. Yet it made for a deadly dull album, one that makes *Infidels* look like *Blonde on Blonde* by comparison.

What went wrong? Well, for one thing, the record does not list a producer, only engineers. Even if Dylan doesn't listen to producers, they usually care enough to try to make sure things turn out right in the end. Its hard to say if Bob Dylan felt a similar commitment while recording his 29th album. If he did, you'd never know it from *Empire Burlesque*. (Album Grade: C+)

Biograph

Produced for reissue by Jeff Rosen for Columbia Records
Released: November 4, 1985

Chart Position   Though *Biograph* only rose as high as No. 33, the stopping point for both *Shot of Love* and *Empire Burlesque,* record industry executives were impressed that an expensive five-record set could sell that well. It was only on the charts two weeks, but sold enough to earn Dylan his 15th gold album. It was only the second time a five-record set was able to break the Top 50.

Singles   No singles were released from this album.

The Cover   It has a nice Daniel Kramer photo of Bob Dylan, circa 1965, tinted red on a gray background, with present-day shots of Dylan in the background.

Liner Notes   If only every music collection were put together the way *Biograph* was. Working with a cooperative Bob Dylan, writer Cameron Crowe did a masterful job annotating this collection and interviewing Dylan about his influences, his career, and rock and roll music. It is interesting and revealing and is a must for any Dylan fan. In fact, if you didn't own a Bob Dylan record and were wondering where to start, this one is it.

The Record   Celebrating Dylan's 24th year as a Columbia recording artist, *Biograph* hit the stores just in time for the Christmas rush of 1985. It is a wonderful compilation of Dylan's greatest hits and an assortment of unreleased oddities and gems, all packaged intelligently by Jeff Rosen of Dylan's publishing company, Ram's Horn Music in New York City.

Considering that Rosen also compiled the exceptional *The Bootleg Tapes, Vols. 1–3* in 1991, Dylan fans owe this guy a huge debt of thanks. Record critics and Dylan devotees had been trying to pry these rarities loose from the Columbia Records vault since the mid–60s. Rosen apparently was able to convince Dylan or the record company that the time was right to put these things out. And Dylan's lagging record sales surely added an incentive.

For Dylan fans, *Biograph* was not the only outstanding Dylan compilation that came out in 1985. On the bootleg market, a five-record set called *The Ten of Swords* included many rare outtakes not included on *Biograph*. Between those two records and the 1991 *The Bootleg Series*, it was clear that Bob Dylan had a lot of outstanding material still in the Columbia vaults. He just didn't seem to want to be bothered picking out the best stuff. Unfortunately, his next two studio albums would leave no doubt about that. But with the release of *Biograph*, Dylan recorded some impressive album sales, paving the way for *The Bootleg Series* six years later.

The positive reviews of *Biograph* helped a great deal. *Rolling Stone* called the compilation "Bob Dylan's Masterpiece," and almost every other prominent musical publication came out with a strongly favorable piece. But an interesting divergence was found from former *Rolling Stone* critic Greil Marcus in *Artforum* magazine.

Taking a look at *Biograph*, along with books on Dylan by Robert Shelton (*No Direction Home: The Life and Music of Bob Dylan*) and by Wilfred Mellers (*A Whiter Shade of Pale*), Marcus made some interesting observations. Comparing "Blowin' in the Wind" with "This Wheel's on Fire," he tried to explain Dylan's achievement and his subsequent failings:

> This great anthem of the civil rights movement ("Blowin' in the Wind"), no matter how profound its effect in the world was ... a song written less about a time and place than by them, an inevitable translation of events into a poeticized reflection. The song itself was blowing in the wind. Dylan simply picked it out.
>
> With "This Wheel's on Fire" from *The Basement Tapes*, something altogether different was going on — in terms of a person creating something that would not have been had that person acted differently....
>
> Real music is a "universal language" because it speaks in many tongues: no matter how effectively the apocalyptic images and tones of "This Wheel's on Fire" translated the apocalyptic moods of 1967, the song could not be held to any fixed, time-and-place meaning. It created its own time and place: one would have heard it in 1967, as one hears it today, as an event, not as a comment on an event, or an incident in a career, or an element of mythos.
>
> A creation, in other words, not a reaction. Marcus continued:
>
> For certain, hard-to-discern reasons, Dylan actually did something

between 1963 and 1968, and what he did then created a standard against which everything he has putatively done since can be measured. There is no way to talk about the possibility that Dylan's career describes not esthetic progress, but the invalidation of the idea of this kind of progress.

Why do some artists seem in touch with the times, then suddenly dated? Marcus went on, discussing the way "It Ain't Me, Babe" stands out on *Biograph*:

> ... remastered, the voice brought forward, allowed to change its shape with every word — it is overwhelming, and it destroys the smeared setting that has been made for it. Here, Dylan moves from certainty to an ambiguity that frightens him back toward a certainty the falsity of which he has just revealed. His whole career comes into focus — as a continuing attempt to tell the truth, supported by economics, mythos, and the lack of anything better to do. His career is an attempt to tell the truth one can discover only in the act of telling what one thinks one already knows, which the act itself exposes as ignorance.
>
> It is foolish to expect that anyone could accomplish such an act by the mere fact of being who one is — at any time, in any place. It makes sense that the confluence of who one is with certain times and places would produce such moments, and that other confluences would not. The question of how the performance of a song makes meaning is raised; so is the question of how a song fakes it.

Was Marcus suggesting that all Dylan's post–1968 work is fake? Or that most of it is? It is an interesting premise to carry into a five-sided collection of 53 Bob Dylan songs.

(Ed. note: Since much of Biograph *is material from previous Dylan albums, the descriptions presented here are only of unreleased material. Descriptions of previously released songs appear on their album of origin.)*

SIDE ONE   **1.** "Lay Lady Lay": From *Nashville Skyline*, 1969. **2.** "Baby, Let Me Follow You Down": From *Bob Dylan*, 1962.   **3.** "If Not for You": From *New Morning*, 1970.   **4.** "I'll Be Your Baby Tonight": From *John Wesley Harding*, 1968.   **5.** "I'll Keep It with Mine": Most of the information on *Biograph* is accurate, but not here. Underneath the title, it says "Recorded in New York City, 1/14/65."

111

Yet in the annotated note underneath, it says "This song was cut on a particularly productive June night in 1964" — the night Dylan cut *Another Side of Bob Dylan*. Since the song wasn't copyrighted until 1965, the first note is probably correct. Whenever it was actually recorded, the song features Dylan alone at the piano. It's a nice performance, sung with confidence. For an interesting comparison, listen to the version of this song released on *The Bootleg Series*, recorded during the preliminary sessions for *Blonde on Blonde*. With Al Kooper on the organ and Dylan's world-weary voice, the song takes on a much more delicate, almost haunted quality. Dylan sounds a lot more than a year older. (B+)

SIDE TWO   5. "The Times They Are a-Changin'": From *The Times They Are a-Changin'*, 1963.   6. "Blowin' in the Wind": From *Freewheelin' Bob Dylan*, 1963.   7. "Masters of War": From *Freewheelin' Bob Dylan*, 1963.   8. "Lonesome Death of Hattie Carroll": From *The Times They Are a-Changin'*, 1963.   9. "Percy's Song": Dylan devotees may recognize this song as the one Joan Baez is seen singing in their hotel room in D. A. Pennebaker's film of Dylan's 1965 tour of England, *Don't Look Back*. This gentle, acoustic version was recorded for *The Times They Are a-Changin'*, but didn't make the record. Too bad, it's a nice song. (B+)

SIDE THREE   10. "Mixed Up Confusion": It's hard to believe, but Dylan recorded this song in November 1962, around the same time as he did "Blowin' in the Wind" and "A Hard Rain's a-Gonna Fall." There doesn't seem to be much of a jump from this one to "Tombstone Blues" (which follows on *Biograph*), but in actuality, it took Dylan three years to start recording with a rock and roll band. Though this cut didn't go anywhere as a single, it's a lively little number, and if you are listening closely, you can hear a great rock and roll singer being born. (A-)   11. "Tombstone Blues": From *Highway 61 Revisited*, 1965. 12. "Groom's Still Waiting at the Altar": Raw, stomping rock and roll, this was one of Dylan's rockingest sides in years, so naturally, he left it off *Shot of Love* in the original release. Talk about a perverse sense of humor. Dylan explained its absence in the *Biograph* liner notes: "I listened back to the song," Dylan said, "and I felt it was too rushed. I felt that we'd lost the original riff to the point where it was non-existent." Maybe Dylan and his band should lose the riff more often. It's a killer. (A)   **13.** "Most Likely You Go Your Way": From *Before the Flood*, 1974.   **14.** "Like a Rolling Stone": From *Highway 61 Revisited*, 1965.   **15.** "Jet Pilot": A studio snippet from the sessions for *Highway 61 Revisited*, it's a humorous look at how Dylan worked. According to the *Biograph* notes, this was the original "Tombstone Blues." (B)

SIDE FOUR   **16.** "Lay Down Your Weary Tune": Recorded for *The Times They Are a-Changin'*, this acoustic track didn't make the cut. Dylan's writing is still developing, and there are some nice lines here. But without any harmonica or instrumental flourishes, it gets a little "weary" by the last verse. (B-)   **17.** "Subterranean Homesick Blues": From *Bringing It All Back Home*, 1965.   **18.** "I Don't Believe You": The second live recording of Dylan and The Band on his 1966 tour of the British Isles to be officially released (the first is "Just Like Tom Thumb's Blues" from the Liverpool date, released on a hard-to-get 1966 single), it's a revealing look at the hard-edged sound Dylan got from The Band (without drummer Levon Helm) on that historic tour. (A)   **19.** "Visions of Johanna": Recorded live in London 20 days after the preceding cut on the same 1966 tour, this one features Dylan alone on acoustic guitar, a regular part of the show. His singing is accurate and powerful. (A)   **20.** "Every Grain of Sand": From *Shot of Love*, 1981.

SIDE FIVE   **21.** "Quinn the Eskimo": From *Self-Portrait*, 1970. **22.** "Mr. Tambourine Man": *From Bringing It All Back Home*, 1965. **23.** "Dear Landlord": From *John Wesley Harding*, 1968.   **24.** "It Ain't Me, Babe": From *Another Side of Bob Dylan*, 1964.   **25.** You Angel You": From *Planet Waves*, 1973.   **26.** Million Dollar Bash": From *The Basement Tapes*, 1975.

SIDE SIX   **27.** "To Ramona": From Another Side of Bob Dylan, 1964.   **28.** "You're a Big Girl Now": This was one of the original cuts on *Blood on the Tracks*, recorded first in September in New York, then recut over the Christmas holidays in Minneapolis. Though this version is nicely done, it's not quite as delicate as the officially released version. What an outtake, though! (A)   **29.** "Abandoned Love": This song sounds like a first take, recorded at the sessions for *Desire*. It's an off-hand lyric but an interesting one. Dylan left this song off the record in favor of "Joey." Bad choice. (B)   **30.** "Tangled Up in Blue": From *Blood on the Tracks*, 1975.   **31.** "It's All Over Now, Baby Blue":

Recorded live in Manchester, England, on that epochal 1966 tour, this is the third live recording to be included on *Biograph*. Hearing it, you can't imagine how Columbia could have permitted Dylan to release the lifeless live tracks from the Isle of Wight concert on *Self-Portrait* while keeping these in the vaults for 20 years. Dylan performs the song a little faster than on the record, but sings it with intensity. His harmonica breaks are brilliant. (A)

SIDE SEVEN   32. "Can You Please Crawl Out Your Window": Recorded twice in 1965, once with Al Kooper and Mike Bloomfield, the backing band he worked with on *Highway 61 Revisited,* and later with the Hawks (later to be The Band), it was released as a single. This is the later version with the Hawks. With its absurdist lyrics, it immediately went nowhere on the charts. However, it would have fit nicely on Side One of *Highway 61 Revisited.* The version with Bloomfield and Kooper is nice also, but this one is better, especially with Dylan's clever quip at the finish, paraphrasing his "Positively Fourth Street" single. (A-)   33. "Positively Fourth Street": From *Bob Dylan's Greatest Hits,* 1967.   34. "Isis": Recorded live on the "Rolling Thunder Revue" in 1975, it's a more dramatic rendition than the one on *Desire.* Dylan explains in the introduction that it's a song "about marriage" then dedicates it to Leonard Cohen, "if he's still here." Fun. (B+)   35. "Caribbean Wind": Recorded for, but not included on, *Shot of Love,* it's a curious, complicated tale that would have made for an interesting pairing with "Every Grain of Sand" and "The Groom's Still Waiting at the Altar," but it didn't get released until four years later. Dylan's voice should be up front more to help us decipher the complex lyrics. (A-)   36. "Up to Me": A remarkable song of artistic dedication — or is it compulsion? — Dylan has rarely sounded so vulnerable, so honest, so unflinching as he does on this outtake from *Blood on the Tracks.* A sound-alike to "Shelter from the Storm," it's courageous where that song is fearful, relentless where that song is resigned. Essential. (A+)

SIDE EIGHT   37. "Baby, I'm in the Mood for You": On this outtake from *Freewheelin' Bob Dylan,* Dylan sounds as if he was having the time of his life in the studio, and he probably was. He said in subsequent interviews that his second record was one of his favorites. This delightful cut gives you an idea of what the recording sessions must have been like. (B+)   **38.** "I Wanna Be Your Lover": Recorded around the time of "Can You Please Crawl Out Your Window" in October 1965, it's a basic blues romp that Dylan roars through. There's a better version of this song on the bootleg *Ten of Swords,* with some of Dylan's wildest rock singing with what sounds like the Al Kooper–Michael Bloomfield *Highway 61 Revisited* backing band. This, "Can You Please Crawl Out Your Window," "Positively Fourth Street," and "Sitting on a Barbed Wire Fence" could have made another fierce side for *Highway 61 Revisited.* (B+)   **39.** "I Want You": From *Blonde on Blonde,* 1966.   **40.** "Heart of Mine": Another song Dylan says his band lost the riff on, this live recording from a New Orleans date in August 1981 is nice. However, there seems to be another factual error. On Dylan's 1989 single "Everything Is Broken," the B side is a live recording of "Dead Man, Dead Man," a track from *Shot of Love.* But the date listed for the song on that record is November 10, 1981. Could Dylan have played New Orleans twice in three months, or is this an error? Either way, look for some live cuts from those November shows someday. (A-)   **41.** "On a Night Like This": From *Planet Waves,* 1973.   **42.** "Just Like a Woman": From *Blonde on Blonde,* 1966.

SIDE NINE   **43.** "Romance in Durango": Recorded the same night as "Isis" on Side Seven, it's an end-of-the-West tale performed enthusiastically by Dylan and his band. (B+)   **44.** "Senor (Tales of Yankee Power)": From *Street Legal,* 1978.   **45.** "Gotta Serve Somebody": From *Slow Train Coming,* 1979.   **46.** "I Believe in You": From Slow Train Coming, 1979.   **47.** "Time Passes Slowly": From *New Morning,* 1970.

SIDE TEN   **48.** "I Shall Be Released": From *Bob Dylan's Greatest Hits, Vol. II,* 1971.   **49.** "Knockin' on Heaven's Door": From Pat Garrett and Billy the Kid Soundtrack, 1973.   **50.** "All Along the Watchtower": From *Before the Flood,* 1974.   **51.** "Solid Rock": From *Saved,* 1980.   **52.** "Forever Young": Recorded for his New York publishers, it's a raw, solo acoustic performance of one of his most played songs of his later career. A nice signoff to a great collection of his work. (B+)

Dylan himself told Mikal Gilmore of the Los Angeles *Herald-Examiner* in 1985 that *Biograph* was no big deal: "I didn't put it together and I haven't been very excited about this thing. All it is, really, is repackaging, and it'll just cost a lot of money." Was Dylan showing concern for his listening audience or resentment that someone else could find a better way to present him to his audience? I vote for No. 2. (Album Grade: A)

Knocked Out Loaded

Produced by Bob Dylan (uncredited) for Columbia Records
Recorded: July 1984–May 1986
Released: June 14, 1986

Chart Position   *Knocked Out Loaded*, a collection of studio tracks, was a poor seller. It did not make the charts, Dylan's first studio album to miss since the 1963 *The Times They Are a-Changin'.*

Singles   Though no singles from the album were officially released, a song Dylan cut with Tom Petty and the Heartbreakers during a tour of Australia called "The Band of the Hand" was released in April.

Outtakes   Since much of the material for this album was culled from several sessions, no outtakes from this record have been officially released.

The Cover   An unusually silly color drawing by Charles Sappington, it shows a sarong-wrapped woman with a large ceramic vase, about to smash it on the head of a man with a sombrero and a gun belt who is choking another man. The words "Knocked Out Loaded," a phrase from the old song "Junco Partner" and from the album's closing song, "Under Your Spell," are stamped above the men. It looks tacky enough to be a bootleg cover, which is probably the idea.

Liner Notes   There are no liner notes to this album. On the inner sleeve, there's a color shot of Dylan on stage. On the flip side is a list of 120 names, people Dylan singled out for "special thanks," including Jack Nicholson, former Dodger pitcher Steve Howe, New York Met Sid Fernandez, and Martin Sheen.

The Record   In a twisted sort of way, you could say that Bob

Dylan used the same method to make *Knocked Out Loaded* that Jeff
Rosen did for the highly acclaimed *Biograph*. He scoured through previously recorded tracks and threw some together. Except Rosen seemed
to have a purpose. If Dylan did with this unseemly conglomeration,
he must really be working for a higher purpose.

There is one terrific track, "Brownsville Girl," and a couple of
others that are interesting. But any hopes for a Dylan renaissance to
follow on the success of *Biograph* were dashed immediately when this
album came out in June 1986. Within a few months, it was banished
to the cut-out bins, which is exactly where it belongs.

SIDE ONE   1. "You Wanna Ramble": In this uptempo blues
standard, Dylan's voice is far back in the mix. It's a decent song and
probably fun to do in concert, but on record, it's certainly nothing
special. (C+)   2. "They Killed Him": It's hard to say which is funnier,
Dylan doing a Kris Kristofferson number or the use of a children's chorus. Somebody like Neil Diamond can pull that off, but not Dylan.
(D)   3. "Driftin' Too Far from Shore": Rolling Stones guitarist Ron
Wood insists that the original track is great. Quoted in an interview
with John Bauldie, he said: "the stuff he [Dylan] was coming out with
was just earth-shattering, but to hear the way he's let producers take
his stuff and bury it has surprised me. 'Driftin' Too Far from Shore' is
a good example of this, a brilliant, fantastic, really vibrant rock 'n' roll
track — but when you hear it on the record ... when he played the record
to me, I went, 'Bob!!! What happened? What happened to your piano?
What happened to the drums?'" And Dylan will just shrug it off. So
should you. (C)   4. "Precious Memories": An old song rearranged by
Dylan with a reggae flavor, it's a standard Dylan remake. The female
chorus is nice enough and the steel drums are well suited to the song.
If you like spirituals, you'll like this song. (B-)   5. "Maybe Someday":
It's difficult to say exactly what this song is about, since these profuse
lyrics are Dylan's densest since "Foot of Pride," an outtake from *Infidels*.
Judging from the way the band kicks in about halfway through it, the
song is probably a first take. But Dylan's vocal, spitting out dozens of
words per line, is inspired. By the end of the song, he's really rolling.
Another artist would have rerecorded this until he had it right. With
Bob, this is what we get. And it's one of the best tracks here. (B+)

SIDE TWO **6.** "Brownsville Girl": An 11-minute opus Dylan co-wrote with Sam Shepard, it's wonderfully conceived and written. You laugh, you don't understand, you keep listening. The song seems to be about a Gregory Peck movie and, perhaps, how the hero finds himself in a similar situation to Peck's character in the film. A great song. It's a shame that it's on such a ragged record. (A) **7.** "Got My Mind Made Up": A tough rocker recorded with Tom Petty and the Heartbreakers, it's not a bad song. Not as good as "Jammin' Me," which Dylan also co-wrote with Petty and appears on the Heartbreakers' *Let Me Up (I've Had Enough)*, but it's still a decent song. (B+) **8.** "Under Your Spell": Written with Carole Bayer Sager, it's a strange love song, unlike anything else Dylan has ever written. Which isn't necessarily a compliment or an insult. (B-)

If it weren't for "Brownsville Girl" and perhaps "Got My Mind Made Up" and "Maybe Someday," you could say there was no reason for this record to exist. But these three songs save it from being the worst album of his career. That Dylan had to resort to a succession of outtakes to follow up his most successful record in several years is sad, indeed. (Album Grade: C+)

Down in the Groove

Produced by Bob Dylan (uncredited) for Columbia Records
Recorded: April 24–May 1987
Released: May 31, 1988

Chart Position   Like its predecessor, *Knocked Out Loaded, Down in the Groove* did not make the charts, Dylan's second straight studio-album flop. Except for *Infidels* in 1983 and *Biograph* in 1985, Dylan had six straight albums that failed to go gold, including three in a row that didn't even make the charts.

Singles   The clever "Silvio," backed with an outtake from *Empire Burlesque* called "Drifting Too Far from Shore," was released in June 1988. It was not a hit.

Outtakes There have been no officially released outtakes from the sessions for this album.

The Cover   This is another soft focus shot of Dylan in the spotlight, playing the guitar.

Liner Notes   There are no liner notes for this album.

The Record   You could call this album "Self-Portrait II," and you wouldn't be far off. Though he hadn't written an album of entirely new material in three years, he was able to muster only two originals and two collaborations for this, his 32nd record release.

Like *Knocked Out Loaded,* it features a variety of bands from different sessions. Unlike *Knocked Out Loaded,* the cuts here are better recorded, and some are better performed. But on the whole, it's a disappointing effort from someone who seems to have been getting bored with the whole idea of making records.

SIDE ONE   **1.** "Let's Stick Together": A good, solid version of Wilbert Harrison's old rock and roll classic, Dylan lays into it, and the band follows capably enough. (B)   **2.** "When Did You Leave Heaven?": This is lame, cornball stuff. Dylan and Madelyn Quebec supposedly harmonize, except that you can't quite hear her. You can hear him, and it doesn't help. (D)   **3.** "Sally Sue Brown": In this standard uptempo blues in the vein of "You Wanna Ramble" or "Let's Stick Together," Madelyn Quebec tries to keep up with Dylan, and fails. (C)   **4.** "Death Is Not the End": A pitiful outtake from *Infidels* that should have stayed that way, this half-baked treatise on life ever after is frightening when you consider that if Bob's right, someday you might have to hear this song again. (F)   **5.** "Had a Dream About You, Baby": A song Dylan performed (well, sort of:) in Richard Marquand's feature film *Hearts of Fire,* it's yet another blues shuffle that shuffles nowhere. (C+)

SIDE TWO   **6.** "Ugliest Girl in the World": Co-written with Robert Hunter, sometime lyricist for the Grateful Dead, it's a little bit outrageous, a little bit silly, and a little bit fun. (B)   **7.** "Silvio": Dylan sings this simple song with a gusto you don't hear much on this record. It was released as a single and got minimal airplay. The backing chorus ought to be shot. (B+)   **8.** "Ninety Miles an Hour (Down a Dead End Street)": This song contains a little more corny harmonizing, though this time you can hear the backing vocalists. It's probably the kind of thing that sounds best in the studio, in warm-ups. (C+)   **9.** "Shenandoah":

Out of nowhere comes this respectful, lovely rearrangement of the old classic. Dylan sings and plays it with surprising care, and the result is one of the better cover versions he's ever done. (A-)　**10.** "Rank Strangers to Me": Dylan has continued to perform this sad song in concert. Few songs in Dylan's repertoire match the sense of isolation he gives to this number. Listening to the closing verse, you can't help but think that the guy actually feels like this. (A-)

These last two studio records are undeniably the worst of Dylan's recording career: uninspired, haphazard, lifeless, and shoddy. After these two nosedives, Columbia had to be concerned about finding someone who could put some life in the old guy. And wouldn't you know it, along came the Grateful Dead. (Album Grade: C)

Dylan and the Dead

Produced by Jerry Garcia and John Cutler for Columbia Records
Recorded: July 1987
Released: February 6, 1989

Chart Position　Dylan's first gold album since *Infidels* was also his fifth live album in the past 15 years. It went to No. 37 and was on the charts for three weeks.

Singles　No singles were released from this album.

Outtakes　No outtakes from these live recordings with the Grateful Dead have been officially released.

The Cover　A nice drawing of a '60s Dylan head and a Grateful Dead Skull and Roses logo flank an approaching train.

Liner Notes　There are no liner notes to this album.

The Record　Recorded on Dylan's brief summer tour with the Grateful Dead in 1987, it wasn't released until two years later, another indication of the problems Dylan was apparently having coming up with new material. His fifth live album since 1974, it's about what you'd expect from touring veterans like the Grateful Dead and Dylan: erratic singing and uncertain beginnings and endings marked by Jerry Garcia's quicksilver guitar.

The record includes Dylan standards like "All Along the Watchtower," the fourth officially released version of that song, and "Knockin' on Heaven's Door," the third officially released version of that one. Unfortunately, the record also includes Dylan's much-maligned "Joey," clocking in at 9:23, filling up a good part of Side Two.

The fact that it sold well despite some harsh reviews hints that when Dylan and Columbia Records decided to release it — two years after the fact — they knew what kind of a loyal following the Grateful Dead have and saw dollar signs.

As the *Village Voice's* Robert Christgau cleverly pointed out in his capsule review:

> Dylan is Bob, the influential singer-songwriter who's resurfaced as the brains of the Traveling Wilburys; the Dead are Grateful, and not just because charismatic guitarist-antileader Jerry Garcia survived an off stage coma — they're rich men, and they sound it. Like Dylan, Garcia plays hardest and works more playfully when someone pokes him a little — Ornette Coleman, say. But unlike Ornette Coleman, Dylan's not forever young and what he makes of his catalogue here is exactly what he's been making of it for years — money.

SIDE ONE   **1.** "Slow Train": Dylan screws up the words while the Dead lend their light, swingy feel to *Slow Train Coming's* angriest song. All of the sudden, it doesn't sound so angry anymore. (B-)   **2.** "I Want You": You can't really blame the Grateful Dead for this one, for their backing, particularly Garcia's up-front guitar, is perfect for this *Blonde on Blonde* classic. But Dylan's hoarse, tuneless bark ruins the song. If only they could have recorded it together in 1966. (C)   **3.** "Gotta Serve Somebody": Garcia's guitar is fine on this minor-chord brooder. Dylan toys with lyrics again, and, at times, it's hard to make them out. On *Slow Train Coming,* Dylan sang this song as if it were a warning, and the aura of impending doom made it work. It got him a Grammy, in fact. This version lacks that feeling, but it does have Jerry's guitar work, which doesn't quite save it. (C)   **4.** "Queen Jane Approximately": The Grateful Dead have been performing this Dylan oldie for years. Bob hasn't, and that may explain the refreshing interpretation he gives it here. Clearly the best song on the record, the Dead slow it down, letting the beautiful melody take over, and the haunted, burned-out majesty of it all is wonderful. You wonder how impressive this entire tour could have been if Dylan had only taken more than 15 minutes to go over the song list. (A)

SIDE TWO   **5.** "Joey": It was bad on *Desire,* and it's bad here. You get the sense that one of the Dead suggested it almost as a joke, and Dylan thought, "Hey, a 10-minute song. That means there's one less song I'll have to do." He sang it much better on *Desire,* too. Have these guys no shame? (F)   **6.** "All Along the Watchtower": Some songs are so durable, they hold up no matter who sings them, no matter how half-hearted the effort. I've heard Dylan's understated version on *John Wesley Harding,* the hard-charging version with The Band on his 1974 North American Tour on *Before the Flood,* and the conga-flute-violin version on *Bob Dylan at Budokan,* not to mention Jimi Hendrix's definitive space-cadet-glimpses-the-apocalypse rendition and even the impromptu live version by U2 on *Rattle and Hum.* They all worked. So does this one, with, once again, Garcia's silvery runs leading the way. (B+)   **7.** "Knockin' on Heaven's Door": Well, they have to close the show with something, and Dylan picks his archetypal song of the Old West. Except here, it's done slower. Handled a little more introspectively than on *Before the Flood,* the song sounds like a quiet "good night," with Dylan trying to sing out and around the melody. Nice try, but...

(Album Grade: C+)

Oh Mercy

Produced by Daniel Lanois for Columbia Records
Recorded in New Orleans (March–April 1989)
Released: September 19, 1989

Chart Position   Dylan's first solo album to make the charts in four years, *Oh Mercy* went to No. 30. It stayed on the charts for six weeks. Though a fine record, it has not yet gone gold.

Singles   The catchy "Everything Is Broken" was released in October with a live version of "Dead Man, Dead Man" from *Shot of Love.*

Outtakes   Though producer Daniel Lanois has hinted at others, the only outtake so far released from these sessions is the evocative "Series of Dreams," which was included on *The Bootleg Series, Vols. 1–3.*

The Cover   A wall painting by Trotsky depicts a couple embracing on one side while a bespectacled man in a gray suit looks away.

Liner Notes   There are no liner notes to the album, simply recording credits on the inner sleeve.

The Record   Just when you thought you had heard the last of Bob Dylan as a vital recording artist, along comes Daniel Lanois, cohort of U2 and the Neville Brothers.

Recording this album in New Orleans, Lanois not only got Dylan to pay more attention to his craft — which wasn't saying much after the last two disasters — but managed to steer him clear of attempts to sing in a higher register, where his voice drones on. Dylan wrote quite captivatingly of the turbulence of these recording sessions with Lanois in "Chronicles, Vol. 1." It's interesting to read Bob's description of what was going on, then listen to the record.

Dylan told Adrian Deevoy of *Q* magazine that Lanois managed to capture "my stage voice," which means that it's gruff, grizzled, and hard-edged. But on songs like "Man in the Long Black Coat," which is talked as much as sung, it works to great effect.

Dylan and Lanois worked well together, and as quoted in John Bauldie's *Wanted Man: In Search of Bob Dylan*, Lanois told about the sessions:

> It's a blend of his fast approach and my more cautious approach. Quite a few of the things are one take, but care did go into this record. It's not a throwaway, it's got kind of ... if you imagine doing fantastic 70 millimeter filming of simple objects and treating them like jewels, imagine a rugged worker's hand and then closing in on it and examining every pore, every broken fingernail, it's got that kind of quality to it, really in your face. "Ring Them Bells" is just him and his piano and it's a staggering piece of work. His last records had some bad sounds on it and there are no bad sounds on this new record, no cliches. It doesn't take a whole lot to pull the quality out with somebody like Dylan provided he is interested, and he was on this record. You have to show the same kind of interest.

Which is not to say the record came out exactly as Lanois wished:

> I did say that I didn't think that certain songs belonged on the
> record. He took it fine but he bucked me on a few of those decisions.
> And I would never say no to at least trying out his ideas. We did try
> a few things that didn't make the finish line. ... We had four or six
> songs we recorded and didn't use. One track, "Series of Dreams," was
> a fantastic turbulent track that I felt should have been on the record,
> but ... he had the last word.

Like "Blind Willie McTell" left off *Infidels*, "Series of Dreams"
was another extraordinary Bob Dylan song that he decided to keep in
the can. Finally released as the closing song on the 1991 *The Bootleg
Series*, it stands out as one of Dylan's finest post–1970s songs. If it were
added to this record, the album would have been a classic. Without it,
Oh Mercy is still the best album Bob Dylan had made since *Infidels* and
is one of the best albums of his career.

SIDE ONE   **1.** "Political World": With a soft, swirling guitar; a
pulsing bass line; and congas, this churning song of societal discontent
is infectious. Dylan spits out the lyrics with a vengeance, and the beat
drives it home. (A)   **2.** "Where Teardrops Fall": A little sappy, this lonely
song of longing doesn't quite match up to the rest of the record. It's not
as fake as some of the songs on *Empire Burlesque,* but it's close. (C+)   **3.**
"Everything Is Broken": The kind of effortless shuffle Dylan seems to be
able to write in his sleep, this was the single off the record, and it's a
dandy. It's catchy and nicely sung with lyrics of the apocalypse; what
more could you ask? (A)   **4.** "Ring Them Bells": Dylan at the piano
warns of the trappings of modern-day life or something like that. Sung
with the solemnity of a true believer, it is Dylan's most believable religious song in a long time. (A-)   **5.** "Man in the Long Black Coat": A
wonderfully evocative song of the sudden appearance and disappearance
of a man who left everything not quite the same. Recorded and performed with subtlety, it is a terrific, enigmatic song that you can't imagine another singer-songwriter could have written. (A)

SIDE TWO   **6.** "Most of the Time": An understated love song
performed with admirable off-handedness, you can imagine Dylan's
wry sneer, denying he even thinks of the woman he loved and lost
"most of the time." (A-)   **7.** "What Good Am I?": Bob asks himself

the question that record critics had been posing since *Street Legal.* An unflinchingly honest look at himself and his relationship to his muse, it reminds you of the comment by *New York Times* music critic John Rockwell that some of Dylan's songs qualify as "remarkable works of art, miniatures in length but as deeply probing as anything produced by the best American artists in any medium." A song so honest, it takes you by surprise. (A+)   **8.** "Disease of Conceit": From a brilliant song to one markedly less imaginative and preachy, that's the curse of Bob Dylan, post–1975. Dylan again tries on the humble, religious mantle he assumed on *Ring Them Bells,* and it doesn't go down quite as easily this time. (B-)   **9.** "What Was It You Wanted": Toying around with that same chord progression that produced "Gotta Serve Somebody," "Señor," and many others, he gives it a new twist lyrically and pulls it off. Not only that, it would make a great phone message for your tape machine. (B+)   **10.** "Shooting Star": Taking one of the most cliched, hackneyed themes imaginable, Dylan gives it a new twist and closes his most successful record in years in tender, reflective fashion. (B+)

If nothing else, Daniel Lanois proved that under the right circumstances, Bob Dylan can still produce first-rate material and record it intelligently.

As London *Times* critic Richard Williams, quoted in *A Dylan Companion*, noted: "For once in his recent history, though, *Oh Mercy* allows us to listen to a new Bob Dylan album without needing to forgive him anything. It may very well be the Bob Dylan album we want; whether it is the one we need is another matter." (Album Grade: A-)

Under the Red Sky

Produced by Don Was, David Was, and Jack Frost for Columbia Records
Recorded: January 6; March 1990
Released: September 17, 1990

Chart Position   Dylan's second straight studio album to make the charts, *Under the Red Sky* went to No. 76. It was on the charts for eight weeks.

Singles   "Unbelieveable," backed with "10,000 Men," was released as a single and went nowhere.

Outtakes   No outtakes from the sessions for this album have been released.

The Cover   Dylan, dressed in a suit jacket and white alligator shoes, squats in the desert. On the back of the album, he wears a poncho and sits on the front step of a house.

Liner Notes   There are no liner notes to this album, though the lyrics of the songs are included for the first time since the 1985 *Empire Burlesque*.

The Record   After a staggering list of 100 concert dates in 1989, according to *Absolutely Dylan* by Patrick Humphries and John Bauldie, Dylan took December off, then went into the studio in January to cut four tracks — "Handy Dandy"; "10,000 Men"; "Cats in the Well"; and "God Knows," a track left over from *Oh Mercy*.

With an all-star cast, including the late Stevie Ray Vaughan, George Harrison, Slash (from Guns N' Roses), Bruce Hornsby, David Crosby, and even Elton John, the record should have been promising, but it seems that, once again, Dylan fell back into the haphazard recording techniques that have marred most of his recording over the past decade.

Though the record has some interesting songs, it appears that neither Don Was nor David Was nor Jack Frost was able to take the time that Daniel Lanois did to get each track the best it could be. The record is good, but not great.

However, the critics did not think that *Under the Red Sky* was even good and laid into it with characteristic fervor. But in this case, they may have misunderstood Dylan's motives.

He has often talked of doing a children's album, and *Under the Red Sky*, at least some of it, may be exactly that — or at least as close to it as we're likely to get.

Take, for example, the title song, an eerie Grimm Brothers–like horrific fairy tale. When Dylan was asked about it by producer Don Was, he replied: "It's about my hometown." Was went on to explain, in Clinton Heylin's *Behind the Shades:* "It's such a great little fable. These people have all this opportunity and everything and they choose to be led around by a blind horse and they squander it. It's beautiful and it was so simple and he just sang it one time through and it was perfect."

Considering that the first four songs recorded — "Handy Dandy," "God Knows," "Cat's in the Well," and "10,000 Men" — can all be seen in that light, as can the title song and certainly "Wiggle, Wiggle," a children's album of sort may well have been what Dylan had in mind. Naturally, Bob didn't say.

SIDE ONE   **1.** "Wiggle, Wiggle": A clever little protestation about female temptresses, Dylan even throws in some sexual imagery at the end to make sure you get the point. A lot of record critics, of course, didn't. (B)   **2.** "Under the Red Sky": A strange song, even from Dylan, it seems to be about a nuclear holocaust or something similar. But then again, it may not be. (B)   **3.** "Unbelievable": With nice guitar work by Waddy Wachtel and old friend Al Kooper on keyboards, Bob rocks on into the sunset. The song would be a killer live, but he did not incorporate it as a regular feature of his live shows following the album's release. (A-)   **4.** "Born in Time": Not as sappy as Dylan's quiet piano numbers often get, it has somewhat unusual lyrics about the laws of nature and destiny and other such mysticism. (C+)   **5.** "TV Talking Song": You had to wonder when Bob would get around to a diatribe against television. Here it is. Just as he warned us we had invented our doom by going to the moon in "License to Kill" on *Infidels,* here he quotes a man who says that nothing can protect us from TV once we turn it on. He may be right, but the whole idea is kind of laughable, which is not likely to be the way Bob intended it. (C+)

SIDE TWO   **6.** "10,000 Men": Another tune about women and sexuality, it's hilarious, but you have to pay attention to the lyrics and the imagery. (B)   **7.** "2 × 2": Maybe it's a coincidence that Elton John and David Crosby appear on this song, and perhaps it's intended to be a kids' song. But it's almost as silly as "Man Gave Names to All the Animals." (C-)   **8.** "God Knows": All right, Bob. Give us a little religion and rock it. With Stevie Ray Vaughan, Jimmie Vaughan, and old Jackson Browne cohort David Lindley on slide guitar, it's a rockin' little number about the importance of faith. (A-)   **9.** "Handy Dandy":

127

A great cheesy Al Kooper organ riff that kicks it off and Dylan's sly vocal make this the best song on the record. The lyrics seem to be about a man who is, let's see, controversial, haunted by something, unable to admit pain, possessing an impenetrable fortress that no one can break into. (A)   **10.** "Cat's in the Well": With Stevie Ray and Jimmie Vaughan and David Lindley rocking away, Dylan closes out Side Two in fine fashion with yet another look at the end of the world or something like that. For a God-fearing soul, Dylan sure seems to be worried about the end of things. (B+)

It is not a bad record and is maybe a sign that Dylan is once again a step ahead of the critics, if indeed this is intended as an ersatz children's record. It would have been a better record if he had dropped a few of the sappy songs like "Born in Time" and "2 × 2," but at least you get the sense that he is trying. (Album Grade: B+)

The Bootleg Series, Vols. 1–3

Produced and compiled by Jeff Rosen for Columbia Records
Released: March 20, 1991

Chart Position   A three-record set, this album, like *Biograph* before it, drew critical acclaim and reportedly sold very well. It was on the charts for two weeks and went to No. 33.

Singles   No singles were released from this album.

The Cover   A fine Don Hunstein photo from 1965 shows Dylan, wearing dark glasses, harmonica to mouth, blowing into a microphone.

Liner Notes   An especially well-done booklet by longtime Dylan devotee John Bauldie, who talks about each song and its place in the Dylan compendium. Bauldie's booklet, together with Cameron Crowe's booklet for *Biograph,* are must-reads for major-league Dylan fans.

The Record   What can you say about a 58-song three-record set of previously unavailable Dylan material? It's about time. Though a good bit of the set has leaked out over the years on various bootleg albums, there are some real rarities here. And everything has been remastered and cleaned up so the sound quality is impressive.

The series begins with a track recorded in a Minnesota hotel room before Dylan cut his first record and concludes with a track kept off 1979's *Oh Mercy*. In between, you can trace the development of Bob Dylan from folksinger to rock and roll star to recluse and all that's happened to him in the meantime.

More recently, the Bootleg Series has concentrated on live shows recorded earlier in Dylan's career, but unreleased. Only the Bootleg Series, Vol. 7, *No Direction Home: The Soundtrack* has included true outtakes. But who can predict what he'll do next?

VOLUME ONE, SIDE A   **1.** "Hard Times in New York Town": Recorded in a Minnesota hotel room, this song gives you a glimpse of the Dylan of the early days. His delivery is impressive, and he sounds like a promising young singer. (B)   **2.** "He Was a Friend of Mine": With gentle guitar picking and easy harmonica, Dylan handles this personalized variation on an old blues song very well. (B+)   **3.** "Man on the Street": Recorded for but not included on Dylan's debut album, the song borrows the melody from an old frontier song — something Dylan did quite often in the early days — and turns it into his own. (B) **4.** "No More Auction Block": Recorded at New York's Gaslight Cafe in 1962, Dylan turns in a performance of real intimacy on this old spiritual. (B+)   **5.** "House Carpenter": An outtake from *The Freewheelin' Bob Dylan,* reputedly it's an extremely old ballad. Dylan performs it with gusto and enthusiasm. (B+)   **6.** "Talkin' Bear Mountain Picnic Massacre Blues": The second of nine outtakes from *Freewheelin'* to be included on *The Bootleg Series,* it's clear that Dylan was developing at a remarkable rate. A funny talkin' blues, similar to "I Shall Be Free." (B+)   **7.** "Let Me Die in My Footsteps": For such a young man (21 at the time this was recorded), Dylan seemed to be obsessed with death. Three songs on his debut album dealt with it, and here is another one. This one, however, didn't make the cut. (C) **8.** "Rambling, Gambling Willie": A delight. This was originally slated to be included on *Freewheelin'* and was included on some rare test pressings of the record. It's a funny song about a roving gambler, and Dylan does it up nicely. (A-)   **9.** "Talkin' Hava Negeilah Blues": Just a snippet of Dylan goofing around in the studio with a "foreign song" he learned in "Utah." (C)   **10.** "Quit Your Low Down Ways":

Here, Dylan goes for the voice of an old-time blues singer, and the result is surprising. It sure doesn't sound like the hillbilly who sang on Dylan's debut record. (B+)   **11.** "Worried Blues": A somewhat predictable blues number that is notable mostly for Dylan's nifty guitar picking. He doesn't seem to play with that kind of delicacy now. (C+)   **12.** "Kingsport Town": Another outtake from *Freewheelin'*, the melody posed a strain for Dylan's vocal cords. It's OK. (C+)   **13.** "Walking Down the Line": Recorded as a demo for Dylan's publishing company at the time (M. Witmark and Sons), it's a lively tune that was covered by artists as diverse as Glen Campbell, Jackie De Shannon, and Rick Nelson. (B)

VOLUME ONE, SIDE B   **14.** "Walls of Red Wing": Dylan heads into his protest period. This bitter tune about life inside a reform school is a bummer musically and lyrically. (C)   **15.** "Paths of Victory": One of the earliest recordings of Dylan at the piano, it sounds like a sister song to Woody Guthrie's "This Land Is Your Land," which is probably the idea. (B)   **16.** "Talkin' John Birch Paranoid Blues": This is the song Dylan was to have played on "The Ed Sullivan Show" until CBS censors nixed the idea. It's hard to imagine that McCarthy's fear of the Reds was still such a part of American life. Dylan has fun with it, recorded at Carnegie Hall several months after the Sullivan fiasco. (A-)   **17.** "Who Killed Davey Moore?": A hard-edged protest song about the death of boxer Davey Moore, it asks all the important questions and gets all the standard answers. (B)   **18.** "Only a Hobo": Dylan's version of this song is very rough; his singing is a bit over the top. Rod Stewart's gentle rendition on the 1970 *Gasoline Alley* is much preferable. (B-)   **19.** "Moonshiner": An outtake from The Times They Are a-Changin', this beautiful song would have done a lot to lighten the doom and gloom of that album. Dylan's singing is superb. (A)   **20.** "When the Ship Comes In": One of the three songs performed by Dylan at Live Aid, it is biblical in tone and content. Dylan's portrait of doomsday is convincing. (B+)   **21.** "The Times They Are a-Changin'": This is Dylan's piano version of one of his most famous songs, recorded as a demo for his publishing company. He's not exactly Jerry Lee Lewis and takes the song at a slow pace. (B+)   **22.** "Last Thoughts on Woody Guthrie": Dylan's only spoken poem, it was performed at the conclusion of his Town Hall concert in New York City on April 12, 1963. It is a remarkable bit of writing from a young man who apparently was, as Robert Shelton's famous *New York Times* review noted, just "bursting at the seams with talent." (A)

VOLUME TWO, SIDE A   23. "Seven Curses": An outtake from The Times They Are a-Changin', this is a sad, age-old tale of a girl trying to save her father's life. Dylan's performance is fine. (A-)   24. "Eternal Circle": Another outtake from *The Times They Are a-Changin'*, it's a little monotonous. (C)   25. "Suze (the Cough Song)": A hilarious improvisation by Dylan, who tries to play a quiet instrumental but breaks out in a cough at the end and then tries to say that the song was supposed to have ended before he coughed. (B+)   26. "Mama, You've Been on My Mind": Another Dylan song that Rod Stewart treated with a little more care and made an entirely new song. Recorded for *Bringing It All Back Home*. (C+)   27. "Farewell, Angelina": A key song in Dylan's development as a songwriter for its unusual imagery, bootleggers had never been able to locate Dylan performing it anywhere until it came out on *The Bootleg Series*. Listening to it, you can hear Dylan beginning to be less literal and more imaginative with his lyrics, setting the stage for the ground-breaking songs that followed. (A)   28. "Subterranean Homesick Blues": Done acoustically, it doesn't lose a thing from the original, which shows you how much Dylan had improved as a singer. It's a great song. And most Dylan afficionados didn't even know this version existed. (A)   29. "If You've Gotta Go, Go Now": Recorded for *Bringing It All Back Home*, this rock number didn't make the album, but was released as a single, backed with "To Ramona" in the Benelux countries in 1967. Quite a collectible. (A-) 30. "Sitting on a Barbed Wire Fence": Recorded for *Highway 61 Revisited* but not included on the record, it's more hard rock from Dylan and his great band from the same session that produced "Like a Rolling Stone." (A-)   31. "Like a Rolling Stone": History in the making. Dylan hammers out a rough version of his most famous song as his voice cracks. It's interesting to note that the time signature really changed in the official release. Included for historical significance. (B)   32. "It Takes a Lot to Laugh, It Takes a Train to Cry": Another song from that historic session, it's taken at about twice the tempo it ended up at on the record. There's great singing and guitar work from Mike Bloomfield. (A) **33.** "I'll Keep It with Mine": A different version of the song was released on *Biograph*. This later version, recorded during the prelimi- nary sessions for *Blonde on Blonde*, is interesting, particularly for the dramatic change in Dylan's voice. He sounds as if he has aged 30 years in the past two. (B) **34.** "She's Your Lover Now": Another *Blonde on Blonde* outtake that beats practically anything else on the record, it's one of the truly great Bob Dylan songs that, for some reason, he kept in the can for years. His writing and singing are superb, and the back- ing by The Band (then the Hawks) is exemplary. Though the song breaks down near the end when Dylan stumbles over the lyrics, it is still a remarkable piece of work. As a side note, it's significant that in both "official" Dylan lyric books *Writings and Drawings* (1973) and the updated *Lyrics* (1985), the song's last verse is missing. However, John Bauldie came to the rescue, including it in *The Bootleg Tapes* booklet. (A+)

VOLUME TWO, SIDE B　　**35.** "I Shall Be Released": A Dylan classic, it has proved to be one of his most enduring compositions, though his original version of the song was not heard until *Bob Dylan's Greatest Hits, Vol. II* and, then, not too impressively. Dylan's vocal is exceptional on this stately rendition. (A) **36.** "Santa-Fe": A nonsen- sical outtake from the personal collection of The Band's Garth Hud- son, it gives you an indication of the good times and high spirits Dylan and The Band shared in The Band's home, Big Pink, in West Sauger- ties, New York. With Dylan making up the words as he goes along, it's loads of fun. (B+) **37.** "If Not for You": If Dylan sounds like a scared man, he probably was. Recorded with Beatle George Harrison on slide guitar in 1970, it is a much more tentative version than the one that eventually ended up on *New Morning*. For Dylan at this time, new material was really hard to come by. (B) **38.** "Wallflower": A coun- try-flavored waltz, recorded at the same 1971 sessions at which Dylan recorded his protest single "George Jackson," it did not make it onto a Dylan album until now, though Doug Sahm and Band did a cover version in 1972. (B+) **39.** "Nobody 'Cept You": On this outtake from the first day of recording with The Band for *Planet Waves*, Dylan's first album of all-new material in three years, he sounds tentative and somewhat uncomfortable. (B)   **40.** "Tangled Up in Blue": The original version of the song Dylan recut over the Christmas holidays, it sounds good, but lacks the brightness of the official release. A lyrical note: Dylan sings the first verse in the third person, the same way it would later appear on the 1984 album, *Real Live*. (B+)   **41.** "Call Letter Blues": A sound-alike to "Meet Me in the Morning," if record critics had heard the confessional lyrics of this one, they surely would have concluded that this song and, indeed, the entire record was about Dylan's failing marriage. Dylan, of course, has insisted that the record was influenced more by his interest in painting. (A)   **42.** "Idiot Wind": Though done just with acoustic guitar and harmonica, the strange thing is that this angry blast doesn't lose any of its power. Another version of this song, with strange organ music in the background, was widely bootlegged. This one is far better. (A)

VOLUME THREE, SIDE A   **43.** "If You See Her, Say Hello": Another of the *Blood on the Tracks* original cuts, it is beautifully sad and handled exceptionally by Dylan. Though not as delicate as the version on the record, you can still hear the emotion in Dylan's voice. (A)   **44.** "Golden Loom": An outtake from *Desire,* it has a bent sort of mysticism that Dylan was into in those days, hence the tarot cards on the *Desire* jacket. (B)   **45.** "Catfish": A tribute to then–New York Yankees free agent pitcher Jim "Catfish" Hunter, it's a laughable blues. (B)   **46.** "Seven Days": Recorded from Dylan's fiery "Rolling Thunder Revue," this is a fine bit of rock and roll with some surprisingly intricate singing by Bob. (B+)   **47.** "Ye Shall Be Changed": An outtake from the religious album *Slow Train Coming,* it's a standard sermonette. (C+)   **48.** "Every Grain of Sand": A publishing demo for this extraordinary song with Dylan at the piano and Kim Carnes singing harmony (occasionally accompanied by Dylan's dog barking in the background), it's a song of remarkable beauty and sensitivity. Fortunately, it also hinted that Dylan was coming to the end of his religious period. (B+)   **49.** "You Changed My Life": An outtake from *Shot of Love,* it harkens back to his "born-again" period. It is heartfelt, but more than a little predictable. (C+)   **50.** "Need a Woman": This is an outtake from *Shot of Love.* Dylan made a significant change in the published lyrics in 1985's

Lyrics. When it comes to the line about searching for the truth the way God wanted, in the book, Dylan says he might drown before he finds it. On the record, he says the real truth is that he is afraid of God's truth. Quite a shift. (B)   **51.** "Angelina": This third outtake from *Shot of Love* is reminiscent of "Farewell Angelina" in more ways than just the title. Lyrically, it comprises a fascinating collection of images that Bauldie's booklet suggests "heads for the deepest, darkest parts of poetic mystery." Or maybe Dylan's just confused. (A-)

VOLUME THREE, SIDE B   **52.** "Someone's Got a Hold of My Heart": An early version of *Empire Burlesque's* "Tight Connection," it's much more natural sounding and a lot more believable. Recorded for *Infidels,* it's one of three or four terrific cuts that Dylan curiously chose to keep off the record. (B+)   **53.** "Tell Me": A New Orleans–flavor cut with slide guitar and a sly Dylan vocal, it's a nice love song. (B)   **54.** "Lord, Protect My Child": A plaintive prayer, Dylan sings it respectfully. It is exactly what the title implies. (C+)   **55.** "Foot of Pride": One of Dylan's finest, angriest songs, this was another extraordinary song that was kept off *Infidels.* Why? Dylan explained on "*The Bootleg Series*" radio special that the drum machine he was working with got carried away. With remarkable lyrics and in intense, committed vocal, this is the kind of song that helped Dylan establish himself as "the conscience of a generation." (A+)   **56.** "Blind Willie McTell": Delicately, perfectly sung and flawlessly written, this song ranks with Dylan's finest, most perfectly realized songs. That it was left off *Infidels* when it is at least twice as good as anything on the record doesn't say much for Dylan's ability to judge his own material. Mark Knopfler's guitar counterpoint to Dylan's vocal is exquisite. This is a masterpiece. (A+)   **57.** "When the Night Comes Falling from the Sky": On *Empire Burlesque,* this uninspired rewrite of "All Along the Watchtower" was a clunky and stiff. Here, backed by pianist Roy Bittan and Miami Steve Van Zandt from Bruce Springsteen's E Street Band, Dylan sings with power and conviction. (B+)   **58.** "Series of Dreams": Another exceptional song that Dylan refused to include on *Oh Mercy,* it is a penetrating look at his muse, his career, and his life. His singing, not much more than a growl in some places, is perfect. This is one of his best. (A+)

Certainly a major addition to the Dylan catalog, *The Bootleg Series,*

Vols. 1–3 shows the remarkable development of Dylan as a songwriter and a singer. What is surprising is that in the entire three-record set, the voice really doesn't change that much, whereas without these important recordings, the Dylan of *Nashville Skyline* sounds nothing like the Dylan of *Blood on the Tracks* or of *Freewheelin' Bob Dylan*.

Hearing songs like "Blind Willie McTell" and "Series of Dreams," Dylan fans had to be encouraged that their man could still write. Apparently, he just didn't have the confidence — or common sense — to release them. But they clearly are a revelation and make this package irresistible. (Album Grade: A)

Good as I Been to You

Production supervised by Debbie Gold for the Gold Network
Released: November 2, 1992

Chart Position   Dylan's first album of all-acoustic material since *The Times They Are a-Changin'* in 1963, the record debuted at No. 51 and went no higher. It was on the charts for eight weeks.

Singles   No singles were forthcoming off the album at its initial release.

The Cover   The first up-to-date close-up of Bob Dylan's face to appear on one of his album covers since *Empire Burlesque,* Dylan looks old and grizzled, not unlike one of those New Testament prophets. He is wearing a leather jacket, a black T-shirt, and a striped shirt; sporting a three- or four-day growth of beard, he looks quite serious.

The shot of Dylan is in black and white. However, the sky above him, on which "Bob Dylan" is superimposed, is purple and yellowish.

Liner Notes   There are no liner notes to this record, but there is a curious photo on the back of the liner sheet that appeared to be a bunch of clouds. Perhaps it's a visual pun to go along with Dylan's cover of Howlin' Wolf's "Sittin' on Top of the World."

The Record   Maybe the title is a give-away. *Good as I Been to You* sounds like a response from someone who doesn't feel appreciated, someone who can't believe his records don't sell like they used to or that his tours don't fill the largest halls.

Dylan's 37th album is the first one he has done where he did not write a single song. The material is credited to "All songs Traditional. Arranged by Bob Dylan, ASCAP, except 'Hard Times,' 'Tomorrow Night,' and 'You're Gonna Quit Me' Public Domain. Arranged by Bob Dylan ASCAP."

So where did the songs come from? Good question. The song "Sittin' on Top of the World" is normally credited to Chester Burnett, also known as Howlin' Wolf. But the rest are more difficult to pin down.

Even a search through the blues and folk sections at your local record store probably won't turn up any other versions of these songs. But the great thing is, it doesn't matter.

Dylan breathes life into these songs and by the time the record is over, you're wondering why more people haven't covered a great rock and roll song like "Step It Up and Go" and why k.d. lang hasn't tried a sweet old ballad like "Tomorrow Night."

For the first time in a long, long time, Dylan sounds energized doing this new-old material. And it reminds me of what was mentioned in the Introduction: How free Bob Dylan sounds when he isn't singing his own songs. Whether it's with the Traveling Wilburys or doing "Pretty Boy Floyd" for the Folkways record, Dylan can still sound like a vital, exciting artist. It is only when he does his own songs that he seems to get bogged down and hung up. You wonder how the creative process ever got that painful for him.

SIDE ONE   1. "Frankie and Albert": An uptempo blues tune of a love affair gone astray — thanks to Albert's infidelity. Frankie shoots her man in the arms of another. Dylan's guitar work is quite energetic on this number, as is his singing. It's really lively and a lot of fun. (A) 2. "Jim Jones": Written in the "Olde English" ballad style, this is a tale of a man sentenced to work in a prison in New South Wales who vows revenge on the tyrants. You can tell that Dylan really gets a kick out of the old language ("Then says the judge says he...") and offers a delightful rendition of this oldie but goodie. (B+)   3. "Blackjack Davey": A minor-chord ballad of a scandalous scoundrel who makes off with an underage girl and the wild love affair that follows. Included is a self-reference to a Dylan song "Boots of Spanish Leather." The theme of adultery and stolen love is universal and apparently everlasting. This song is similar in lyrical flavor to "The Jack of Hearts" off *Blood on the Tracks.* (B)   **4.** "Canadee-I-O": A ballad of a young girl who falls in love with a sailor and tries to stow away on the ship. The sailor dresses her up in a sailor's suit, the crew threatens to throw her overboard, but the captain comes to her rescue. Of course, the girl marries the captain. (B+)   **5.** "Sittin' on Top of the World": A wailing harmonica kicks off this thumping rendition of Howlin' Wolf's old classic. Dylan usually includes a blues song on every album, and this one stands with his finest. (A)   **6.** "Little Maggie": A nifty little guitar piece about a gun-totin' gal named Maggie. The riff is irresistible, and Dylan's singing is imaginative and captivating. Very different. (A-)

SIDE TWO   **7.** "Hard Times": "Is a song the last sigh of the weary?" Dylan asks in this song, which sounds as old as anything he is ever recorded. He treats it with dignity. (B)   **8.** "Step It Up and Go": It's acoustic, but it rocks harder than just about any Dylan song you can think of since "Groom Still Waiting at the Altar." It sounds like some sort of old gutbucket blues from the early 1920s rocked up plenty. Bob should add this song to his live shows. (A)   **9.** "Tomorrow Night": Written by Will Grodz and Sam Coslow in 1939, one might call this the missing link in the Dylan-Elvis connection. "Tomorrow Night" was one of the songs Elvis Presley recorded but did not officially release on the historic Sun Sessions, Presley's first recordings for Memphis studio legend Sam Phillips. That Dylan would select a song with this kind of historic connection shows his impeccable taste, his keen sense of rock and roll history and his place in it. An old ballad you can picture Al Jolson having recorded, it's a little hokey, but Dylan's singing on this version is as impressive as on anything he's recorded since the mid–1970s. (A-)   **10.** "Arthur McBride": A medium-tempo tale of the life of a soldier named Arthur McBride and his cousin and their subsequent struggle with, a sergeant and then, the horrors of war. It sounds like it was written around the time of World War I and is reminiscent of a Grimm Brothers fairy tale, much like "Under the Red Sky." (B)   **11.** "You're Gonna Quit Me": This is another nifty country blues, reminiscent of "Baby, Let Me Follow You Down" off his first album. Dylan sings and plays it sweetly. (B+)   **12.** "Diamond Joe": Sounding like an outtake from The Times They Are a-Changin', it's the story of an outlaw, scamp, and troublemaker. There's a great line at the finish where Dylan sings "Give my blankets to my buddies. Give the fleas to Diamond Joe." It's very funny. (B+)   **13.** "Froggie Went a Courtin'": A strange old song about the marriage of cousins in the animal kingdom. There's quite a cast of characters, and Dylan's singing makes you feel as if you can picture every one. Some folk musicologist has probably written a lengthy dissertation on the symbolism in this song. It is strange and ultimately somewhat unsettling, yet one could easily interpret it as a children's song. (A-)

It is somehow both poignant and encouraging that to revitalize a singing and recording career that had skidded in recent years, Dylan chose to return to the very types of material that got him interested in singing and writing songs in the first place. That's what you call bringing it all back home. (Album Grade: A-)

Bob Dylan: The 30th Anniversary Concert Celebration

Produced by Jeff Rosen and Don DeVito
Recorded at Madison Square Garden, New York (Oct. 18, 1992)
Released: August 23, 1993

Chart Position   The two CD set debuted at No. 40 on the Billboard charts, its highest position, and went gold after 11 weeks on the charts. It is Dylan's 18th gold album.

Singles   No singles were forthcoming off *Bob Dylan: The 30th Anniversary Concert Celebration* at its initial release.

The Cover   With color photographs of the evening's performers cut into the letters "Bob Dylan" on an all-white background, you can spot Dylan, Eric Clapton, Stevie Wonder, Neil Young, Chrissie Hynde, John Mellencamp, George Harrison, Tom Petty and Eddie Vedder from Pearl Jam.

All are understandable choices, except perhaps Vedder, who was selected over such artists as Willie Nelson, Johnny Cash and Lou Reed. They must have been going for the youth vote.

Liner Notes   Be sure to wear your galoshes as you slog through David Wild's prose on the liner notes to this record. Whether describing Johnny Winter's "monumental display of blues power" on his take of "Highway 61 Revisited" or Stevie Wonder's "endlessly soulful" version of "Blowin' in the Wind," Wild is a guy who shouldn't be allowed near a thesaurus.

The key word, however, was "moving," as in Stevie Wonder's "moving" introduction to "Blowin' in the Wind"; Tracy Chapman's "eloquent and moving" solo acoustic version of "The Times They Are a-Changin'"; Eric Clapton's "startling and moving" performance on two Dylan numbers (one of which was so moving they didn't include it) and Dylan's own "moving composition" "Song to Woody," which, according to the liner notes, was also prevented from being included here for "technical problems."

The hyped tone of the notes almost makes it seem as if the record company needed to make an excuse for releasing yet another Dylan live album of old material. But Columbia needn't apologize. Many of the performances here are keepers.

The Record   In the 30 years since Bob Dylan released his first recording for Columbia Records, there have been times when his influence and perhaps his achievement were doubted or at least, taken for granted.

The noted rock writer Tim White once said the 1950's song "The Book of Love" said more to him than the entire Bob Dylan canon — about as heretical a sentence as any rock critic has ever written about Dylan.

Yet one wonders if White would have wanted to amend his thoughts after witnessing the October 18 "Tribute to Bob Dylan" at Madison Square Garden, which was shown first on pay-per-view. Then released as a live album ten months later.

With 24 different artists performing a wide-ranging selection of Dylan compositions, it was indisputable evidence of Dylan's complete and comprehensive mastery of the various styles of contemporary popular music.

Ranging from the wonderful howling protests of Pearl Jam's Eddie Vedder performing the oldie "Masters of War" to the charming folk/country rendition of "You Ain't Going Nowhere" by the trio of Mary-Chapin Carpenter, Roseanne Cash and Shawn Colvin to the blistering metal guitar work of Neil Young on the venerable "All Along the Watchtower," it is difficult to imagine another artist producing such a vast and varied body of work for such a diverse group of artists to draw from.

There was even a little controversy as Ireland's Sinead O'Connor, fresh off an appearance on NBC's "Saturday Night Live" in which she ripped up a photograph of the Pope, was roundly booed.

She was slated to do "I Believe in You" a song off *Slow Train Coming,* but the boos were so loud, she never acknowledged Booker T.'s piano intro to the song. Instead she performed Bob Marley's angry "War," the same song she had done on "Saturday Night Live."

Since Dylan himself had purportedly been booed off the stage at the Newport Folk Festival in 1965 for daring to play rock and roll music, some were surprised that Dylan himself didn't come out and give O'Connor a measure of support and quiet the crowd down. According to O'Connor, he did tell her later to "keep doing what I'm doing."

Her performance is not included in the two CD set.

That aside, what seemed the most remarkable thing about the night was how malleable Dylan's songs seemed to be.

Opening the show, John Mellencamp seemed to have no trouble adapting Dylan's most popular song, "Like a Rolling Stone" to his own gospel cajun-flavored brand of rock and it set a tone for other artists to follow.

DISC ONE   **1.** "Like a Rolling Stone": With Al Kooper, who played organ on the original recording of this song 28 years earlier joining Mellencamp's band for this one, it would have been hard to foul it up and Mellencamp doesn't. Actually, he adds several nice touches, using two backup singers to help him with the verses, throwing in a nice soft violin break in mid-song. One of the most respectful covers of the night and also one of the best. (A)   **2.** "Leopard-skin Pillbox Hat": As loose and rolling as a Tennessee hillside, Mellencamp has fun with one of Dylan's most playful lyrics. (B)   **3.** "Introduction by Kris Kristofferson": Kris makes the point that it's Bob Dylan's night and of course, it is. But it would have been even better to get Bob out to say a few words.   **4.** "Blowin' in the Wind": While Stevie Wonder's introduction might be long-winded by most people's standards, by Stevie's own it was barely a semi-colon. His rendition of one of Dylan's most enduring songs is fine. (A-)   **5.** "Foot of Pride": You probably had to be a hard-core Dylan fan to recognize this one, an outtake from *Infidels* that simply roars. Though Lou Reed occasionally has a hard time keeping the words matched to the relentless guitar riff, he swaggers through the song with the intensity of an Old Testament scribe and the passion of a religious zealot. But maybe I repeat myself. (A)   **6.** "Masters of War": This sounds nothing like Pearl Jam but lead singer Eddie Vedder and guitarist Mike McCready infuse one of Dylan's angriest lyrics with the kind of intensity you might expect from young, fiery protest rockers. Vedder's vocal muscle, at times almost a howl, is exceptional and the song works as well as any on this magical night at the Garden. (A+)   **7.** "The Times They Are a-Changin'": Tracy Chapman's wavering vibrato voice isn't for everyone but her take on Dylan's alarm for the protest movement is right on the money. And yes, it does sound a bit like she wished she had written. (A-)   **8.** "It Ain't Me, Babe": The night's first miss but a good-natured one. Dylan had to have old pal Johnny Cash included and Cash brought along his wife June Carter to turn in a lively, if somewhat inappropriate, rendition of "It Ain't Me, Babe." The theme of the song has nothing to do with the way these two perform it but, if Sonny and Cher can cover it, so can Johnny and June. (C+)   **9.** "What Was It You Wanted": The erratic Willie Nelson quickly brings the evening back into focus with a subtle reading of one of Dylan's most unusual songs, a cut off the New Orleans–based *Oh Mercy*. Willie gives it his own special brand of talk-singing and it works. (B+)   **10.** "I'll Be Your Baby Tonight": You can't very well invite Kris Kristofferson and not let him sing, so his rendition of Dylan's country-flavored tune off *John Wesley Harding* is harmless though not particularly tuneful. (C)   **11.** "Highway 61 Revisited": Though the scrawny, heavily tattooed arms of guitarist Johnny Winter looked more than a little unhealthy, there's plenty of steam in that ol' guitar. His rockin' workout on the title cut from one of Dylan's greatest records is a textbook of how electric blues slide guitar should be played. (A-)   **12.** "Seven Days": At times, Ron Wood's singing is even worse than Dylan's, which is about as bad on the tonal scale as it can get. But Woody was into the all-star gala and turned on the pipes and did himself proud. (B+) **13.** "Just Like a Woman": Richie Havens' unusual open tuning guitar playing and understated singing style enable him to reinterpret even the most well-known Dylan songs. One of his finest covers is this Dylan classic off *Blonde on Blonde.* Some have said his version is better than Dylan's. (A-)   **14.** "When the Ship Comes in": Though you might not think Bob Dylan aka Zimmerman has much to say to the Irish community, Tommy Makem, Robbie O'Connell and the Clancy Brothers turn this early Dylan number into a song you might expect to hear at an Irish wedding. Which may be a compliment. (B+)   **15.** "You Ain't Going Nowhere": Flawless voices, a perfect melody and ridiculous lyrics provide the ideal vehicle for country-folk singers Mary-Chapin Carpenter, Rosanne Cash and Shawn Colvin. These three should record an entire album of Dylan songs. (A)

DISC TWO   **16.** "Just Like Tom Thumb's Blues": There are a few bootleg recordings of Neil Young's performance of this old Dylan classic circulating but none have the world-weary singing or the guitar fire of this one. Simply an exceptional cover version, one that both cuts and reminds you of the original. (A+)   **17.** "All Along the Watchtower": As if Young's stunning take on "Just Like Tom Thumb's Blues" wasn't enough, he pushed the stakes even higher with a guitar-fueled, sonic strafing run at this oft-covered Dylan classic. U2 have done it, Jimi Hendrix has covered it and so, believe it or not, has Dave Mason. But Young's exceptional guitar work and delicate yet impassioned singing make this the hit of the night. (A+)   **18.** "I Shall Be Released": It takes a major performer to fit in between two legendary guitarists and the Pretenders' great Chrissie Hynde didn't seem to mind a bit. She turns in a slow, thoughtful cover of one of Dylan's most lovely ballads. (A)   **19.** "Don't Think Twice, It's All Right": One of Dylan's early classics turned into a standard blues by the high priest of the wailing guitar, Eric Clapton. Eric's playing is fine, the song's new twist is interesting and you wonder why they cut the other Clapton cover (Love Minus Zero/No Limit) from the record. (A-)   **20.** "Emotionally

Yours": One of Dylan's more tepid ballads from *Empire Burlesque;* the O'Jays invest the song with much more passion than Dylan ever did. It's not the high point of the evening but it was interesting to see a black vocal group take a mediocre Dylan song and find a way to make it a hit. (B+)   **21.** "When I Paint My Masterpiece": It's hardly fair to still call them The Band in a lineup that no longer includes guitarist and songwriter Robbie Robertson or the late piano player Richard Manuel. Nevertheless, Levon Helm, Rick Danko and Garth Hudson were on hand for this night, joined with a half-dozen other players for a nice rendition of this middle-period Dylan tune. (B-)   **22.** "Absolutely Sweet Marie": Unfortunately, former Beatle George Harrison's enthusiasm for Dylan's songs does not match his ability to sing them. He loves Dylan and he's done some great songs over the years. This isn't one of them. (C+)   **23.** "License to Kill": An unusual choice for Tom Petty and the Heartbreakers to cover, this tune from *Infidels* is haunting in its imagery and tone. The Heartbreakers, however, always sound much better rockin' down the house so this is just OK. (B)   **24.** "Rainy Day Women #12 & 35": This is more like it. Raucous, fun, tinkling piano and pounding drums, the Heartbreakers sound as if they're enjoying themselves on this one. Petty's singing is a little too restrained, though. (B+)   **25.** "Mr. Tambourine Man": Petty stayed on stage to introduce and join ex–Byrd Roger McGuinn for a fine rendition of the Byrds' first hit, an electric 12-string guitar-led cover of "Mr. Tambourine Man." McGuinn even sings a couple more verses than on the two-minute-plus original hit. (A-)   **26.** "It's Alright, Ma (I'm Only Bleeding)": After a heartfelt reading of "Song to Woody" which isn't included here, Dylan roars into perhaps his finest sustained sermon, the powerful "It's Alright, Ma." Though not done at the breakneck speed of the *Before the Flood* version or as grotesquely as on the "Hard to Handle" video from his Australian tour with Tom Petty and the Heartbreakers, Dylan still manages to make the song sound alive. (A)   **27.** "My Back Pages": An inspired choice for the perfunctory set closer, particularly for the ironic twist of the chorus. Everyone gets a turn at the mike: McGuinn, Petty, Young, Clapton, Harrison and our Bobby, who had to have overdubbed his foghorn vocal for the release of the record. But it is a good thing he did, because everything else about the song, including the fine Clapton and Young guitar solos, make this worth buying the record. (A+)   **28.** "Knockin' on Heaven's Door": Dylan's concerts apparently have to end with this due to federal regulations, or so it seems. This is a cursory run-through. It is a song that has been sung to death. (C+)   **29.** "Girl of the North Country": With the credits rolling on the pay-per-view broadcast, you could hear the early strums of Dylan's guitar, long after it seemed like the show was over. It was his final encore in Madison Square Garden, probably the last time he'd play such a big place. His choice was a gentle, early number off *Freewheelin'* and though his voice is too shot to make himself sound wistful, it's a nice thought. And the effort is there. (B)

By their nature, all-star reunions are a mixed bag. Some stars are out of it, some are into it and some are way past their prime. The Band's farewell concert documented on *The Last Waltz* probably remains the definitive all-star get-together — there are more classic performances on that recording than on *Anniversary.*

But this record is still a very listenable tribute to Dylan and his music. There really is not a terrible song on the record — something you cannot say about *The Last Waltz* (remember Neil Diamond's constipated "Dry Your Eyes"?). Neil Young and Eric Clapton's performances are exemplary and the finale "My Back Pages" is guaranteed to get you singing along.

At the same time, there's a bit of sadness to the whole thing. For at the time, you wondered if Dylan would ever do anything this musically significant again. (Album Grade: A-)

World Gone Wrong

Produced by Bob Dylan for Columbia Records
Recorded and mixed by Micajah Ryan
Release date: October 26, 1993

Chart Position   "World Gone Wrong" peaked at 70, its debut position on the charts. It was on the charts for only four weeks.
Singles   No singles were released from this album.

World Gone Wrong (1993)

The Cover In a jaunty top hat, Dylan sits at a table with a turquoise plastic tablecloth. He is wearing a long dark coat and his dark-gloved left hand holds another chair or perhaps an umbrella. The cover shot is slightly off-center, as if the world has gone wrong.

On the green painted wall behind Dylan, you can see part of a painting — probably by Dylan himself— of a tortured face. The title, in black and white lower case typewriter script, is stripped sideways on the cover picture. The overall effect brings back a long-ago description of the songs on the album *Blonde on Blonde*. It was called a record of "dandy's blues."

At 52, Dylan still looks like a dandy.

On the inside photo, Dylan, wearing a white cowboy hat, is shown in sepia-toned close-up. He looks somber.

The Liner Notes For the first time since the short jacket notes to *Desire,* Dylan has written some prose for one of his records. It's terrific.

The notes were very possibly written at the behest of his record company, who were almost certainly deluged with questions from journalists and fans about the sources of the obscure material Dylan used on *Good as I Been to You.*

On that record, about the only song rock audiences were reasonably familiar with was Howlin' Wolf's "Sittin' on Top of the World," which Dylan later credited to Public Domain.

Here, no songs are familiar. So the liner notes are titled simply "About the Songs" (what they're about).

Beginning with "Broken Down Engine," a song Dylan calls Blind Willie McTell's "masterpiece," Dylan goes into a mystical, poetic, hard-charging rant, discussing the songs a little and society a lot.

The prose style is somewhat similar to his novel, *Tarantula,* except his writing seems sharper. It's delightful to read.

And of course, Dylan slips in a few read-between-the-lines tidbits.

The song "Stack a Lee," is a much-analyzed tune that is sometimes seen as a precursor of Lloyd Price's hit "Stagger Lee." It has already been discussed in some length by Greil Marcus in the appendix of *Mystery Train,* his outstanding book on American popular music.

Dylan explains in the liner notes that the song tells us "no man gains immortality thru public acclaim." Who could Bob be talking about?

A few lines later, Dylan jokes about hats, as he's depicted on the album's cover and jacket photo wearing one. A hat is also the reason Stack a Lee got into his historic fight with Billy Lyons.

"A man's hat is his crown," Dylan says.

There are many other memorable turns of phrase in the notes. Dylan refers to "these modern times" as "(the New Dark Ages)" and makes a cry for the "Authentic alternative lifestyle, the Agrarian one."

The writing is vivid, imaginative and gives Dylan the opportunity to use words like "effete," "hegemony," and "rectitude," — very likely the first time an artist associated with rock and roll has ever displayed such a well-armed vocabulary.

The Record   The story goes that Bob Dylan walked into the Columbia Records office in Los Angeles, strolled up to the receptionist and handed her a cassette.

"This is my new album," Dylan said.

"Oh," said the receptionist, wondering who the scruffy little guy was. "Thank you."

The cassette, his 40th album, *World Gone Wrong,* stayed on her desk until the end of the day, when she finally remembered to hand it over to someone.

There is no way to confirm this story — it was told at a record convention — but if it's true, Bob Dylan must have been delighted.

After years of having fans sleeping outside his house, pawing through his garbage, asking for a sign, *the* sign, Dylan finally may have gotten his wish.

At last, he was anonymous.

It took some work. Years of haphazard recording techniques, willfully — some might say, gleefully — perverse decision-making, unpredictable concert performances and just plain weird behavior painted him as a sort of gifted screwball.

He was still seen as an artist who might write and record a song as fresh and sharp as a cool summer morning rain, yet not release it because "he didn't record it right."

146

Naturally, there is a limit to how much of this people are willing to tolerate. And since Dylan had been acting this way at least since 1975's *Desire,* his last major solo success with all-new material, their patience had worn thin.

So until the big comeback with *Time Out of Mind* in 1997, the music business showed him little respect and less attention. And though at times it must gall an artist of Dylan's stature to have been treated with the same status as Simon LeBon, he knew better than anyone the price to be paid for notoriety.

For years, he felt the strain of being, in Jack Nicholson's words at Live Aid, an artist "whose work speaks for his generation." Dylan seemed to delight taking a different path as long as he stayed out of the limelight.

In the early '90s, his latest kick, as revealed on 1992's *Good as I Been to You* and his new record, *World Gone Wrong,* was reaching back into his kit bag of ancient, half-remembered obscurities.

Working only with his acoustic guitar and occasional harmonica, Dylan tries to breathe new life into these old songs.

Though he is delivering these songs to an audience that knows nothing of their heritage (which is probably what the liner notes are for), Dylan is giving us his own *Basement Tapes,* a look at the rich and largely unexplored lower shelf of American music — material he freely admits shaped his writing and performing style.

By re-recording songs originally done by such largely unfamiliar artists as Blind Willie McTell, Tom Paley, Frank Hutchinson, the Mississippi Sheiks, Willie Brown and Doc Watson, Dylan is both bringing their work to a somewhat larger audience and illustrating an important point.

As D.H. Lawrence put it: "Trust the tale, never the artist."

Though his audience would certainly prefer to hear him sing his own work, Dylan is again defiant. Telling them, in so many words, don't pay so much attention to *who* is writing the words, pay attention to *what* the words say.

If you want to keep hearing from me, Dylan says, then you're going to have to listen to what I feel like singing.

Which right then was not his own songs.

THE SONGS   **1.** "World Gone Wrong": A mournful ballad Dylan credits to the Mississippi Sheiks, it is a haunting tune, one that would not have been out of place on any of Dylan's cover-laden early albums. A theme Dylan has used many times, it is particularly well-suited for an album opener and is very well done. (A)   **2.** "Love Henry": A lovely little girl from Cornersville kills her lover and dumps him down a well. Her parrot is a witness to the whole thing but refuses to squawk. Ain't it just the way? (B)   **3.** "Ragged & Dirty": A sassy little blues number, Dylan's deft acoustic guitar work and appropriately ragged ending suit this one just fine. It's a come-on song and Dylan sings it with surprising subtlety. (A-)   **4.** "Blood in My Eyes": Another Mississippi Sheiks tune and a dark one. The singer is drawn to a hooker. It is performed with tender persistence by Dylan. (B+)   **5.** "Broke Down Engine": Described by Dylan as "a Blind Willie McTell masterpiece," it's a lively blues tune, reminiscent of *Good as I Been to You*'s "Step It Up and Go." And when Dylan raps the face of his guitar to depict knocking on a door, it sounds like he's having more fun than he has had in a recording studio in years. (A)   **6.** "Delia": Dylan turns in a fine, tender vocal performance on this soft-spoken ballad sung by a man who loved a gamblin' girl shot down by Cutty, a girl who never had time for the singer. (B+)   **7.** "Stack a Lee": A tale of the legendary fight between Stack a Lee and Billy Lyons. Stack a Lee, later to be Stagger Lee in the song Lloyd Price made famous, wins the fight. He shoots Billy, who'd stolen his John B. Stetson hat — his crown, Dylan says — through the head. There's a public outcry over Billy's death but Stack a Lee gets away with it. In the notes, Dylan writes: "in the preindustrial age, victims of violence were allowed (in fact it was their duty) to be judges over their offenders — parents were punished for their children's crimes (we've come a long way since then)." Such a card. (A)   **8.** "Two Soldiers": A song Dylan calls "a battle song extraordinaire," it was taught to him by Jerry Garcia of the Grateful Dead. Dylan plays and sings it with dignity. Though it's a nice song, it's kind of boring. (C)   **9.** "Jack-a-Roe": An up-tempo, minor-chord folk ballad that Dylan has always done well. Somewhat reminiscent in tone of "Seven Curses" on *The Bootleg Series, Vols. 1–3*, Dylan sings this tale of deception and love gone astray with just the right mix of verve and foreboding. (B+)   **10.** "Lone Pilgrim": This Doc Watson tune, written by G.F. White and Adger M. Pace, is delicate and Dylan sings it that way. His voice isn't pretty, but the guitar-playing is tender and his delivery has rarely been so gentle. This could be a lullaby. Beautifully done. (A)

Whether it was the perverse burst of freedom Dylan felt in recording an entire album of obscure covers — knowing they were songs that most journalists couldn't track down — or the sense that he was taking some great undiscovered songs and bringing them to a new audience or finally, that he could still do a record in this day and age that would get good reviews, Dylan stuck with the same formula that made *Good as I Been to You* a success on *World Gone Wrong*. And again, he delivered a very nice, solidly performed album.

But that said, the question remained, would he ever want to write again? The liner notes showed he still could. (Album Grade: A-)

Bob Dylan's Greatest Hits, Vol. III

Released: November 15, 1994

The release of *Bob Dylan's Greatest Hits, Vol. III*, comprising 13 previously available tracks and "Dignity," a five-year-old outtake from the sessions for *Oh Mercy*, was apparently intended to be representative of Dylan's finest work over the last 21 years — the oldest song on it is 1973's "Knockin' on Heaven's Door" — but it fails by a wide margin.

Four songs on this record ("Gotta Serve Somebody," "Tangled Up in Blue," "Knockin' on Heaven's Door," "Groom Still Waiting at the Altar") were previously released on *Biograph*. And the "Forever Young" included here from *Planet Waves* was also on *Biograph* in demo form.

The one "new" track, "Dignity," is five years old. A mid-tempo number, it's nothing more than glorified filler. Considering Dylan fans haven't heard a freshly written song from their man in four years, including that is just plain exploitation.

Looking at the other songs — "Jokerman," "Hurricane" — it would be interesting to know who actually made the song selection. Was it

Dylan or *Biograph* compiler Jeff Rosen or someone else? The song selection is curious.

There is no "Blind Willie McTell," easily the finest single Dylan recording since 1974's "Tangled Up in Blue," although "Series of Dreams" is included. If you're a Bob Dylan fan, you'll have a hard time understanding why *Street Legal*'s "Changing of the Guard" was chosen instead of "Where Are You Tonight (:Journey Through Dark Heat)."

Or how can you figure the bizarre choice of *Oh Mercy*'s "Ring Them Bells" instead of "What Good Am I?" or "Most of the Time" or even "Political World?"

Greatest Hits, Vol. III does rescue the clever "Silvio" from the dreck of *Down in the Groove* and "Brownsville Girl" from the dismal *Knocked Out Loaded*.

But one has to wonder why Columbia chose to re-release songs like "Tangled Up in Blue" one more time. This studio version of the song is already on *Biograph* and *Blood on the Tracks* and the song was also released in a live version on *Real Live*.

Similarly, you can find "Knockin' on Heaven's Door" on the *Pat Garrett and Billy the Kid Soundtrack* and *Biograph* in the studio version that's included here and if you want a live version, it's on *Before the Flood* as well as *Bob Dylan: The 30th Anniversary Concert Celebration* and *MTV Unplugged*.

MTV Unplugged

Executive Producers were Jeff Kramer and Jeff Rosen for Columbia
　　Records
Recorded in Sony Music Studios in New York (November 17, 1994)
Released: June 30, 1995

Chart Position　*MTV Unplugged*, in something of a surprise, roared to No. 23 on the Billboard charts and as high as No. 10 in the British charts.

Outtakes　Dylan performed a number of songs that were not included in the MTV telecast or included on the CD/DVD. These included "Love Minus Zero/No Limit," "Tonight I'll Be Staying Here with You," "I Want You," "Everything Is Broken," "Don't Think Twice, It's All Right," "Hazel," "Absolutely Sweet Marie," and "My Back Pages."

Singles   No singles were released from this album.

The Cover   With the old dark sunglasses, a black and white polka dot shirt, circa 1965, Bob Dylan leans into the microphone.

The Liner Notes   There are none offered for this live recording.

The Record   Apparently, Columbia Records decided it was time for Bob Dylan to cash in on the *Unplugged* craze and this show, recorded at the Sony Music Studios in New York, is nice enough. Unlike many of the *Unplugged* shows where the artist goes on to explain why he or she wrote the song, Dylan is silent between songs.

Oddly, Bob has a stool to sit on but he never quite does. He sort of leans against the stool at varying points, but never sits down and gets comfortable. Only Bob would find a creative way to use a stool.

Dylan's choice of material is interesting and he performs them pretty well. The arrangements, however, are relatively similar to the actual recordings of these songs, unlike the roustabout treatment they generally get in concert. It might have been a lot more fun to hear some of these arrangements re-thought for posterity.

My favorite part of the show is when they screw up "Like a Rolling Stone" and Dylan stops the show, says they're going to get this right and they start up again. And they left it all in!

THE SONGS   **1.** "Tombstone Blues": Almost a rockabilly version of this classic from *Highway 61 Revisited*, Bob and his band breezily rumble through this chestnut. (B)   **2.** "Shooting Star": With a steel guitar lead in, this version of the album closer from *Oh Mercy* doesn't quite have the poignancy and delicacy of the original. Dylan's voice is rougher. (B-)   **3.** "All Along the Watchtower": One of his most played songs, according to Dylan maniacs, this tune from *John Wesley Harding* is usually a concert closer. Dylan's singing here is weird, yet it gets a standing ovation from the crowd. My guess is it was performed near the end of the set and later fit in here. (C+)   **4.** "The Times They Are a-Changin'": A slowed and stately version of Bob's early anthem from the album of the same name. He sort of talks through the lyrics at points, which is effective. The original sounded like a warning. This sounds like he's sad he was correct　(A-)　**5.** "John Brown": An inspired choice, written in 1963 but never included on an official album, its anti-war sentiments seemed particularly appropriate. And let's face it, it is pretty amazing that the guy can remember all the words to an obscure song he wrote some 30-plus years earlier. (A)　**6.** "Desolation Row": Another inspired choice. The backing is gently bouncy, which helps Dylan sail through the verses. As you listen to the extraordinarily creative lyrics, you wonder if we'll ever hear another songwriter with such a profound imagination, so willing to take chances. (A)　**7.** "Rainy Day Women #12 & 35": A crowd favorite, it usually gives Dylan a chance to mumble as much as he wants through the early bits. Here he sticks to the original lyrics and yes, the crowd loves it. (B+)　**8.** "Love Minus Zero/No Limit": A surprisingly delicate version of this oldie. Dylan sings it with some passion and plays a gentle harmonica. Nice (A)　**9.** "Dignity": An outtake that Dylan revived for this show — and as a selling point for all those fans who have these other songs in innumerable versions. It's a good song. (B)　**10.** "Knockin' on Heaven's Door": One of Dylan's most famous songs gets a sing-song version here. Lousy. (C)　**11.** "Like a Rolling Stone": Slow and stately, sung with some intensity, it's a nice resigned version of Dylan's greatest song. He screws around a little holding notes longer than is recommended, but there is unusual sincerity in the "How does it feel." And he's only sung this how many times? (A)　**12.** "With God on Our Side": A most unusual choice for an encore, Dylan lays into this oldie with intensity. Sung slowly and with real emotion, you can't help but think about how far he's come. And that he's still out there, singing. (A)

(Album Grade: B)

Time Out of Mind

Produced by Daniel Lanois in association with Jack Frost Productions for Columbia Records
Recorded in Miami (January and February, 1997)
Released: September 30, 1997

Chart Position   *Time Out of Mind* climbed to No. 10 on the Billboard charts.

Outtakes   "Mississippi" (later released on *Love and Theft* in 2001) and "Girl from the Red River Shore."

Singles   No singles were released from this album.

The Cover   An old, grim-faced Bob Dylan poses with an acoustic guitar in a darkened recording studio in the round. The black and white picture, probably taken by Daniel Lanois, is not particularly sharply focused, which fits the dark, isolated feel of the album, Dylan's second with Lanois.

The Liner Notes   There are none, only a considerably long list of fellow musicians and who played on what. The album's two other photographs — a black and white inside the jacket and a colored, truly out-of-focus shot on the back — lend to the somber mood. It looks as if Bob doesn't want anybody to get a really good look at him.

The Record   Recorded in Miami with Daniel Lanois, Dylan's old *Oh Mercy* producer, it seems as if Bob came into this project with a particular sound, a concept in mind. According to interviews with Lanois and others, he actually read the songs aloud before they even went in to try and record them.

Consequently, this brought about some radical changes when it came to actually putting these words to music. For example, the one song from here that seems to immediately rank with Dylan's greatest numbers, "Not Dark Yet," was altered in style and tempo when it came to actually recording it.

Whether Dylan had as difficult a time with this album as *Oh Mercy*— described so vividly in *Chronicles, Vol. 1,* we'll likely never know. All implications are that it took a tremendous amount of effort from everyone involved. And Dylan's final calls on what songs made it and what didn't were, as always, up for debate. Dylan even mentioned that when, some months later, he stepped on stage to accept his Grammy.

Any way you look at it, though, this clearly was Bob's finest, most focused record in a very long time. It was good to have him back.

THE SONGS   1. "Love Sick": Haunting, spooky, almost hypnotic. You can hear Dylan — and see him — as a truly old man, lamenting his lost loves, his awful decisions, his wrong turns. It is the sound of a man who has really lived. (A). **2.** "Dirt Road Blues": A sprightly, neo-rockabilly number, it's a light-hearted relief to the woe of "Lovesick." (B+) **3.** "Standing in the Doorway": Not a lot has been written about Dylan's sumptuous melodies, but on this album and the two that would follow, they are lovely. Augie Myers' organ is seductive and supportive at the same time. (A-) **4.** "Million Miles": It wouldn't be a Bob Dylan album without some blues-based songs on it and "Million Miles" qualifies. There are some great lines here and Dylan's phrasing, especially when he has time to get creative with it, is beautiful. (A) **5.** "Tryin' to Get to Heaven": Another absolutely epic song on this album full of loss, regret and determination. Bob will have you in the palm of his weathered hand from the majestic opening two chords. Rarely has Bob sounded so genuinely wounded. Wow. (A+) **6.** "'Till I Fell in Love with You": A cute romp through a bluesy number. (B) **7.** "Not Dark Yet": One of the truly landmark Dylan songs. Even if you didn't hear the words, the stately, mountaintop melody would grab you. Then you hear ol' Bob come in with the voice of time and experience, sharing his life experiences with us. Absolutely wonderful. And so unexpected. Who would think the guy who wrote "Wiggle, Wiggle" still had this in him? (A+) **8.** "Cold Irons Bound": A crunching rocker, one of Dylan's finest, with cryptic, scary lyrics that capture the depth of love and desperation. Just a killer track. (A) **9.** "Make You Feel My Love": After two absolute stone classics, we get this offering, covered by Billy Joel among others. It's nice enough but is as out of place on this album as Jimi Hendrix' "Star-Spangled Banner" would be on a Toby Keith record. (C+) **10.** "Can't Wait": Another slow, lurching melody, a song written by a man in the depths of obsession, croaking the lyrics with determination and passion. (A) **11.** "Highlands": Could anybody else in recorded history have thought of this song? Would anyone else have dared try it? In some ways, it's a typical Bob Dylan shaggy dog story. Yet in another way, rarely has he tried to put us in his skin, his existence as a performer, superstar, folk idol, aging chronicler of the times that have now changed. The story of him flirting with the waitress and her sassy answers back is classic —

and HAD to have happened. I don't know that there is a song he's ever written that makes you feel what it's like to actually *be* Bob Dylan more precisely than this one. It is long and weird, hence some can't make it through it. But for the initiated, it's one of Bob's most revealing gems. (A)

(Album Grade: A)

Live 1966, the Bootleg Series, Vol. 4

Produced by Jeff Rosen for Columbia Records
Recorded at Free Trade Hall at Manchester, England, May 17, 1966
Released: October 13, 1998

Chart Position   *Live 1966, the Bootleg Series, Vol. 4* , made its first appearance on the charts at the No. 31 position. It became a gold album for Dylan in 2005.

Outtakes   There aren't any outtakes per se from this release. However, since the release of *No Direction Home,* there are other examples of Dylan and the Hawks playing live. There are some great shows. But this one sounds like the best.

Singles   No singles were released from this album.

The Cover   A young, fresh-faced Bob Dylan, who looks like he's had some sleep (must have been before the tour started) looks at the camera.

The Liner Notes   The accompanying booklet essay by long-time Dylan friend Tony Glover along with period photos and rare concert photos is outstanding. Glover truly does a remarkable job in capturing the chaos, the excitement and the angry reaction to Dylan's monumental change. It has taken Columbia Records a damn long time to finally release this epic set. But at least when they finally did, after bootlegs of this remarkable evening in Manchester, England had circulated around the world, they did it right...

The Record   Perhaps the stunning success of *Time Out of Mind* made Dylan feel it was finally OK to release this long sought-after set that had been the single most important bootleg record ever released.

The first I read about it was in Greil Marcus's review in *Rolling Stone*, where he made it sound as if the entire world stopped spinning long enough to hear Bob Dylan sing.

Acquiring the record though a mail-order company was surprisingly easy and when the discs arrived, I was shocked to hear how clear and sharp the recording was. My first thought was somebody at Columbia Records leaked this, perhaps for money or perhaps because they wanted to show the world just how great these shows were.

Remember, the only official release of any of the Bob Dylan and the Hawks' material was a raucous version of "Just Like Tom Thumb's Blues" on the B-Side of a single. So though writers who had heard the set raved about it, the general listening public did not know what awaited them.

DISC ONE   **1.** "She Belongs to Me": Though some critics, namely Robert Christgau, formerly of *The Village Voice*, hated the acoustic set, it sounds pretty intense. It is still amazing how quiet and respectful the crowd is. (B)   **2.** "Fourth Time Around": A song from as-yet unreleased *Blonde on Blonde*, this supposedly was influenced by the Beatles' "Norwegian Wood." Only Dylan says he wrote his first. It's an intricate song, done well here. (B+)   **3.** "Visions of Johanna": One of Dylan's classics, nicely, respectfully done, true to the previous versions of this. (A)   **4.** "It's All Over Now, Baby Blue": A song that Dylan has used a varying times in his career to make a point. For example, this is the song he came out and played acoustically after being booed at Newport. Here, he sounds as if he's way past the song already, something that's from his past. Heck, he's barely 25 (A)   **5.** "Desolation Row": Welcome to the kaleidoscopic world of Bob Dylan. Can you imagine another singer holding an audience spellbound for 11 minutes with a single song? Didn't they have ADD then? A wonderful version of the song, filled with all those characters we know and love (Dr. Filth, Einstein, Robin Hood, etc.) (A+)   **6.** "Just Like a Woman": Another song from the unreleased *Blonde on Blonde* that Dylan dared to debut. He doesn't do that anymore. In fact, sometimes he'll go on tour to support a new record and not play a single song from it for months and months. This is a gentle version of one of his best-loved songs. He sounds so very vulnerable. (A)   **7.** "Mr. Tambourine Man":

Yet another classic rendition of one of his finest songs and most infectious melodies. It was interesting to note that in *No Direction Home* when Scorsese used cuts of the angry crowd from Dylan's British concerts, basically saying how boring and tuneless his new acoustic music was, this is the song they cut back to. (A+)

DISC TWO   **8.** "Tell Me, Momma": Never officially recorded, this powerful, irresistible rocker opens the concert with a rifle shot. Powerful stuff and it offers a great opportunity for the band to open the show at full throttle. Essential. (A)   **9.** "I Don't Believe You": A re-done version of the acoustic number from *Another Side of Bob Dylan* that you would not recognize. Call them distant relatives. Dylan sounds like he's having a blast. (A)   **10.** "Baby, Let Me Follow You Down": Taking an old song from his first album and turning into a wild, thunderous rocker is a cool idea. This is also the song that Dylan would play with The Band at The Last Waltz, twice, even. Note Rick Danko's bass. As Greil Marcus might put it, he hits notes that nobody knew existed. (A)   **11.** "Just Like Tom Thumb's Blues": A wonderfully colorful, descriptive song from *Highway 61 Revisited* is done with richness and splendor. The Hawks, soon to be The Band, seemed to really understand Dylan's music. (A+)   **12.** "Leopard-Skin Pillbox Hat": An unreleased — as yet — song from *Blonde on Blonde* is an out and out stomp. It's amazing how easily the Hawks soar into this song and Dylan rips through the lyrics with joy. (A)   **13.** "One Too Many Mornings": Superbly accompanied by the Hawks on this one, another reworking of an early song off *The Times They Are a-Changin',* Dylan and his mates truly sound as if they have traveled a million miles — to steal a song title from a later album — and this world-weary version of the song shows it. (A)   **14.** "Ballad of a Thin Man": Find another rock and roll song that's as scary/eerie as this one, go ahead. With audiences hollering at him, newspaper writers and music critics wondering where the old Protest Singer went, Dylan used this song to enact revenge, singing it with vengeance. A classic. (A.)   **15.** "Like a Rolling Stone": The famous "Judas" moment (you have to let "Ballad of a Thin Man" play through to hear it) finally officially released, it captures Dylan and the Hawks at the absolute height of their onstage fury. Hearing this, you can understand why Robbie Robertson once described the music they made on this tour as "violent." The studio recording is very likely Bob's greatest recording and his finest song. Yet this version, full of fire and anger and intensity, takes the song even further. If you are a Bob Dylan fan and you have not heard this, put the book down right now and go get it. (A+)

Album Grade: (A)

The Essential Bob Dylan

Produced for Columbia Records from July 1962 to July 1999
Released on October 31, 2000

Details   One of a Columbia-wide series of releases for major artists, *The Essential Bob Dylan* was yet another greatest hits package designed to introduce his work (and rake in a few more chips) on some of his greatest — if previously released long ago — material. The song list is what you would expect, from "Blowin' in the Wind" to "Things Have Changed" with all your Dylan faves, arranged in chronological — if not musicological — order. You could almost come up with as good a two-disc set using the songs that *didn't* make this — not to sound like Clinton Heylin.

But with an artist as prolific and as unpredictable as Dylan, that's to be expected. To leave "Rainy Day Women #12 and #35" and "You Ain't Goin' Nowhere" on and "Stuck Inside of Mobile" or "Blind Willie McTell" off seems silly. This is about record sales, that's all. Give us the hits, kid. Yeah, I know we've put a lot of these out before. Some of them appear — in the same version — on six or seven albums. But this is what the kids want...

THE SONGS, DISC ONE   **1.** "Blowin' in the Wind."   **2.** "Don't Think Twice, It's All Right."   **3.** "The Times They Are a-Changin'."   **4.** "It Ain't Me, Babe."   **5.** "Maggie's Farm."   **6.** "It's All Over Now, Baby Blue."   **7.** "Mr. Tambourine Man."   **8.** "Subterranean Homesick Blues."   **9.** "Like a Rolling Stone."   **10.** "Positively 4th Street."   **11.** "Just Like a Woman."   **12.** "Rainy Day Women #12 & 35."   **13.** "All Along the Watchtower."   **14.** "Quinn the Eskimo (the Mighty Quinn)."   **15.** "I'll Be Your Baby Tonight."

DISC TWO   **16.** "Lay, Lady, Lay."   **17.** "If Not for You."   **18.**

"I Shall Be Released." **19.** "You Ain't Goin Nowhere." **20.** "Knockin' On Heaven's Door." **21.** "Forever Young." **22.** "Tangled Up in Blue." **23.** "Shelter from the Storm." **24.** "Hurricane." **25.** "Gotta Serve Somebody." **26.** "Jokerman." **27.** "Silvio." **28.** "Everything is Broken." **29.** "Not Dark Yet." **30.** Oscar-winner, "Things Have Changed."

Love and Theft

Produced by Jack Frost (Bob Dylan) for Columbia Records
Recorded in May 2001
Released: Sept. 11, 2001

Chart Position *Love and Theft,* a title that would later seem to be considerably more prophetic than perhaps even Dylan intended when it was released on 9/11, climbed all the way to No. 5 on the Billboard charts. It became a gold album about a month later.

Outtakes There are no outtakes from *Love and Theft* that have leaked out to the general public.

Singles No singles were released from this album.

The Cover A simple cover, just a black and white close-up photo of Bob in the studio, looking old and drawn.

The Liner Notes There are no liner notes. The deluxe edition includes a separate disc with a 1961 recording of "I Was Young When I Left Home" and a 1963 demo of "The Times They Are a-Changin.'"

The Record As fate would have it, Columbia Records decided to release this album on the fateful day the twin towers were attacked in New York City. There was at least one Bob Dylan fan driving to work, listening to the CD instead of following the horror on CNN. Released with little fanfare and even fewer rumors about its actual conception, the record/CD just about leaps out of the CD player, full of confidence, imagination, daring and the exuberance of creation.

Or perhaps of getting away with something. Dylan mischievously titled the record *Love and Theft* which is also the title of an Eric Lott book on American blackface minstrelsy. He also, according to some people, borrowed some of the ideas for his lyrics from an obscure book titled "Confessions of a Yakuza" by a doctor from Japan named Dr. Junichi Saga. Why Dylan chose that book, who knows? But there are some startling similarities.

In his book "20 Years of Isis," Derek Barker recounts just about all of the near-matches between the Dylan lyric and the Saga book and it is too extraordinary to have happened without Dylan reading the book.

Yet since Dylan has never acknowledged reading the book about a Japanese crime lord, the album as a whole doesn't appear to have any relation to the book itself. Except perhaps the odd tale of Tweedle Dum and Tweedle Dee. It's not exactly plagiarism, since Dylan's use of a phrase or two is part of a completely different whole, the context is quite different.

Interestingly, this issue would arise again with his most recent album, "Modern Times" with an obscure poet of the Confederacy named Henry Timrod. Dylan has not responded.

Controversy aside — and it wasn't much of one — for the first time since *Blood on the Tracks* and maybe even further back, Bob Dylan had released two great records back-to-back. There are those critics who insist that this record is better than the more celebrated *Time Out of Mind*. While it's difficult to make a call on that one — they *both* are great, if very different — it's amazing to actually have that debate over the latest recordings from a guy who's been recording since 1963. What is encouraging to Dylan fans is after the success of *Time Out of Mind*, the old guy went in the studio determined to surpass it. Some say he did.

THE SONGS 1. "Tweedle Dee and Tweedle Dum": An extraordinarily strange song about two oddballs and their oddball relationship. Not exactly sure what Bob was getting at here, but it's fun to listen to. (B+) 2. "Mississippi": Reportedly an outtake from *Time Out of Mind*, it's another of those late-in-life killer melodies that Dylan keeps coming up with. Full of great, soaring lines and fascinating thoughts. (A) 3. "Summer Days": This is swing. Never heard a song like this on any previous rock album. Written like a blues with a repetitive verse, it's a fun romp. But as entertaining as it is, how

Columbia Records could pick THIS song instead of "Mississippi" or "Honest with Me" or "Highwater (for Charlie Patton)" or "Sugar Baby" for inclusion on *The Best of Bob Dylan* is beyond me. (B+) **4.** "Bye and Bye": Again, Bob finds a gentle, soothing organ sound and grooves along. It's funny and playful. (B)   **5.** "Lonesome Day Blues": A real raw blues here, it comes as a bit a of a shock after the easy rolling songs like "Summer Days" and "Bye and Bye" which was, no doubt, Bob's intention. Some great lines here. (A)   **6.** "Floater (Too Much to Ask)": Sort of a sister tune to "Summer Days" and "Bye and Bye," this could have been written in 1925. (B+)   **7.** "High Water (for Charlie Patton)": Funny how hearing a bit of banjo seems a revelation for a Bob Dylan song. Maybe there's one on "Shenandoah" off *Down in the Groove,* but it's sort of odd that such an authentic folk instrument is so rare on Dylan albums. From the opening notes, you can tell that Dylan has something to say here. With evocations of Robert Johnson, Charles Darwin, the old South, it's one of his nicest bits of writing. (A)   **8.** "Moonlight": A song so incredibly effortless, you're sure you've heard it before. Another old-timey sounding number, Dylan's voice is full of emotion, power and believe it or not, seduction. The old guy can still get romantic. (A)   **9.** "Honest with Me": One thing about later Bob Dylan works. There may not be as many rockers but the ones included are terrific. That's the case with this one, sparked by a great riff and some clever lyrics; it reminds you of the kind of song Dylan and the Hawks wowed England with in 1966. (A)   **10.** "Po' Boy": Funny, playful, boastful, this is a song that you could hear in a Tennessee kitchen, a Mississippi parlor or Louisiana sitting room. You can't hear it without smiling. (A-)   **11.** "Cry a While": Another blues-based cut where Bob gets his snarl up, talking about Don Pasquale's booty call. Plenty of life in the old boy yet. (A-) **12.** "Sugar Baby": Perhaps influenced by the old Dock Boggs number, Dylan's gentle putdown of the world and his woman is delivered with such world-weary resignedness, you can picture taking that curly mop in her arms, kissing his forehead and telling him it'll be OK. (A)

(Album Grade: A)

Live 1975, the Bootleg Series, Vol. 5

Produced by Jeff Rosen and Steve Berkowitz for Columbia Records
Recorded on Rolling Thunder Revue from Nov. 19 through Dec. 4, 1975
Released: November 26, 2002

Chart Position   *Live 1975, the Bootleg Series, Vol. 5,* made its
first appearance on the charts at the No. 56 position. It became a gold
album for Dylan a year later.

Outtakes   There aren't any outtakes per se from this release.
However, the hard-to-find film *Renaldo and Clara* has plenty of
Rolling Thunder Revue music running through it. Many Rolling
Thunder Revue shows were bootlegged with varying degrees of audio
quality.

Singles   No singles were released from this album.

The Cover   Bob Dylan, resplendent with scarf, *Desire*-style
Stetson with flowers around the brim, glowers back at the camera.

The Liner Notes   The accompanying booklet essay by long-time
Dylan friend Larry "Ratso" Sloman, he of the fabled paperback *On the
Road with Bob Dylan*— Dylan called it the "War and Peace of Rock and
Roll"— is as well-done and fun to read as all of the *Bootleg Series* book-
lets. There are all sorts of very nice color shots and details from the
memorable tour.

The Record   Leave it to Columbia Records to decide that, oh,
let's say um ... 27 years after the actual event is the ideal time to
release a Bob Dylan live album from the Rolling Thunder Revue
Tour.

The good news is that the two-record set is fantastic, extremely
well-recorded and performed with intensity and delight by one and
all. Having witnessed the second of the Rolling Thunder Revue shows
at Southeastern Massachusetts University, I can attest that this two-record
set is a pretty good replica, even if it's not a complete show. It's pretty
close though, offering a wide range of Dylan favorites, new material and
a few obscurities.

Bob seemed to be having a very good time and so did everyone
else, regardless of how things looked on *Renaldo and Clara*.

DISC ONE   1. "Tonight I'll Be Staying Here with You": Well, Bob is back. From the gentle promise on *Nashville Skyline* to this challenge, Dylan roars through this. OK. (B+)   2. "It Ain't Me, Babe": Sung to a Tex-Mex sort of beat, when the chorus comes, Dylan starts galloping and the song rumbles into the chorus. This is a very different interpretation of one of Dylan's most famous songs, capped by a neat harmonica solo. (A)   3. "A Hard Rain's a Gonna Fall": Perhaps influenced by the version on Bryan Ferry's first solo album (a hit in England), Dylan turns his most apocalyptic song into a stomp. Never has the apocalypse seemed like such fun. (A)   4. "The Lonesome Death of Hattie Carroll": Sometimes taking a well-known acoustic classic and re-interpreting it as a wild crowd-pleasing rocker works. Sometimes, it doesn't. It's a nice thought to revive the song. But this doesn't make it. (C)   5. "Romance in Durango": You'll remember this one from its memorable opening line, sung like this: "Hotchilipeppersintheblistering sunnn." It's similar to the version on *Desire*. Nice. (B)   6. "Isis": Another Desire number, sung with appropriate drama and intensity. (B+)   7. "Mr. Tambourine Man": Bob opens the acoustic part of his Rolling Thunder show with perhaps his most beloved acoustic song. His voice sounds a bit strained but he shows a lot more respect for the original recording than usual. It was probably interesting for him to get reacquainted with songs he hadn't sung in a decade. (B)   8. "Simple Twist of Fate": A lovely, intense version of one of *Blood on the Tracks* most famous cuts with a few new verses. (A)   9. "Blowin' in the Wind": Accompanied by unannounced ex-girlfriend, folk music idol Joan Baez , Dylan takes a long, affectionate look back at his very first popular hit. (B+)   10. "Mama, You Been on My Mind": A song Dylan reportedly wrote in California, staying with Baez, it's a very nice, up-tempo countrified version. Not as good as Rod Stewart's version on *Never a Dull Moment*, though. (B+)   11. "I Shall Be Released": This Basement Tapes number has found a new life as a set closer. Dylan and Baez sing well together on this. (A-)

SIDE TWO   12. "It's All Over Now, Baby Blue": Another acoustic number, delivered with intensity and a good deal of respect towards the original version. Dylan, I think, is very proud of this particular song. (A)   13. "Love Minus Zero/No Limit": Delicate, reflective, Dylan sings this one with care and reverence. Most unlike him. (B+) **14.** "Tangled Up in Blue": The most popular song on *Blood on the Tracks* is fun live and the video version of this, with Bob in whiteface, shows how intense he can be onstage. He's not going to top the studio version, though, and he knows it. There's an interesting story about that take of the song. According to a story in "20 Years of Isis," musician Kevin Odegard, who was there, said Dylan played him an early version of "Tangled Up in Blue" and asked for his opinion. Odegard told him it was "passable." Dylan was indignant. After Odegard suggested they move it up a key for a livelier sound, Dylan agreed and then delivered the version we've come to love. (A) **15.** "The Water Is Wide": This old Irish tune is nicely delivered by Dylan and Baez. (B+) **16.** "It Takes a Lot to Laugh, It Takes a Train to Cry": You won't recognize this tune, which is OK. It sounds like Bob and company are having a good time rediscovering his songbook. He called it "a biographical song." Sure, Bob. (B+) **17.** "Oh Sister": Asked for a protest song by a leather-lunged fan, Dylan complies with a nicely done version of the cut from *Desire.* (A-) **18.** "Hurricane": With Bob's impassioned introduction, this is a solid version of the hit track from Desire. You can bet it was fun in concert. (A) **19.** "One More Cup of Coffee (Valley Below)": A sister song, so to speak, of "Romance in Durango; Bob gets to play a little gypsy. (B+) **20.** "Sara": A powerful version of the closing cut from *Desire,* some people have said this is a little too sentimental. She left him anyway. (A-) **21.** "Just Like a Woman": Having seen these two songs performed back-to-back, you can see how deeply Bob was in love and also, how desperate he was to make things right. But it didn't work. (A) **22.** "Knockin' on Heaven's Door": What else could he end the concert with? Though the song was only out for a short time, it already had the makings of a classic. (A)

    (Album Grade: A-)

Bob Dylan: Live 1964, the Bootleg Series, Vol. 6

Produced by Jeff Rosen and Steve Berkowitz for Columbia Records
Original Recording supervised by Tom Wilson.
Recorded on Oct. 31, 1964 at Philharmonic Hall, New York City, NY
Released: March 30, 2004

Chart Position *Bob Dylan Live 1964, the Bootleg Series, Vol. 6,*
began a four-week stay on the Billboard charts at No. 28. This album,
like the original *"Bob Dylan: The Bootleg Series, Vol. I-III,"* has not yet
achieved gold record status, the only two of *The Bootleg Series* releases
not to make it.

Outtakes This is a complete show, hence there aren't any outtakes.

Singles No singles were released from this album.

The Cover A color portrait of a very young Bob Dylan, pale
blue eyes and thoughtful demeanor, stares back at the camera.

The Liner Notes The accompanying booklet essay by historian
and author Sean Wilentz was nominated for a Grammy Award and
deservedly so. Wilentz, who went on to write a book on show-busi-
ness minstrelry called *Love and Theft*, does a superb job of capturing
American life in 1964 and how Dylan seemed to come along at precisely the right moment in history.

The Record Well, since Columbia Records opted to release the
Rolling Thunder Revue in 2002, why not go back to 1964 two years later?

Once again, the happy news is that this two-record set is a fascinating document and a very good portrait of what it must have been
like to see a young Bob Dylan on stage and in command. There is
charm, intelligence, power and a depth that few performers can match.
You can easily imagine someone attending this show and remembering it the rest of their life. What is amazing to the modern listener is
Dylan in 1964 vs. Dylan in 1975. It sounds as if he's a completely
different person, you would never guess one led to the other. As Daniel
Lanois has suggested Bob has had many lives. You really get that sense,
listening to this wonderful recording. You also wonder why it was never
officially released until now. It's that impressive a statement.

DISC ONE   **1.** "The Times They Are a-Changin'": A fine performance of Dylan's introductory charge, the first line gets a hand all by itself. There is such authority in his voice and he's just a kid. (A) **2.** "Spanish Harlem Incident": Fresh off the recording of *Another Side of Bob Dylan* this isn't a song Dylan performs in concert very often. It's OK. (C+)   **3.** "John Birch Society Blues": Yes, the very famous song that censors on The Ed Sullivan Show would not let Dylan perform. He makes note of that, too... "This is 'Talking John Birch PARANOID Blues' it's a fictitious story." (B+)   **4.** "To Ramona": Another new song from *Another Side of Bob Dylan,* Dylan sings and enunciates this very well. (B+)   **5.** "Who Killed Davey Moore?": One of Dylan's early "newspaper" songs, it tells a sad tale about one of the victims of the sport of boxing. (B+)   **6.** "Gates of Eden": One of the deeper lyrical explorations by Bob, it's an interesting lyrical contrast to the matter-of-fact Davey Moore saga. It's a little bit out of tune (one string) but Dylan is clearly trying to go somewhere else.(B+)   **7.** "If You Gotta Go, Go Now (or Else You Gotta Stay All Night.)": A delightfully light and sassy acoustic number to change the mood after the somber tunes that preceded it. It's funny and Bob opens it with a laugh. (A-)   **8.** "It's Alright, Ma (I'm Only Bleeding)": Fresh, new, powerful and penetrating, Bob lets it all go. Go ahead, tell me Gordon Lightfoot could have written this. Or Jackson Browne. Or the Beatles. "Yes, it's a very funny song," Bob says. Right. (A)   **9.** "I Don't Believe You (She Acts Like We Never Have Met)": Another irresistible acoustic mood-lightener, later to become a potent blast from the stages of England with the Hawks. Bob has rarely sounded more playful. Especially when he can't remember the beginning lines of the song. (A)   **10.** "Mr. Tambourine Man": Clearly, one of Dylan's most famous, most mystical and yet most appealing songs. (A)   **11.** "A Hard Rain's a-Gonna Fall": One of Dylan's most apocalyptic songs opens with a little bit of humor, he begins another song, then changes to this. It gets an enormous ovation. You can sense that this is a guy who is headed for the top. (A)

DISC TWO   **12.** "Talkin' World War III Blues": A little harmonica, a few laughs, it's a lightweight intro to the second half of the concert. The leader of the pack? (B)   **13.** "Don't Think Twice, It's All Right": One of Dylan's early acoustic classics. He's trying to break glass, hitting some of those high notes. (B).   **14.** "The Lonesome Death of Hattie Carroll": Powerful, evocative version of this song from Dylan's second album. Another newspaper song, this song has always stirred Dylan's audiences of any age. (A)   **15.** "Mama, You've Been on My Mind": A song written in California with his girlfriend at the time, Joan Baez, Dylan brings her onstage to sing these next few numbers. It's cute. Baez sings "But Daddy you've been on my mind." Dylan as daddy? (B+)   **16.** "Silver Dagger": An old song done by Baez on her own albums, this was a nice version with Bob on guitar and harmonica. (A)   **17.** "With God on Our Side": Dylan and Baez have often duetted on this. It's an interesting song, one of Dylan's most political, which is no doubt why Baez liked it so.   **18.** "It Ain't Me, Babe": For his first encore (with Baez) he offers a classic that they sing well together." You wonder if, as Baez was singing with Bob, she knew that he was singing this to her. (A)   **19.** "All I Really Want to Do." After listening to several requests, including "Mary Had a Little Lamb," Dylan returns alone to offer the leadoff track of *Another Side of Bob Dylan*, a lighthearted way to wind up a remarkable night of music (A-).

(Album Grade: A-)

Bob Dylan: Live at the Gaslight (1962)

Produced by Jeff Rosen and Steve Berkowitz for Columbia Records
Recorded in New York City (October 1962)
Released through Starbucks coffee shops, August 2005

Details: *Bob Dylan: Live at the Gaslight (1962)* was released exclusively at Starbucks coffee shops all across America in conjunction with the release of Martin Scorsese's magnificent documentary *No Direction Home.*

Not considered an "official" release by Dylan's management — neither this album or the EP from Carnegie Hall released a few months later are listed on the www.bobdylan.com album page — the record came as a bit of a surprise to Dylan fans all over the world.

Though it had been bootlegged some over the years, the clarity of the sound and the quality of the performances themselves were surprising.

The album, a 10-song live disc, likely compiled from shows at the Gaslight, gave listeners a nice earful of the young Dylan in fine voice. The song list is imaginative, giving fans a chance to sample the early Dylan's tastes in song, which he would later revisit with his back-to-back acoustic albums in 1992 and 1993 (*Good as I Been to You* and *World Gone Wrong.*)

The song list includes just four Dylan songs: "A Hard Rain's a-Gonna Fall," "Rocks and Gravel," "Don't Think Twice, It's All Right," and "John Brown." The rest, "The Cuckoo (Is a Pretty Bird)," "Moonshiner," "Handsome Molly," "Cocaine," "Barbara Allen" and "West Texas," were traditional numbers that Dylan put his own stamp on. Dylan diehards will note that one song included on the disc, "Handsome Molly," had been previously released on the rare Japanese import with the oh-so-debatable title *Live 1961–2000: Thirty-Nine Years of Great Concert Performances.* The other Gaslight song that had previously leaked out was "No More Auction Block," which was included on Dylan's successful *The Bootleg Series, Vol. I* in 1991.

Later, this album and the *Bob Dylan: Live at Carnegie Hall* EP would be included as gift with the purchase of a new Dylan album.

(Album Grade: B)

No Direction Home, the Bootleg Series, Vol. 7

Produced by Jeff Rosen, Steve Berkowitz, Bruce Dickinson and Martin Scorsese for Columbia's Legacy Records
Recorded at various locations 1959–1966
Released: August 30, 2005, in conjunction with the release of the Martin Scorsese film *No Direction Home.*

Chart Position   *No Direction Home, the Bootleg Series, Vol .7,* made an 11-week visit to the Billboard charts, beginning at No. 16. By October, it was a gold record.

Outtakes   A collection of Bob Dylan's various outtakes, a few of which have never been heard or bootlegged before.

Singles   No singles were released from this album.

The Cover   Yet another black and white portrait of a wild-haired Bob Dylan from 1966 on tour in England, wearing dark glasses and looking annoyed as he waits at a ferry.

The Liner Notes   The accompanying booklet essay by Al Kooper and Andrew Loog Oldham is interesting, though Loog Oldham's piece shows the effects of too much acid. Kooper's piece is funny and engaging and offers just the proper sense of historical perspective for what turned out to be groundbreaking material for Bob Dylan. It's funny and insightful and just reverent enough. Clearly, there isn't a whole lot that hasn't already been written about. But it's worth checking out.

The Record   After all the pilfering of the Bob Dylan Archives for *Biograph, The Bootleg Series, Vol. 1–6,* what could possibly be left?

Well, how about some pristine outtakes from *Blonde on Blonde?* Or some fine live material, really old and good recordings of some of those oh-so-controversial electric dates? And just for the heck of it, how about some alternate takes that some will contend — don't you just know it — are *better than* the actual releases.

Granted, the Dylan Archives may not have many more surprises left. But there are a few gems on here that any real Dylan fan will want to hear.

You wouldn't exactly say this was a soundtrack. But that's splitting hairs, really. If you're a Bob Dylan fan, you'll definitely want the DVD and probably this CD, too.

DISC ONE   **1.** "When I Got Troubles": As far as we know, the earliest record of Bob Dylan, as a youngster. The bad note is funny. Historic, I suppose. And possibly it may also be encouraging to any youngster who also sounds bad on a home tape recorder. (C+)   **2.** "Rambler, Gambler": A considerable improvement from the year before. Not quite hit material, however. (C+)   **3.** "This Land Is Your Land": Woody Guthrie's classic, performed in 1961 with great reverence and not as a sing-along. Interesting. (B+)   **4.** "Song to Woody": Dylan's first official song on his debut album. He's modest and purportedly swiped the tune from another Guthrie number. Woody wouldn't mind. (B)   **5.** "Dink's Song": The young Dylan is learning how to play, how to vary his music and his singing. (B)   **6.** "I Was Young When I Left Home": A surprisingly effective song from Bob's early days, this was also released as a two-sided single with the deluxe version of *Love and Theft*. Recorded in Minnesota two days before Christmas, you can imagine the artist growing before your very eyes. He is learning his craft. (B+)   **7.** "Sally Gal": No less a Dylan expert than Clinton Heylin ripped into Columbia for including this Greenwich Village leftover on the Soundtrack instead of some other Dylan outtake. It's a cute song, with Bob still in his hillbilly stage. (C+)   **8.** "Don't Think Twice, It's All Right,": A demo version of this early Dylan classic tune. It's amazing how well-crafted it sounds, even in this early stage. (A)   **9.** "Man of Constant Sorrow": Humorless version of this oldie. Well-performed but not one of his greatest. (C+)   **10.** "Blowin' in the Wind": Of course, Dylan archival material has to include one of his most-covered songs, here included in a non–sing-along version from his 1963 Town Hall performance. (B)   **11.** "Masters of War": Another fiery song from the same show. You hear him introduce the song, he sounds like a very young man, then boom.... (B)   **12.** "A Hard Rain's a-Gonna Fall": Recorded at Dylan's concert at Carnegie Hall, it's a prime example of the young artist realizing the power of the written/sung word (A.)   **13.** "When the Ship Comes in": In "No Direction Home," Baez tells a great story about Dylan writing this song to get back at the people who refused to allow him to stay in the same motel as Baez — until she interceded. Dylan first sang this in public, apparently, at the March on Washington, probably just before Martin Luther King's epic speech. He also sang this song at "Live Aid." (A-)   **14.** "Mr. Tambourine Man": The first complete take of this song, it's sort of a goof-off with Ramblin' Jack Elliott singing what is claimed by various people to be harmony. Dylan made a good call to retake this epic number. (C+)   **15.** "Chimes of Freedom": Dylan is reaching for the very outer fringes of his vocabulary galaxy here and if you listen closely, sometimes he hits, sometimes he misses. But the sentiment behind this is potent stuff. (A-)   **16.** "It's All Over Now, Baby Blue": An outtake and to some people, perhaps a preferable version of this Dylan mid-sixties classic. The original, on *Bringing It All Back Home*, is still a little sharper. (A-)

DISC TWO   **17.** "She Belongs to Me": An alternate take of one of Dylan's sweetest love songs. Nice. (B+)   **18.** "Maggie's Farm": Where the trouble started. After Peter Yarrow (of Peter, Paul and Mary) makes a gentle, restrained introduction, Dylan and company roar into rock and roll at the Newport Folk Festival. Bob is mostly yelling but it's a lot of fun. (A-)   **19.** "It Takes a Lot to Laugh, It Takes a Train to Cry": An alternate take of a song that was always one of Dylan's easiest rolling numbers. It's a little more strident here. Which makes it better. It rocks. (A)   **20.** "Tombstone Blues": Great version of this classic tune. Rocking out. Dylan goofs at the end, which makes it funnier. (A-)   **21.** "Just Like Tom Thumb's Blues": Very good alternate take. You can tell Dylan is on a roll. Nice harmonica work. (A-)   **22.** "Desolation Row": Al Kooper's liner notes describe this as a "punked out version" of one of Dylan's most lyrically imaginative numbers. It's an accurate description. (A)   **23.** "Highway 61 Revisited": A terrific version of a rocking number that was plenty of fun to sing and play. (A)   **24.** "Leopard-Skin Pillbox Hat": The first take of one of Dylan's more loopy numbers on *Blonde on Blonde*. Outtakes from this album have NEVER been bootlegged. Cool. (A)   **25.** "Stuck Inside of Mobile with the Memphis Blues Again": Bob doesn't yet have this where he'll get it in a few more takes (this is Take 5) but it's still really neat to hear the song being born. (A)   **26.** "Visions of Johanna": This is a more rocking version of Dylan's epic to (possibly) Joan Baez and their love affair. This version has been around. (A-)   **27.** "Ballad of a Thin Man": Recorded live in Scotland on the famous 1966 Tour, Dylan scares the bejesus out of everybody in the hall. Great. (A)"   **28.** "Like a Rolling Stone": Already issued on "Live 1966" this is the definitive, legendary, epic version of his greatest song, performed with precision, élan, passion and intensity for a contentious audience in the Manchester Trade Hall. Yes, the "Judas" moment is here. And unlike on "Live 1966" you don't have to hear "Ballad of a Thin Man" to get to it. (A+)

(Album Grade: B+)

Bob Dylan: Live at Carnegie Hall (1963)

Recorded in New York City (October 26, 1963)
Released by Columbia Records, November 2005

Details *Bob Dylan: Live at Carnegie Hall (1963)* was released in time for the Christmas rush at record stores, sometimes as part of a gift package with Scorsese's *No Direction Home* or other Dylan material.

As it turned out, the soundtrack to the Scorsese documentary *(No Direction Home: The Bootleg Series, Vol. 7)* included two songs from this show, "A Hard Rain's a-Gonna Fall" and "When the Ship Comes in." The remaining songs were "The Times They Are a-Changin'," "Ballad of Hollis Brown," "Boots of Spanish Leather," "Lay Down Your Weary Tune," "North Country Blues" and "With God on Our Side."

Dylan is in good voice, and hearing a 22-year-old singing his own stunning material, songs of such gravity and import, working through each and every verse as if the future of the world were hanging on his next syllable, remains intriguing. There is no questioning his commitment to his material. A few months down the line, we will be hearing him sing "but I was so much older then, I'm younger than that now." Hearing these two discs, we know precisely what he means.

(Album Grade: B+)

Modern Times

Produced by Jack Frost for Columbia Records
Recorded in February 2006
Released: August 29, 2006

Chart Position *Modern Times,* amazingly, became Bob Dylan's first No. 1 album since 1976's *Desire* selling, according to some sources, 192,000 copies in the first week. This was due, in part, to Dylan's clever iTunes television campaign, where he performed "Someday, Baby," a song that would later earn him a Grammy nomination. The album went platinum, Dylan's 16th platinum album.

And by the way, for those purists out there who insist album sales don't tell you anything about an album's quality, Dylan's platinum studio albums are: *The Freewheelin' Bob Dylan, Bringing It All Back Home, Highway 61 Revisited, Blonde on Blonde, John Wesley Harding, Nashville*

Skyline, Blood on the Tracks, Desire, Slow Train Coming, and *Time Out of Mind.*

With the possible exception of *The Basement Tapes* and *Live 1966: The Bootleg Series, Vol. 4,* these are the essential Bob Dylan releases — so maybe the buying public does know something after all. (Unless, of course, you subscribe to the Heylin-esque theory that the only reason people bought *these* albums instead of a *Down in the Groove* or *Under the Red Sky* was because so many critics had recommended them.)

Of the many Dylan compilations, *Bob Dylan's Greatest Hits I* and *II* are multi-platinum releases. Both *Biograph* and *The Essential Bob Dylan* are platinum albums as is the live *Before the Flood* with The Band.

Outtakes   No outtakes from *Modern Times* have leaked out. Yet.

Singles   "Someday Baby," Dylan's first single release in 11 years, since "Dignity" off the *MTV Unplugged* set was released shortly after the album came out but did not chart.

The Cover   Ted Croner's famous black and white portrait of New York City — "Taxi, New York at Night" from 1947 is the front cover. On the deluxe edition, there are several color shots that feature an old, pinched-looking Bob and there's also a nice shot of him with his band.

The Liner Notes   There are no liner notes to this album, though the deluxe edition includes four wonderful DVD videos, Bob Dylan doing "Lovesick" at the Grammy Awards and videos for "Things Have Changed," and "Blood in My Eyes" and a "Masked and Anonymous" performance clip "Cold Irons Bound." Happily, the version of "Lovesick" from the 1998 Grammy Awards has the weird — but somehow appropriately named — Michael Portnoy "Soy Bomb's" writhing performance edited out. Who says Columbia Records isn't looking out for you?

The Record   There wasn't much information available about the recording of this album. Dylan is getting good at keeping people silent about this sort of thing after all these years. Recording with the bulk of his current touring outfit — Tony Garnier on bass, George Receli on drums, Denny Freeman and Stu Kimball on guitar and Donnie Herron on all sorts of other instruments, Dylan produced the record as "Jack Frost."

Supposedly recorded in Manhattan in February of 2006 and rehearsed at the Bardavon 1869 Opera House in Poughkeepsie, N.Y. a few weeks earlier, the record, Dylan's 32nd studio effort, roared to the top of the Billboard charts, a first for a performer of Dylan's age. The record was also supported by a TV advertising campaign, including a brief Dylan iTunes video for the song "Someday Baby," a number that earned him a Grammy. Who said Dylan couldn't change with the times? Heck, he wrote the song.

THE SONGS   1. "Thunder on the Mountain": A great open-the-album song. Everybody's always wanted to hear Bob rewrite "Johnny B. Goode" which he sort of does here. Yes, he does mention Alicia Keys just to show how "current" he is. Oh. (A)   2. "Spirit on the Water": Gentle, semi-swing version of Dylan in a reflective mode. (B)   3. "Rollin' and Tumblin'": Borrowing the title — if not the tune — from Muddy Waters, Dylan and his band roar through this one with ease. Impressive. (A.)   4. "When the Deal Goes Down": A devout Dylan love song that somebody at Columbia Records thought should have an accompanying video (starring Scarlett Johannson). It's very nicely done, superbly sung by a guy with a fragment of a singing voice. (A)   5. "Someday Baby": One of those Dylan songs you're sure you heard before, it was catchy and was the only song from this album that I heard on regular radio. It won him a Grammy. (A)   6. "Working-man's Blues #2": Borrowing a title from Merle Haggard, Dylan's beautiful piano melody sweeps you away. Even though the opening line's mention of the proletariat is somewhat, uh, startling. (A)   7. "Beyond the Horizon": One of those old-timey sounding tunes, this is nicely written and performed. You just know Bing Crosby would have had a hit with it — if he was still around. (A-)   8. "Nettie Moore,": Dylan has said that this song, more than any other on this album, gave him trouble in the studio. It sounds impassioned, well-thought out and superbly performed by a guy who, after all, has been doing this a long time. (A)   9. "The Levee's Gonna Break": The official set-closer, a nice fast song to set the stage for the apocalyptic ending. The guitar work is simple, direct and lively. The old man is smiling through this one. (A)   10. "Ain't Talkin'": Dylan closes his most successful commercial album in many years with a sermon from the mountaintop, another State of the Nation address from our favorite wacky prophet. Except he doesn't seem so wacky. Harrowing, penetrating and dead-honest, it's a wonderful way to close out a terrific album. Let's hope that Dylan has a few more in him. But if he doesn't, this is a helluva note to go out on. (A)

(Album Grade: A)

Dylan 07: His Greatest Songs

Produced by (many) for Columbia Records
Released October 1, 2007, in three formats

Details   *Dylan 07: His Greatest Songs* was released just as Todd Haynes' remarkable film *I'm Not There* was hitting movie screens and Murray Lerner's *The Other Side of the Mirror* was filling DVD racks across America. Sounds like a perfect marketing strategy, doesn't it?

What was different about this particular greatest hits compilation — there are several others — is that this time, Dylan's management came up with the idea of including fan videos, stories, photographs or paintings and other sorts of things to enable Dylan Nation to partic-ipate in this release. Others may see what Columbia did as a diversion-ary tactic to distract attention from what many would see as a rip-off. How many times are they going to re-issue "Like a Rolling Stone?"

Of course, Columbia Records could argue that Dylan's recent commercial successes have brought him a new audience, folks who need some sort of catch-up compilation. And here it is. The collec-tion — which features no previously unreleased tracks (i.e., nothing for Dylan devotees) — came in three versions: a one-disc greatest hits pack-age; a three-disc digipack set which features 51 Dylan hits; and the most expensive version, a deluxe box set that included postcards and a detailed booklet. It also added a bonus disc that included Mark Ron-son's interesting remix of Dylan's *Blonde on Blonde* cut "Most Likely You Go Your Way (and I'll Go Mine)" and three live tracks. This was, it was duly noted, the first time Dylan had allowed a remix to be done with one of his master tracks. Essentially, Ronson merely moved Dylan's voice up a little higher in the mix and added a trumpet. The track's impact fell a bit short of the remix's goal, likely set by the radical remix Junkie XL did for Elvis Presley's single "A Little Less Conversation" in 2002, turning that old forgotten song into a No. 1 hit decades after the King's death. The bonus disc's live tracks were oldie "Blowin' in the Wind" plus "Tryin' to Get to Heaven" and "Can't Wait," whose studio versions were on *Time Out of Mind*.

As for the one-disc record itself, here's the song list: "Blowin' in the Wind," "The Times They Are a-Changin," "Maggie's Farm," "Mr. Tambourine Man," "Subterranean Homesick Blues," "Like a Rolling Stone," "Positively 4th Street," "Just Like a Woman," "Rainy Day Women #12 & 35," "All Along the Watchtower," "Lay, Lady, Lay," "Knockin' On Heaven's Door," "Tangled Up in Blue," "Hurricane," "Things Have Changed," "To Make You Feel My Love," "Someday Baby" and "Forever Young." You can quibble with the selections, of course, but the idea of selecting "To Make You Feel My Love" from *Time Out of Mind* instead of "Not Dark Yet" or even "Cold Irons Bound" seems utterly ridiculous. But there will be another compilation soon.

Album Grade: U (Unnecessary)

TWO

Singles and Recorded Collaborations

In his lengthy recording career, Bob Dylan has appeared on dozens of other artists' records, sometimes playing harmonica, sometimes singing backup. Since his contributions to these recordings are minimal, they're not included here.

What follows are the remaining Bob Dylan songs and collaborations (like with the Traveling Wilburys) that are officially available, either as official singles, on live albums, or as add-ons to soundtracks. Dylan has done several of these in recent years, including his Academy-Award winner, "Things Have Changed."

SINGLES AND ODD TRACKS

"Just Like Tom Thumb's Blues": Shuffled onto the B side of 1966's "I Want You," this raw rock and roll version performed in The Beatles' hometown of Liverpool is amazing. Today, it sounds like a forerunner of punk rock. Back then, Dylan and The Hawks were just ahead of their time. It is available only on the single and on the three-record set import album *Masterpieces*, released in Australia, New Zealand, and Japan in 1978. (A)

"George Jackson": Released in November 1971, this was Dylan's first plain "protest song" since his folkie days. It is a simple tune, and Dylan sings it with directness. This single, incidentally, remains one of the best-known Dylan cuts never included on any American album. (B)

"George Jackson" (Big Band Version): This alternative to the folkie version seems an honest expression of emotion. It is available on the import album *Masterpieces.* (B)

"Rita May": An outtake from the sessions for *Desire,* it retains much of that album's easygoing feel. Released in February 1977 as the B side of a live version of "Stuck Inside of Mobile" from *Hard Rain,* it's cute. (B+)

"Trouble in Mind": A bluesy outtake from *Slow Train Coming,* it beats the hell out of "Man Gave Names to All the Animals." Released as the B side to "Gotta Serve Somebody." (B)

"Let It Be Me": This is a *real* rarity. Dylan and his *Shot of Love* band recut this oldie, which also appears on Dylan's 1970 album *Self-Portrait.* Dylan and Clydie King sing it with tenderness. It was released in Europe as the B side of "Heart of Mine." (B+)

"Band of the Hand": Recorded in Australia with Tom Petty and The Heartbreakers on their world tour, it's a fire-and-brimstone, hell-hounds on your trail, gospel chorus, the whole nine yards. Released as a single in August 1986, it also ended up being the title track to a really bad B movie. (B-)

"Dead Man, Dead Man": Recorded live in New Orleans in 1981, this lively track wasn't released until eight years later, when it was the B side for "Everything Is Broken," a single off *Oh Mercy.* The song, from Dylan's *Shot of Love* album, really comes alive in concert, if you'll pardon the pun. (B+)

"Angel Flying Too Close to the Ground": Recorded during the sessions for *Infidels,* this easy-listening track was released in 1983 as the B side of "Union Sundown." Dylan does a decent job with this Willie Nelson classic. (C+)

"Things Have Changed": Included on the soundtrack for the film *Wonder Boys* in 2000, this struck some critics as Dylan's finest song in years. Not an official single, it won him an Academy Award, a Golden Globe and now is included on *The Essential Bob Dylan* compilation. A stark look at his life and all that swirls around him; he's scarcely been in better form. Looking back, it may have been the song that pointed him in the right direction. (A+)

"Cross the Green Mountain": Written for the *Gods and Generals* Civil War epic in 2002, Dylan himself appears in the video that accompanies the DVD release. Not an official single, it's a sad, country-styled weeper, fitting for the historical moment. (B+)

"Down in the Flood," (C+) "Dixie," (B) "Diamond Joe" (C+) and "Cold Irons Bound" (B+) were four Bob Dylan tracks added to sweeten up the soundtrack for the film oddity *Masked and Anonymous*. The rest of the soundtrack consists of cover versions of Dylan hits, many in other languages. The four Dylan tracks were recorded with Bob's crack touring band at the time and they're pretty good versions of some pretty obscure stuff and of course, "Dixie." Dylan's "Cold Irons Bound" vocal is interesting and particularly unusual since the video of that performance is shot by a single camera in a single spot, focused in tightly on an expressionless Bob Dylan. It's as if he's daring us to come as close as we want, we still can't get in.

"Tell Ol' Bill": Written for the soundtrack for the film *North Country* in 2005, it's a nice enough, piano-driven, ol' tune. But Bob's voice is rougher than usual. Which few thought was possible. (C+)

"Huck's Tune": Written for the film *Lucky You* in 2006, it's sort of a cross between "Standing in the Doorway" from *Time Out of Mind* and "Things Have Changed." Nicely done. This is the most recent new Bob Dylan song we have. Let's hope there are more to come.(A-)

"I'm Not There": Often written about, often bootlegged but never before officially released; Bob Dylan broke down and allowed director Todd Haynes to include this mysterious *Basement Tapes* number in the film and on the film's soundtrack, which includes lots of Dylan cover versions by an array of performers. The title song itself is certainly an interesting, if not nearly finished, performance that Dylan figured — correctly — he'd never capture again. (A)

179

Bob Dylan as Blind Boy Grunt

Recorded for Broadside Records, 1962–63
Re-released as *The Best of Broadside 1962–1988: Anthems of the American Underground from the Pages of Broadside Magazine* on Folkways Records in 2000

In 1962 and 1963, Bob Dylan recorded about a dozen songs for Broadside Records under the pseudonym Blind Boy Grunt. One of the worst-kept secrets in the music industry was the identity of the mysterious singer who wrote these powerful topical ballads. The Dylan songs re-released on the award-winning compilation were "John Brown" and "The Ballad of Donald White."

Billed as Blind Boy Grunt on these Smithsonian Folkways recordings, Dylan sings "John Brown," "Talkin' Devil" and "Only a Hobo" and harmonizes with Happy Traum on "Let Me Die in My Footsteps" on *Broadside Ballads, Volume 1*, which was released in September of 1963.

Dylan also appears — as Blind Boy Grunt — doing a version of "Only a Pawn in Their Game" in the version of *We Shall Overcome: Documentary of the March on Washington*, which was released in August 1963.

You can find the Dylan obscurities "Train A' Travelin,'" "Dreadful Day," "The Ballad of Emmett Till" and "The Ballad of Donald White" on *Broadside Ballads, Vol. 6*, which was released in 1972 when Dylan fans were starved for any new material out of their hero.

WITH GEORGE HARRISON

The Concert for Bangladesh

Recorded: August 1, 1971
Released: December 1, 1971

In this, Dylan's fourth post-accident appearance in five years, he was the surprise guest and turned in one of the finest, most heartfelt sets of his career.

"Right up to the moment he stepped onstage, I wasn't sure he was going to come on," George Harrison said in a 1976 BBC radio interview. "So it was kind of nerve-wracking. I had a little list on my guitar and I had a point after "Here Comes the Sun"— it just said, "Bob?" with a question mark. So it got to the point, I turned around to see if Bob was there, to see if he was going to come on ... and he was all ready, he was so nervous, he had his harmonica on and his guitar in his hand and he was walking on stage, like it was now or never."

    1. "A Hard Rain's a-Gonna Fall": A wonderful rendition of one of his oldest "protest" songs, it seemed especially poignant on this night. (A)   **2.** "It Takes a Lot to Laugh, It Takes a Train to Cry": A personal favorite of Harrison, who lent some nice slide guitar to the tune. Dylan sings it with affection. (B+)   **3.** "Blowin' in the Wind": According to those who were backstage at the concert, it was a great surprise when Dylan broke into this golden oldie. Phil Spector told the *Rolling Stone* in 1972 of the time at rehearsals when Harrison asked Dylan to sing this song. "The audience would love it," he said. "You interested in 'Blowin' in the Wind'?" Dylan asked. "Are you gonna sing 'I Want to Hold Your Hand'?" (A)   **4.** "Mr. Tambourine Man": An exquisitely sung, beautifully performed version of one of his greatest songs. This is the one the audience was waiting to hear, and Dylan didn't let them down. (A+)   **5.** "Just Like a Woman": A sentimental choice to wind up his set. Dylan harmonizes with Leon Russell and Harrison on a crowd favorite, and it's touching. Rarely has he been so generous since his return to performance after his accident. (A)

WITH THE TRAVELING WILBURYS

Traveling Wilburys, Vol. 1

Produced by Otis and Nelson Wilbury (Jeff Lynne and George Harrison) for Wilbury Records
Recorded at Garage Studio, Malibu, California (April and May 7–16, 1988)
Released: November 1988

The Record　Recorded as a lark, the *Traveling Wilburys* brought Dylan his best record sales in over a decade, giving him his first platinum album since *Desire*.

The combined talents of Tom Petty, George Harrison, Jeff Lynne, Roy Orbison, and Bob Dylan produced a record that was as much fun as any rock and roll release in years.

George Harrison's record company, Warners, needed another song to be released on a 12-inch single. As Harrison explained to BBC radio interviewer Roger Scott:

> I didn't have another song, so I just said to Jeff[Lynne] — I was in Los Angeles and he was producing Roy Orbison — we having dinner one night, and I said, I'm just going to have to write a song tomorrow and just do it. And I said, Where can we get a studio? And he said, Well, maybe Bob, 'cos he's got this little studio in his garage. And it was that instant, you know. We just phoned up Bob and he said, Sure, come on over. Tom Petty had my guitar and I went to pick it up; he said, Oh, I was wondering what I was going to do tomorrow! And Roy Orbison said, Give us a call tomorrow if you're going to do anything. I'd love to come along. And that was it.

Once the record company heard "Handle with Care," with all these famous voices on it, they wouldn't let Harrison put it on the single. So, "the only thing I could think of was to do another nine — to make an album," Harrison said. "And as it happened, they all said yeah — they all loved the idea."

Who didn't?

SIDE ONE　**1.** "Handle with Care": You can hear Dylan's gruff voice harmonizing with Tom Petty on the chorus on this Beatle-like tune. Harrison and Roy Orbison share the lead vocals. (A)　**2.** "Dirty World": This tune was Dylan's idea, and he sings the lead vocal. It's one of Harrison's favorites. "Bob's very funny, he said. "I mean, a lot of people take him seriously and yet if you know Dylan and his songs, he's such a joker, really.... Bob said, 'Let's do one like Prince!' And he just started banging away. 'Love your sexy body. — I love that track, it's just so funny." (A-)　**3.** "Rattled": Former Electric Light Orchestra leader Jeff Lynne takes the lead on this Sun Studio–style rocker. (B-)　**4.** "Last Night": Tom Petty takes over the lead mike for this one, a humorous look at romance on the road. (B+)   **5.** "Not Alone Any More": Roy Orbison's showcase, it's one of the few times you can tell a song was written specifically with one singer in mind, and it works. (A-)

SIDE TWO • **6.** "Congratulations": Dylan's blackest lyrics are bitter, yet not without his wry sense of humor. As Harrison said, "I'm a huge Bob Dylan fan, I've got all his records and I like him and I'll go on liking him regardless of how bad his records are, but I was pleased that he was so into the mood. He really got into it and was comic — even "Congratulations" has some comical things in there." (B)   **7.** "Heading for the Light": A George Harrison–Jeff Lynne collaboration, and it sounds it. It's light, bright, and breezy. (C+)   **8.** "Margarita": Considering how little time these guys had to prepare for this record, it's amazing there wasn't more filler like this. When Dylan's vocal comes in halfway through the song, you wonder where he came from. (C+) **9.** "Tweeter and the Monkey Man": An amazing takeoff on Bruce Springsteen, done as only Dylan could do it. There are a half dozen Springsteen references sprinkled throughout the song, and Dylan performs it with mock seriousness — much like *Nebraska*. Hilarious. And also great. (A)   **10.** "End of the Line": A fond pat on the back by the boys, it turned out to be an eerily prophetic second single from the record. Just before they were to do a video, Orbison died of a heart attack. (A)

Funny, refreshing, enjoyable, and entertaining — all these adjectives apply to this delightful record. It's definitely worth buying. (Album Grade: A-)

Nobody's Child: Romanian Angel Appeal

Collection of various tracks to benefit Romanian orphans
Released: August 1989

1. "Nobody's Child": Nobody seems to know where the Wilburys came up with this oldie, written by Cy Coben and Mel Foree. Tom Petty, George Harrison, Jeff Lynne, and Dylan take their turn at this sob story. (A-)

Traveling Wilburys, Vol. 3

Produced by Spike and Clayton Wilbury (George Harrison and Jeff
  Lynne)
Recorded in Mobile Studio (April 1990) and Friar Park, England (July
  1990)
Released: October 1990

The Record   An album as successful as *Traveling Wilburys* needed
a sequel, and this one didn't disappoint. (There was no Vol. 2.) The
group was a foursome since Orbison had died, and for this record,
Dylan was dominant, taking a turn on seven of the record's 11 songs.
  SIDE ONE • **1.** "She's My Baby": Perhaps the hardest rockin'
song Dylan has sung on since "Groom's Still Waiting at the Altar," it's
a riot from start to finish. Everyone gets a turn, but Bob gets the best
lines. (A)   **2.** "Inside Out": Dylan harmonizes nicely with George
Harrison on this song of confusion. Tom Petty is fine on the chorus.
(A-)   **3.** "If You Belonged to Me": A wonderfully simple song, Dylan
sings it perfectly, throwing in a spirited harmonica solo for the heck of
it. Who said the guy couldn't sing? (A)   **4.** "The Devil's Been Busy":
Tom Petty sings about life on the fairway, with Dylan on the bridge.
The nicest ecological warning you ever heard. (B+)   **5.** "Seven Deadly
Sins": In this song, which sounds like a 1950s single that the Flamin-
gos might have recorded, Dylan takes the lead and does a decent job.
(C+)   **6.** "Poor House": Tom Petty and Jeff Lynne meet Flatt and
Scruggs; this hillbilly ditty is a howler. (A-)
  SIDE TWO • **7.** "Where Were You Last Night?" Dylan takes
over the lead mike with help from George Harrison for this easygoing
song of accusation. (B+)   **8.** "Cool Dry Place": Tom Petty does a marvelous take-off of a vintage Dylan number, replete with tight-lipped
humor. Listening to it, a story told to interviewer Thomas Lasarik in
1983 about Dylan in the studio producing Lone Justice comes to mind.
Maria McKee was getting frustrated because she couldn't seem to find
a way to sing the song that satisfied Dylan. So she cranked up her best
Bob Dylan imitation and Dylan said, "That's it, now you're really
singing." (B+)   **9.** "New Blue Moon": In another song with 1950s

184

flavor, Jeff Lynne handles the lead vocals as the rest of the Wilburys harmonize. Dylan steps in on the bridge and sounds like the Old Man of the Mountains. It's cute. (C+)   **10.** "You Took My Breath Away": Tom Petty handles lead vocals, with harmony help from George Harrison; Jeff Lynne sings the bridge on this tender tribute to the late Roy Orbison. It's very nice, with Harrison's fine slide guitar setting the mood. (B+)   **11.** "Wilbury Twist": Everybody gets a turn in this playful romp, sort of an English version of "Whole Lotta Shakin' Goin' On." Dylan gets the last verse, and they wind the song up in style. (A-)

A delight. *Traveling Wilburys, Vol. 3* is one of the most enjoyable albums you could find. Every one of the artists has done better, more serious work elsewhere, but that's not the idea here. It is one of those rare occasions in which a bunch of rock stars get together and come up with something memorable. Shortly before this book was finished, Rhino Records re-released the Wilburys' work, including two outtakes from the original recordings and a DVD of some home movies. An extremely well-done BBC Special aired the two outtakes " Maxine" and "Like a Ship" as well as many interviews with band members. Lots of fun.

(Album Grade: A-)

WITH THE BAND

A Tribute to Woody Guthrie, Part One

Produced for Columbia Records by Harold Leventhal
Recorded: January 20, 1968
Released: January 1971

The Record   After taking most of 1967 off, recuperating from his 1966 motorcycle accident, Dylan released *John Wesley Harding* in December 1967. On January 20, 1968, he made his first public appearance since his 1966 tour of England when he appeared at New York's Carnegie Chapter Hall at the Woody Guthrie Memorial Concert.

185

These recordings, which weren't released until three years later, are historic for those reasons, not so much for the performances, which are OK.

Contrasted with the recordings from "The Isle of Wight" concert the following summer that were released on *Self-Portrait* a year before this came out, there's still an edge to Dylan's work. The mellowness of "Nashville Skyline" hadn't hit him yet.

1. "I Ain't Got No Home": Dylan and The Band approach this song as a modified blues, a little up-tempo. His singing comes close to hollering, but it's nice the way The Band's voices all come in at the end of each verse. (B-) **2.** "Dear Mrs. Roosevelt": Somebody's guitar sounds out of tune, and Dylan's singing is sincere, but a little wild on this song, adapted by Woody Guthrie. The Band pitches in on the chorus. (C+) **3.** "Grand Coulee Dam": This song, the most up-tempo of all three, seems to suit Dylan and The Band best. His singing is high pitched, above the melody, and guitarist Robbie Robertson plays some stinging notes that probably shocked an audience of folkies. It's almost rockabilly. (B+)

The Last Waltz

Recorded at Winterland (November 25, 1976)
Released: April 1978

The Record   Filmed on Thanksgiving night by Martin Scorsese at San Francisco's Winterland, The Band's final performance, high lighted by all sorts of special guests (including Eric Clapton, Van Morrison, Joni Mitchell, and Muddy Waters) was extraordinary.

To close the show, they brought out their old friend Bob Dylan. Together, they did two songs they had performed together on their thunderous tour of England in 1966 — "Baby, Let Me Follow You Down" and "I Don't Believe You" — and two songs from their 1973 *Planet Waves* album with Dylan — "Hazel" and "Forever Young."

"Hazel" did not make the Warner Bros. soundtrack, released two years later, but the rest of the set did.

In the film, Dylan and The Band do "Forever Young"; the reprise of "Baby, Let Me Follow You Down"; and the encore, "I Shall Be Released."

The video is available and outstanding. The soundtrack, which includes performances not included in the film, is recommended.

1. "Baby, Let Me Follow You Down": To open their set, Dylan picks a chestnut from his first album that he and The Band revived on his 1966 tour. It's rockin'. (A)   **2.** "I Don't Believe You": Another song from the 1966 tour, it doesn't lose any of its original ferocity here. Dylan once said that he liked singing with The Band because he "could drill his songs into people." This gives you an idea what he meant. (A) **3.** "Forever Young": A benediction from *Planet Waves*. Dylan and The Band summon a lot of passion on this rendition, perhaps because they recognized it was the last time they would play it together. The singing is impressive, and Robertson's guitar work is inspired. (A)   **4.** "Baby, Let Me Follow You Down": To close out his set, Dylan reprises the song that opened it, the same technique he used in 1975, when he appeared on a PBS special honoring John Hammond, the man who had signed him to Columbia Records. On that show, he opened with "Hurricane," did "Oh Sister" and "Simple Twist of Fate," and then closed with another version of "Hurricane." This version of "Baby, Let Me Follow You Down" is as exciting as you'd imagine it to be, closing one of the finest concerts Dylan had ever been a part of. (A+)   **5.** "I Shall Be Released": A nice way to wind up the night. Dylan leads everyone through one of his most graceful, uplifting numbers from *The Basement Tapes*. (A-)

Rock of Ages

Recorded at New York's Academy of Music, December 31, 1971–January 1, 1972
Released: April 2001

If you purchased The Band's original double live album *Rock of Ages,* there was a nice little tease in the upper right hand corner of the centerfold. It was a picture of Bob Dylan, who, at the time, was eschewing any concert appearances. Reports of the concert included news of

Dylan singing a few songs with the Band. But they had never leaked out. Until now.

With the re-release of The Band's spectacular live album, Capitol Records also included the four songs done with Bob Dylan. Dylan is in pre–"Before the Flood" yell/voice and seems like he's having a ball.

The songs include a somewhat raggedy "Down in the Flood" (B), a raucous "When I Paint My Masterpiece" (B+), a wild "Don't Ya Tell Henry"—(A) and, as an encore, a playful if rough version of "Like a Rolling Stone." (B).

It's an interesting experiment to play this harmless live version right after the matchless version from the Free Trade Hall in Manchester, England just five years earlier. Amazing how things change in five years.

CONTRIBUTIONS TO OTHER ALBUMS

Hearts of Fire Soundtrack

Recorded at Townhouse Studios, London (August 27–28, 1987)
Released: October 1987

The Record   A forgettable effort on everyone's part. Dylan is uninspired in the film, and only the cover version of John Hiatt's "The Usual" is worth holding on to.

1. "The Usual": A nice version of John Hiatt's song that Dylan handles with more care than he devotes to his own material. (B+)   2. "Had a Dream About You, Baby": It sounds like Dylan had about 15 minutes to spare in the studio and came up with this. (C)   3. "Night After Night": Ditto. (C)

A Tribute to Woody Guthrie and Leadbelly

Recorded for Folkways Records
Released: August 1988

1. "Pretty Boy Floyd": In this terrific rendition of the Woody Guthrie classic, Dylan's singing is inspired, committed, and uplifting. Just great. (A)

For Our Children

Recorded for Walt Disney Records
Released: 1991

1. "This Old Man": With harmonica, acoustic guitar, and organ, Dylan has a ball with this old children's classic, recorded for a benefit record to help children with AIDS. Dylan really has fun with this. A collector's item, for sure. (B+)

THREE
Bootlegs

Beginning with *The Great White Wonder* in 1970, no popular recording artist has been bootlegged more than Bob Dylan. And with the explosion of the Internet, with YouTube and all the various and sundry websites — all of which have happened since the release of my first book — let's just say there is more Bob Dylan out there than you can possibly imagine. Just a click away. We can't cover it all. Just as I was completing the manuscript, I checked YouTube and found 20-plus pages of Bob Dylan songs. There is so much out there and more coming.

And let's be honest about something. Though Dylan has been critical of the bootleggers, who have, perhaps, cost him money and privacy (there are *how* many great songs we never would have heard?) the bootleg industry has also been essential in perpetuating and sustaining his myth.

Particularly so in the early seventies, when Dylan was recording *Nashville Skyline, Self-Portrait,* and even *New Morning,* it was a discouraging time for most Dylan aficionados.

Maybe Bob was happier singing country songs but much of his audience wanted rebellion, defiance, music with substance. They found that music on bootlegs, whether it was early material that never was released or in the extraordinary *Basement Tapes,* recorded in the summer of 1967 with The Band or in other outtakes from *Blonde on Blonde* or *Highway 61 Revisited.*

After *John Wesley Harding,* it became clear that Dylan was having a tremendously difficult time coming up with new, first-rate material.

Nashville Skyline, for example, was barely a half-hour long. Since Dylan couldn't keep up with the demand, the alternative of releasing old material was certainly discussed. But Dylan balked every time.

His audience, however, wanted to hear that seminal work. Much of what was later officially released on *Biograph* in 1985 and on *The Bootleg Series, Vols. 1–3* in 1991 can be found on an assortment of bootleg records that have been trickling out since the early 1970s.

Obviously, there are too many Dylan bootlegs available for this section of the book to cover them all. However, Paul Cable, among others, wrote a good book on that very topic: *Bob Dylan: His Unreleased Recordings.* And there are any number of other Dylan guides out there. Bob, apparently, doesn't attract lukewarm fans.

Some that I have stumbled over and enjoyed are: For historic purposes, *The Great White Wonder* is interesting; the marvelous *Ten of Swords,* which was released around the same time as *Biograph* and, according to some people, is better; *Passed Over and Rolling Thunder,* a collection of early live tracks from the Newport Folk Festival, outtakes from *Blood on the Tracks,* and Dylan's live appearance on the John Hammond tribute; and the most impressive of all, *The Royal Albert Hall Concert* material, which is simply extraordinary.

This concert was later released on *The Bootleg Series, Vol. 4* but the actual concert was from the Free Trade Hall in Manchester, not the Albert Hall as it had said on bootlegs for years.

The 1964 Halloween concert (mentioned in the first edition) has been released in *The Bootleg Series, Vol. 6.*

Bob Dylan and the Hawks II

Berkeley, California (December 4, 1965)

This extraordinary show from 1965 popped up on bootleg CDs. Titled "Long Distance Operator," it comprises nine songs featuring Dylan and The Band (minus Levon Helm) at their peak. The recording is pretty good and the set list includes such rarely heard live Dylan-Band cuts as "Tombstone Blues," "It Ain't Me, Babe," "Positively Fourth

Street" and a basement tape track "Long Distance Operator." If there's more of this stuff out there, let's hear it. Worth looking for.

Bob Dylan 1966 World Tour

In Melbourne, Australia

Dylan and the Hawks visited Australia in April 1966, and Dylan's acoustic sets were remarkable. Utterly exhausted, Dylan sounded as if the songs were playing him, not vice versa, and it made for revelatory listening.

A good-quality bootleg is available from the April 19 show at the Festival Hall that features all acoustic versions of "Fourth Time Around"; "It's All Over Now, Baby Blue"; "Desolation Row"; and "Visions of Johanna," somewhat wryly retitled "Mother Revisited" by Dylan on stage.

On these recordings, it is as if Dylan was tapped into something he didn't quite understand but had to let out. We need to hear more of them, especially since they were not included in the wonderful "No Direction Home."

The Basement Tapes

Recorded with The Band in West Saugerties, New York (June–October 1967)

You may have read that there was some sort of conspiracy regarding the official release of *The Basement Tapes* in 1975. Some contend that the best material was omitted, as if Dylan or The Band were trying to hold some ultimate trump card. Don't believe it. By and large, they put out the best songs. Greil Marcus, who wrote a whole book on them, *Invisible Republic*, would not agree. But there's more on Greil's book in the book section.

And there are reasons for not including the ones they left out. One of the songs that should have been included — "Quinn the Eskimo" — was on the 1985 *Biograph*. It probably was not included on the 1975 *The Basement Tapes* because Dylan had just released the live version of the song, performed with The Band at the Isle of Wight, on the 1970 *Self-Portrait*.

Another song that should have been included, the original "I Shall Be Released," was released as part of *The Bootleg Series Vols. 1–3*. But even that omission can be explained. On the 1971 *Bob Dylan's Greatest Hits,* Dylan and old pal Happy Traum had recut the song and included it as "new material." Dylan wasn't about to re-release a superior version four years later. A more pertinent question was, Why didn't he release the original version earlier?

Though the four-record set of material from those sessions that didn't make it onto the official release is interesting, and perhaps a must for a diehard Dylan fan, the rest of the world isn't missing anything extraordinary. However, you wouldn't know that, to read some of the comments written by Dylan devotees about some of this material. These devotees think that Columbia's *Basement Tapes* are a ripoff.

The key song seems to be "Sign on the Cross," a slow, mock-spiritual that Dylan performed with tongue firmly in cheek, particularly the closing bits, which are spoken. It is funny, but the listener isn't quite sure that it is intended to be so, much like Roxy Music's "Psalm," a song you get halfway through before you recognize the mock sincerity and campy humor of it all. Some reviewers haven't gotten the joke. The gushy liner notes to the bootleg say that the final side opens with

> ... perhaps the finest song of all the Basement Tapes, officially released songs included.
>
> The seven-minute "Sign on the Cross" is a beautiful tune, enhanced stunningly by a rich, swelling organ that gives you the impression Garth [Hudson] could not play a note a microsecond out of place even if he tried. And the lead guitar playing is of such mellowness, restraint and sympathy that it must put Robbie [Robertson] aside Bruce Langhorne [who played on "Mr. Tambourine Man"] for the award of best lead guitar on any of Bob's tracks.
>
> Whether "Sign on the Cross" is a religious song is ambiguous [Note: the title is hardly ambiguous]. Either way, the lyrics are weirdly evocative. The last verse and the break preceding it where a passage of the

lyric is spoken to the music are put across in an uncharacteristically manic and euphoric manner.

Manic and euphoric? It sounds like a good description of the author of these liner notes.

Even Paul Williams, whose book *Performing Artist: The Music of Bob Dylan* is well done, seemed to be snapping at this bait. He wrote:

> "Sign on the Cross" is built like a symphony, with four separate movements. The first is deliberate and elegant, Dylan singing with sublime slowness while Robbie Robertson plays gorgeous grace notes all around him.
>
> The second movement starts with an inspired bridge [could be the chorus, but we never hear it again], rousing and passionate, transitioning into a restatement of the musical theme from the first movement.
>
> The third movement is spoken/sung monologue — Dylan's vocal performance on this is nothing short of genius, and the improvised music is dazzling in its complexity and accuracy.
>
> Another great segue takes us to the concluding movement, which starts with echoes of the bridge but immediately moves onto new structural ground, the music just as fresh and surprising now as when the song started, while successfully incorporating everything that's happened so far.

It sounds more like Dylan and The Band were attempting another parody, much like "Fourth Time Around," a parody that actually surpasses its model "Norwegian Wood" (Dylan actually claims to have written his first) or "Clothes Line Saga," a hilarious *Basement Tape* number that is a take-off of Bobbie Gentry's popular "Ode to Billie Joe," as documented by Marcus in "Invisible Republic."

For a few verses, it sounds as if Dylan and The Band are seriously attempting some unusual sort of spiritual. But by the end, you can hear Dylan's voice cracking; he's about to start laughing. And it's not hard to understand why this was never released. Most people take their religion seriously, as Bob well knows. To put this out in 1967 would have been an outrage.

What's intriguing is how many Dylan "experts" took this playful number far more seriously than Dylan did. One of the greatest attributes of *The Basement Tapes* is Dylan's rollicking sense of humor. "Yea, Heavy and a Bottle of Bread"— now there's a title for you.

As Garth Hudson, told Clinton Heylin in *Bob Dylan: Behind the Shades*:

> We were doing seven, eight, ten, sometimes 15 songs a day. Some were old ballads and traditional songs, some were already written by Bob and Richard [Manuel], but others Bob would make up as he went along.... "Sign on the Cross" would have been a good one but Bob never finished it. We'd play the melody, he'd sing a few words he'd written, and then make up some more, or else mouth the words or even syllables as he went along. It's a pretty good way to write songs.

But not symphonies. Which is not to say that there aren't some songs worth hearing. "I'm Not There" with its' wistful melody and curious singing is interesting and the minor chord ballad "The Hills of Mexico" is worth listening to.

Dylan even tries out oldies "A Fool Such as I" and "I Don't Hurt Any More," and they're fun. One side of the four-record set features Tiny Tim singing with The Band as they stomp through "Be My Baby"; "Memphis, Tennessee"; and "I Got You Babe."

Though they are not exactly the Rosetta stone of rock and roll as some critics would have you believe, some of these outtakes from *Basement Tapes* are entertaining. It may be worth putting them out so people don't think they are getting ripped off.

Bob Dylan–Johnny Cash Recordings

In Nashville (1969)

There is nothing really extraordinary here, but it is fun to listen to Dylan and Cash spin through song after song, trying to find something they can do together.

Dylan sounds as if he is really searching hard for something new and is unable to find it. Cash just tags along. They do "I Walk the Line" and "Ring of Fire" and several others. Very loose.

Before the Flood: Bob Dylan and The Band

1974 Tour

A double-album set titled *Before the Flood* was released from this tour, and it is a nice souvenir. But true Dylan collectors will want to hear the historic tour's opening song, the rarely performed "Hero Blues," and perhaps other cuts not included on the album.

In reviewing "No Direction Home," National Public Radio's Ken Tucker talks about a 1978 documentary called "Before the Flood" made by Martin Scorsese about the comeback tour with The Band. I've never heard of it, but would love to see it — if there is such a thing.

iTunes: The Collection

Since most Bob Dylan fans already have all the "essential" recordings already, new forms of media attempting to get new customers have to find ways to attract them. With CDs, that means "bonus tracks" which used to be called outtakes. With Bob Dylan's entire recording career available on computer on iTunes, they had to find a way to attract Dylan fanatics.

So, what they offered is the Collection, is a grab bag of live recordings, B-sides and other assorted Dylan material that real collectors may have picked up already.

For example, "I Was Young When I Left Home" — a 1961 recording — was issued as a bonus disc with *Love and Theft*. There are a handful of cuts from the Gaslight Tape that Dylan made available at Starbucks, a couple from the limited edition Dylan at Carnegie Hall CD and various and sundry soundtrack cuts and live performances.

The one real gem here is a live version of "Just Like Tom Thumb's Blues" recorded in Liverpool, England, on the historic 1966 tour. This is actually the first live recording of Dylan and the Hawks to leak out and it is 5:37 of pure, raucous Dylan singing his skinny butt off. "Blackmailed the sergeant of arms intogettingupandleavinghis pooooooost." Great stuff. I have the original 45 (it's the B-Side for "I Want You") and it's a classic.

FOUR
On Film

Don't Look Back

Filmed by D.A. Pennebaker on Bob Dylan's tour of England (April–May 1965)
Released: September 6, 1967
Available on videocassette

If you are a Bob Dylan fan and you have not seen *Don't Look Back*, get yourself to a store now. The film remains the definitive portrait of early Bob Dylan and may well be the finest, most honest portrait of a popular recording artist ever done.

Working with a low budget, New York filmmaker D.A. Pennebaker was invited along on Dylan's tour of England. At the time, Dylan was perhaps more popular in England than in the United States. As you'll see in the film, his song "The Times They Are a-Changin'," though two years old, was a hit single (it was never released as a single here), as was his 1965 release "Subterranean Homesick Blues," a rock and roll track off the soon-to-be released *Bringing It All Back Home.*

With big crowds greeting Dylan everywhere, he was encountering true celebrity for the first time. Since he was venturing away from folk singing into rock music, it was a time of tremendous change in his artistic and personal life. Having Pennebaker on hand to record Dylan's reactions to all these events is our great fortune.

The film begins with a clip of Dylan holding up cue cards to help illustrate his latest single, "Subterranean Homesick Blues." After a short

clip of him walking on stage as the credits roll, Dylan and pal Bob
Neuwirth arrive at London's Heathrow Airport.

As an enormous crowd greets him, Dylan is reminded that he came
to London two years earlier. Then he is asked why he is so big this time.
"I've absolutely no idea," he says, a hint of excitement in his voice. "I don't
even know about it if it is. I figure just do the same thing I did before."

From there, we see Dylan in press conferences, on stage, and in
his hotel room. There are arguments, fights, songs, pranks, and dozens
and dozens of cigarettes.

What we see is someone who seems fearless, an artist who is totally
convinced that what he's doing is important and necessary. Dylan
relentlessly questions everything — every single word — and it makes
for some funny moments.

> REPORTER: "Would you say you cared about people particularly?"
> DYLAN: "Well, yeah, but you know ... I mean, we all have our own
>   definitions of all those words ... care and people."
> REPORTER: "Well, but surely we know what people are."
> DYLAN: "Do we?"

Moments later, a man arrives at Dylan's hotel door with an award
for the best-selling folk album *Freewheelin' Bob Dylan*. "I don't even
want to see 'em," Dylan says, turning away. There's a thought that
hadn't even occurred to 1965 America: When someone gives you an
award, you don't have to accept it.

Two of the most famous encounters in the film are Dylan confronting
Terry Ellis, a "science student," who subsequently went on to found
Chrysalis Records, and Horace Judson, a reporter for *Time* magazine.

In the first encounter Dylan's barbed wit is playful. Twisting and
turning in all sorts of unpredictable ways, he refuses to be pinned down,
and Ellis doesn't like it:

> ELLIS: "The whole thing that gets me about you is that you're knock-
>   ing from the minute I come in."
> DYLAN: "I don't think you know when you're liked, that's all...."

The duel with Judson reveals an angry, hostile Dylan challenging
a reporter who dared to question Dylan's integrity. After four or five
vicious blasts at Dylan, the reporters tries again. "Do you care about

what you sing?" he asks rather timidly. Dylan explodes: "How could I answer that if you've got the nerve to ask me?" he says. "I mean, you've got a lot of nerve asking me a question like that. Do you ask the Beatles that?"

Though the interview ends with a bit of a joke, Dylan comparing himself with Enrico Caruso, the point is made. This is someone who is not going to sit back and be interrogated, even for a national magazine.

By the end of the film, we can understand why Dylan had to move into rock and roll. We get a sense of his anger and resentment; of why he felt misunderstood; and of why he felt he had to go on into rock and roll, even if it infuriated many of his fans.

The remarkable thing about Pennebaker's film is that, even now, you get a sense of an artist who was tired of performing the same old songs in the same old order every night, who refused to give pat answers to interviewers, and who did exactly what he wanted to do and no more.

The scene that closes the film is absolutely perfect. As Pennebaker told interviewer John Bauldie, as quoted in *Wanted Man: In Search of Bob Dylan,* "That final, incredible scene you just fall on — the moment when you can't make a mistake, and you know you're right in the center and you just shoot everything that moves, and you don't even think about why or how, you just shoot it, it's in your lap.... Fantastic! It's just fantastic! Just one shot. You didn't have to edit anything."

The scene takes place in a cab, Dylan riding away from his final acoustic concert, moving ahead into the unknown world of rock. As he looks out the window, Dylan says "God, I feel like I've been through some kind of ... thing, man.... There was, something was special about it, that's all."

Indeed. (A)

Eat the Document

Filmed by D. A. Pennebaker on Bob Dylan and the Hawks' 1966 tour of England
First shown: February 8, 1971
Not currently available

If *Don't Look Back* was a revealing glimpse of Bob Dylan hitting the big time, *Eat the Document* may be considered the dark side. This film is in color, and the setting is similar — Dylan and The Band (then the Hawks) on tour in England — but otherwise the films — and Dylan — are markedly different.

In *Don't Look Back*, Dylan is bold, aggressive, and fun loving, an artist trying to take a bite out of the world. The film is filled with Dylan's confrontations with a loud drunk at a party, a reporter, a teenager, and a cute fan. Bob never backs down once.

In *Eat the Document,* he is a man beginning to be isolated by his fame, a man dabbling in drugs, a troubled man who seems to find release only on stage. In this film, there are no confrontations and not really much dialogue. We see Dylan on stage and offstage, and if we thought we were coming to know him from *Don't Look Back,* we have lost him again.

Perhaps the one similarity between the films is the live performances. Both films have a lot of jump cuts in the middle of songs. But whereas the cutaways seem well planned and flow with the rest of the film in *Don't Look Back,* in *Eat the Document,* every cutaway is a jolt (probably Dylan and Howard Alk's intention).

For example, we hear the grand opening notes to "Like a Rolling Stone" from the Royal Albert Hall concert, then the film abruptly cuts away to the song's end. At another point, we see Dylan and his band roaring through "Tell Me Mama," an unreleased song from that time, when suddenly the song ends and Dylan and his band walk offstage.

The film was an experiment. It is unfortunate, however, that they picked such a momentous time in rock and roll history to try something new. A straight concert film, even a *Don't Look Back II,* like the one D.A. Pennebaker made but was never able to release, would have been priceless.

This film doesn't quite work. Dylan made it for an ABC television special and it was rejected.

The film opens with someone snorting something off the surface of the piano. Then he pounds out an ominous chord sequence. "Are we ready to move on?" he asks.

First, the troupe is on a train, traveling through the English countryside. Next, they're in London and Dylan is in the back seat of a cab. Then the camera zooms in. "I'm sorry for everything I've done," he says. "And I hope to remedy it soon." The film cuts immediately to Dylan and the Hawks on stage, roaring through "Tell Me Mama."

After a quick clip of Dylan and the band on the bus, showing Dylan reading an astrological magazine, it jumps to Dylan at a press conference where a reporter asks him why he isn't singing protest songs anymore. "Every one of them is a protest song," Dylan says. "All I do is protest."

Next, he is in the hotel room, playing an unreleased acoustic love song ("What Kind of Friend Is This?") with Robbie Robertson, when the film suddenly cuts away to Dylan, back on the bus forlornly strumming the Everly Brothers' "When Will I Be Loved?" before it cuts back to the song in the hotel room.

In the next scene, Dylan, attired in a natty white suit and vest and sporting a Dali-esque mustache, flirts with a French woman. "You're not the type to hypnotize, you must be the type to do something else," Dylan says, a hint of eroticism in the air.

The next song is another unreleased acoustic song, "I Can't Leave Her Behind," giving us a pretty fair hint at what happened in the meantime.

From there, the film moves into an examination of Dylan and his fans, as Dylan cuts from live performances to mostly critical comments from his fans as the music blares in the background. The songs "I Don't Believe You" and "One Too Many Mornings" are filmed almost in their entirety. There are also bits of "Like a Rolling Stone"; "Just Like Tom Thumb's Blues"; "Ballad of a Thin Man"; and "Baby, Let Me Follow You Down."

The footage of Dylan on stage is revealing. You can see why Dylan said he and The Band felt as if they "were drilling these songs into people." The songs carry an extraordinary power, and Dylan performs them with a sense of abandon even if he's so hopped up on drugs that he can barely keep his hands still.

It has been suggested that the reason his hands were shaking and trembling was merely nervous creative energy. Maybe it was. But Dylan looks more like a speed freak trying to keep it all together. Interestingly, almost none of the music seen in *Eat the Document* shows up in the Scorsese documentary *No Direction Home*, which shows you all the great material that Bob had before him — and you see what he chose.

As the film, which lasts about an hour, winds down, one of the more interesting moments is a spooky version of the harmonica solo on "Mr. Tambourine Man." Fans are shown lined up outside, and the recording seems to be from the back of the hall. Suddenly we're on stage with Dylan; then we see him backstage as the music keeps on playing. It's as if his music is omnipresent, even if he isn't.

Beatles fans will enjoy the quick glimpse of John Lennon riding in the back seat of the car with Dylan, who seems to be feeling the effects of so many drugs.

> "Are you troubled by sore eyes, a groovy forehead and curly hair? Try zoomdom," Lennon says. Then he tries to cheer Dylan up: "Come, come, it's only a film." When Dylan doesn't respond, we understand why the film cuts to "One Too Many Mornings."

The film concludes with Dylan and Robbie in the hotel room, working on another unreleased acoustic song. Dylan finally turns and notices the cameraman. "Hey, why don't you move around, man," he says, gesturing. "Unless you're comfortable in that chair."

The frame freezes. End of film. (B+)

The Concert for Bangladesh

Filmed at Madison Square Garden (August 1, 1971)
Released: March 1, 1972
Available on videocassette and DVD

Bob Dylan is not the featured performer in this film; ex–Beatle George Harrison is. But like *The Last Waltz,* leave it to Bob to steal the show.

His live performance at the Concert for Bangladesh was his first solo public appearance in years. He appeared with The Band at the

Isle of Wight Festival in 1970 and at the Woody Guthrie Memorial Concert.

But after George Harrison's introduction, "I'd like to bring out a friend of us all, Mr. Bob Dylan," out he strode, looking cool and casual in a dungaree jacket and jeans. Dylan is on screen for about 20 minutes, performs "A Hard Rain's a-Gonna Fall"; "It Takes a Lot to Laugh, It Takes a Train to Cry"; "Blowin' in the Wind"; "Mr. Tambourine Man"; and "Just Like a Woman." He is brilliant. The film is not to be missed. (A+)

Pat Garrett and Billy the Kid

Directed by Sam Peckinpaugh
Released: May 1, 1973
Available on videocassette

This retelling of the old Billy the Kid story is interesting enough. Dylan's role in the film, a character named Alias, is minor, but he brings an unusual quality to it.

Perhaps the most memorable scene is where Pat Garrett, played by James Coburn, kills a man in a saloon. Alias is there, and to keep him out of harm's way, Garrett orders him to go over to a row of canned goods and start reading. So Dylan puts on his granny glasses and starts to read: "Uh, beans. Succotash. Sweet potatoes, beans."

It's a funny scene. Other than that, his moments in the film are few, except for one particularly awkward knife-throwing incident that should have been cut out.

Dylan also did the soundtrack for the film, but when the film was recut at the studio, the soundtrack was switched around, so it was unrecognizable even to the guy who wrote it.

"I can't say as I recognized anything I'd done [as] ... being in the place I'd done it for," Dylan told Cameron Crowe for the liner notes for *Biograph* in 1985. (C+)

Hard Rain

Filmed by Top Value Television for the NBC Special "Hard Rain,"
  broadcast September 14, 1976
Not currently available

In 1976, the name Bob Dylan was all over the place. He had a
number 1 album with *Desire;* his Rolling Thunder Revue was winning
critical acclaim all over the country; and he was hot, commercially. The
problem was that by the time they got around to filming the Rolling
Thunder Revue, the troupe had lost much of its original steam.

During the early part of the tour, Dylan and Joan Baez sang duets
as if it were 1964, and then Dylan performed mostly acoustic numbers. But by the time of the filming, the enthusiasm and genuine joy
in performance had become an exorcism. Dylan's marriage was in trouble, and when his wife, Sara, showed up to celebrate his birthday, she
found her husband with two girlfriends in tow.

As you might expect, the show that resulted from all this chaos
was spotty. It's intense, loud, annoying, touching, and heartbreaking.

Dylan performs 10 songs, some of which are different from those
released on the live record *Hard Rain.*

The show opens with a white-turbaned, bearded Dylan singing a
slow, mournful version of "A Hard Rain's a-Gonna Fall." Next, Joan
Baez joins him for four songs, "Blowin' in the Wind," "Railroad Boy,"
"Deportee," and a wild "I Pity the Poor Immigrant." None of these
songs made the live record. Next Dylan straps on a white electric guitar and plays a little slide guitar on a remarkable "Shelter from the
Storm." It is easily the best song in the show, and one of Dylan's finest
live performances ever.

But the show loses steam from there. "Maggie's Farm" is sloppy;
"One Too Many Mornings" is solid, if somewhat plodding; the slight
"Mozambique" was probably included because it was the single Dylan
had out at the time; and, finally, "Idiot Wind" was pretty fair.

It certainly wasn't "Bob Dylan for mainstream consumption"
which is probably the special the NBC was hoping for. Instead, it was
difficult, frustrating, and challenging. Just like the artist. (B-)

Renaldo and Clara

Filmed by Bob Dylan and Howard Alk in 1975
First shown: January 25, 1978
Not currently available

Even Dylan's devoted cult of bootleggers have had a difficult time
acquiring the only feature film he has ever made. As of 1991, Dylan's
good friend D. A. Pennebaker had never seen the four-hour opus, which
perhaps is just as well.

The film was roundly criticized by nearly every film critic — or so
it seemed — in the Western Hemisphere. Writing for the *New Yorker*
(February 13, 1978), the noted film critic Pauline Kael called it "The
Calvary Gig" and slammed the film and its filmmaker:

> He has given himself more tight close-ups than any actor can have
> had in the whole history of movies.
> They are so close you don't see the whole face — only from under
> the brims of his hats down to midway across the chin. His eyes are
> heavily lined in black, for a haunting, androgynous effect, and you
> get the skin blemishes, the face hair, the sweat and the bad capillar-
> ies, and, when he sings, the upper lip pulling back in a snarl and the
> yellow teeth like a crumbling mountain range.

Though the film is currently unavailable for home viewing,
Leonard Maltin included it in his book *Home Video Guide,* rating it "a
bomb."

Not everyone hated it. In his book *Dylan,* Jonathan Cott called
it "an ambitious, fascinating and illuminating movie." In *Performing
Artist: The Music of Bob Dylan,* former *Crawdaddy* critic Paul Williams
called it "a masterpiece." According to Williams, Dylan's other masterpieces so far are "Don't Think Twice, It's All Right," "A Hard Rain's
a-Gonna Fall," "Mr. Tambourine Man," "Like a Rolling Stone" and
"Blind Willie McTell."

Those who saw the film twice, once in its original four-hour length
and then in the shortened version (which was essentially just dynamic
concert footage) had to wonder. There were some great concerts and
perhaps some interesting bits of dialogue and plenty of toying with the

207

Bob Dylan myth. But there was no way anyone, even a devoted Bob Dylan fan, would walk away from the film understanding it on one viewing.

Since Dylan's ex-wife Sara is in the film, it is perhaps unlikely that he will ever permit it to be released to the general public. This is unfortunate because if Dylan's career has taught us anything, it's that sometimes, it takes us a few years to catch up with him. At other times, he's just way out there in left field.

Until the film becomes available again for continued study, we have to leave it like it seemed on first viewing — a mystery.

Hard to Handle

Filmed by Gillian Armstrong on Dylan's 1986 world tour with Tom
    Petty and the Heartbreakers
Recorded in Sydney, Australia (February 24–25, 1986)
Shown on HBO: June 20, 1986

Bob Dylan's first full-fledged concert film in 10 years was filmed in Australia on his tour with Tom Petty and the Heartbreakers. It is nicely filmed, using several unusual camera angles, and Dylan's performances are, by turns, enthusiastic, playful, and intense.

The show begins with a Dylan speech (and a burp): "I want to do a song about my hero," he says, strumming his electric guitar. "Everybody's got their own hero. I don't know who your hero is. Mel Gibson, maybe? Let's hear it for Mel Gibson.

"If you're where I come from, you might say Michael Jackson or Bruce Springsteen. Well, I've known a few of them and I don't care nothing about those people. I want to do a song about my hero."

And the band swings into "In the Garden," a lively song from Dylan's religious album *Saved.* The band plays with fire, and Dylan seems to enjoy playing with them.

Next is an old favorite, "Just Like a Woman," with lots of piano flourishes by Heartbreaker Benmont Tench. Dylan sticks to the original melody and sings it sweetly. "Like a Rolling Stone" follows, and again, Dylan sticks to the original rendition. Petty and the band sound great, and this version of the song is one of the best available since the original.

Dylan next takes the stage for two solo numbers, a fast, intense version of "It's All Right, Ma," followed by a wistful "Girl from the North Country," a rarely performed number off Dylan's second album *Freewheelin'*.

When the band returns, Dylan offers a stately rendition of "Lenny Bruce," his tribute to the controversial comedian; a hard-rockin' "When the Night Comes Falling from the Sky"; a superb "Ballad of a Thin Man"; and a somewhat soggy "I'll Remember You," which closes the set.

The encore, during which the credits start rolling, is "Knockin' on Heaven's Door." Certainly the best concert footage of Dylan in a long time, *Hard to Handle* is a worthwhile investment and a pleasant, enjoyable show. It is not particularly daring, but it is not intended to be. (B+)

Hearts of Fire

Filmed in Canada, London, and Wales (Fall 1986)
Premiered at Marble Arch Odeon, London (October 9, 1987)
Currently available on videocassette

If you're a Bob Dylan fan — and why else would you want to watch this movie — there isn't much here that should make you want to rush out and rent the video. It's a standard B movie.

Dylan plays Billy Parker, an aging rock star who happens to catch Fiona and her band at a roadhouse and eventually joins them onstage for a good rendition of John Hiatt's "The Usual." Parker is supposedly burned out by the business, but is going to London for an oldies show and asks Fiona to go with him. Since her day job as a tolltaker is a drag and the band she's been playing with is taking a job at the Holiday Inn, she decides to go.

Once she gets to London, she runs into her favorite British pop star James Colt (Rupert Everett), who steals her away from Parker for a while before fame and his egomania drive him (and her) wacky, and she decides to go it on her own.

There are many humorous moments, some of which are even intentional. Dylan fans will note that the theater that Dylan and Fiona drive by is playing *Pat Garrett and Billy the Kid*, Dylan's other "straight" Hollywood film release.

There's also a moment at Colt's house when he is watching footage of Dylan strumming an acoustic guitar at the Concert for Bangladesh while the rocking sounds of "When the Night Comes Falling from the Sky" play on the soundtrack.

There really isn't much of Dylan, who is so skinny he looks unhealthy, on stage. He sings "The Usual"; a pretty lame rewrite called "Had a Dream About You, Baby"; and later, at the end of the film in the hayloft with Fiona, Shel Silverstein's "Couple More Years."

He has some funny lines, he throws the most awkward punch since Leon Spinks's pro debut, and his wooden delivery is straight out of *Terminator*. But his unusual appearance and quirky manner make the film interesting viewing for Dylan fans. Maybe once. (C-)

Masked and Anonymous

Directed by Larry Charles.
Written by Sergei Petrov and Rene Fontaine
Starring Bob Dylan, John Goodman, Jessica Lange, Luke Wilson, Jeff
    Bridges, Penelope Cruz.
Filmed in Los Angeles, Summer 2002
Released: July 25, 2003

After the debacle of *Hearts of Fire* and Dylan's well-noted film woes with what came to be seen as very expensive vanity projects like *Renaldo and Clara* and *Eat the Document,* nobody in their right mind would have expected Bob Dylan to undertake a starring role (well, sort of) in his own film.

You could say *Masked and Anonymous* is unpredictable but that would be undercutting the out-and-out weirdness of it. You've probably read about the plot by now.

Dylan, a has-been superstar who may or may not be the son of a dying president, is freed from jail to participate in a benefit concert in a country that's overrun by Latin American-styled dictators. In the process of preparing for the actual show — which doesn't exactly happen — Dylan or Jack Fate as he's called runs into all sorts of unusual folks, exchanges some sassy or nebulous lines and moves on.

Dylan has several interesting scenes in the film. In his first important scene, Fate returns to the run-down hotel he used to stay at. As he enters his room, he flashes back to when he was a young man, having a fling with Angela Bassett, who, apparently, was the mistress of his dying father. He calls the President's home, gets a recording. Tries again, gets his room but does not speak to his nurse/wife.

Then Fate offers an ominous voiceover: "Some of us pursue perfection and virtue and if we're lucky, we catch up to it. But happiness can't be pursued. It either comes to you or it don't.... In my father's world, you do not take what is his. Not his gold. Not his silver. Not his woman. I thought I was doing it for my mother. I thought I was doing it for my country. Ultimately, I was doing it for me. In the end, it's the strongest arm that stretches the bow."

Well, OK.

Fate is then hooked up with a Jack Fate cover band, called "Simple Twist of Fate" and with one camera zooming in on Dylan (Fate), his bandmates all in frame, they roar through an oldie, "Down in the Flood," one of a handful of unusual selections, including Bob's version of "Dixie," "I'll Remember You" "The Wicked Messenger" and "Cold Irons Bound."

There are some yuk-yuk in-jokes. First, Jessica Lange asks (Fate's manager) John Goodman if (Fate's) songs are going to be recognizable (a common complaint of Dylan fans.) Goodman says "All of his songs are recognizable even when they're not recognizable." Later, a rock journalist (Jeff Bridges) asks Fate why HE wasn't at Woodstock? (Dylan LIVED there, for goodness sakes, but ducked the concert.)

The film continues and you do wonder what will happen to Fate. On screen, Dylan is a skinny and weatherbeaten as you might expect.

He delivers a line a little better than he did in *Hearts of Fire* but let's face it, we're not watching him expecting Robert DeNiro.

Fate's big dramatic scene comes after he visits his mother's grave. He bucks up and decides to go to see Angela Bassett, who urges him to try and straighten things out with his father. Fate says he wants to go see his father. They almost kiss, then Fate leaves to go see his father.

He greets his brother, the long-haired, bespectacled Mickey Rourke, who is about to take over the country. As "Senor" plays, Fate comes in to visit his dying dad, hat in hand, tears in his eyes. He does not speak.

After his father dies, Rourke takes over the country, just as Fate is in the middle of a rousing "Cold Irons Bound." Shortly after that, an argument between Goodman and Bridges winds up with Bridges getting killed by a guitar. And Fate, of course, is framed, arrested and sent back to jail.

The final scene is a close-up of the wizened old face of Bob Dylan, riding by his lonesome on the back of a beaten down jeep, echoing the final scene of D.A. Pennebaker's *"Don't Look Back."*

Bob Dylan: 1965 Revisited

A film by D.A. Pennebaker
Released 2005 with Deluxe Edition of "Don't Look Back"

Many film critics have suggested that D.A. Pennebaker's "Don't Look Back" is the finest, most honest documentary ever made about a popular musician. Granted, that list may be quite short.

For the 40th anniversary of the release of that classic about Bob Dylan's final all-acoustic tour in 1965, what can Pennebaker do for an encore?

Well, he can plow back through 20 hours of unreleased footage shot on Dylan's 1965 British Tour (his final all-acoustic tour) and see what he can find of interest.

That's that Bob Dylan 1965 Revisited is all about, the companion disc to the re-released "Don't Look Back" luxury box set. And it's very nice to have.

The film opens with Dylan alone at the piano, cuts to a concert performance of "Don't Think Twice, It's All Right" and traces the familiar route of the 1967 original, Dylan with fans, Dylan with the press, Dylan posing with Joan Baez.

Whereas in "Don't Look Back" Pennebaker showed snippets of performances, here he tries to include complete performances. There's Dylan and Baez harmonizing in a hotel room on "Wild Mountain Thyme" (Dylan does not let her perform with him), Dylan trying out a verse of "Love Minus Zero" in a soundcheck, singing "To Ramona," delicately refusing a request from a rowdy Liverpool audience (foreshadowing the fireworks the following year) and singing instead "It's All Over Now, Baby Blue," the final verse of "The Lonesome Death of Hattie Carroll" and Joan Baez singing "What a Friend I Have in Jesus" over Bob's typing.

We also hear Bob's turn at Willie Nelson's "Remember Me" in a hotel room, then a stunning "It's All Right, Ma" before an absolutely spellbound Liverpool audience. We also see a nice "It Ain't Me, Babe," shot from the side in Newcastle, a view that reveals Dylan's riveting intensity.

We also get the playful "If You've Gotta Go, Go Now" in concert and in a hotel room, Dylan forgetting the words to his own "Let Me Die in My Footsteps."

There's also a brief clip of "She Belongs to Me" and a backstage rehearsal piano version of "I'll Keep It with Mine"—a song he supposedly wrote for Nico (who is shown chatting with Albert Grossman.)

And with his fans, Dylan is much warmer than you'd expect. There's one moment where a star-struck teen-ager, stumbling over his sentences in front of Dylan, put his hands in his pockets, shrugs and says "I don't know what to say."

Off camera, Dylan gently offers a reply.

"Me, neither," he says.

As a final throw-in, there's also an alternate take of the "Subterreanean Homesick Blues" video with producer Tom Wilson and road manager Bob Neuwirth on the roof of a hotel.

If you're a fan of "Don't Look Back"—and it's hard to imagine anyone reading this book who isn't—you'll enjoy "Bob Dylan: 1965

Revisited," particularly the commentary by Pennebaker and Neuwirth, two eyewitnesses to history who now, aren't afraid to look back.

No Direction Home

A Martin Scorsese picture
Directed by Martin Scorsese. Produced by Martin Scorsese, Susan Lacy, Jeff Rosen, Nigel Sinclair and Anthony Wall.
Released: July 21, 2005
Available on DVD and VHS

Superbly packaged, elegantly filmed and crisply edited, if Martin Scorsese's *No Direction Home* isn't the Holy Grail of Bob Dylan movies, it's hard to imagine one that will surpass it.

Using rarely — and sometimes never — seen footage culled from various performances on various stages throughout the world in the early years of Dylan's career — including the JUDAS moment — Scorsese takes the very bold step of attempting to connect Dylan to his times.

In addition, Dylan himself, of all people, actually contributes to the film, providing relatively straightforward interviews, timely voiceovers and sharp commentary from start to finish.

Aired on American and British television, the documentary was an enormous success and almost certainly sparked record sales for all of Dylan's work. Columbia Legacy also issued a "Soundtrack" along with the release of the film, though only a handful of songs on the actual CD appear in the movie in the same form.

The film opens with a brief recent interview with Dylan, saying something about starting off very far from where he was supposed to be and now he was on his way home.

Jump to a stage in Newcastle, England nearly 40 years earlier where the young Dylan, all wild curls and toothy snarl accompanied by explosive sound of the Hawks, are winging their way through an ear-splitting version of "Like a Rolling Stone."

Even though the film is 40 years old, its rich color and clarity are stunning. And revelatory. The very real sense of anger and disillusionment between the crowd and the performer is there. You can sense it, even all these years later. Can you imagine what it must have felt like onstage?

As the film continues, Scorsese makes generous concert footage stops throughout the film, telling his tale through flashbacks that Dylan, in some cases, helps narrate.

Since so little of this footage has ever been seen — Dylan's strange documentary from that tour *Eat the Document* seems mostly to use different shots — you find yourself waiting for the next concert break through all the personal biography. Not that the biography stuff is poorly done, it's just that the concert footage is so explosive, you want more of it. Particularly so in Part II, where the crowds are getting increasingly upset and quite vocal ("What happened to Woody Guthrie, Bob?") and most famously, "Judas." You can see why it happened.

Yet Scorsese's film (actually 1966 footage shot by D.A. Pennebaker) also reveals a Bob Dylan, caught up in creating the greatest music of his life, who just couldn't give a damn what anybody said.

On film, you see a ferocity that you don't really get on record. Nobody will confuse this film with *A Hard Day's Night*. Because of all the emotion and anger, when we learn Al Kooper decides to leave Dylan's band upon learning the tour itinerary takes them through Dallas, just three short years after John F. Kennedy was assassinated, nobody laughs.

As the film treks through Dylan's early career, there's a marvelous moment where someone, it doesn't say who, takes some film footage of a very young Bob Dylan, just arriving in New York City for the first time. The footage is black and white and moves a little jumpily, like an old newsreel. Tellingly, it shows Dylan opening a guitar case and trying on a wide assortment of hats, perhaps unwittingly foreshadowing the many changes he would go through in the next several years.

Dylan, of course, is his wry self throughout, noting at one point that two girls that he was fond of "brought out the poet in me." The magic bohemian lifestyle of Greenwich Village is brought back extremely well and one can see how an ambitious "sponge" like Bob Dylan flourished in such a wild, free-spirited environment.

About midway through the film, Dylan correctly notes that

through all his amazing changes, he found a way to go on — because he had to.

"I felt like I had discovered something no one else had discovered," he says.

"And I was in a certain arena that no one had ever been in, though I might be wrong about that." All the great early Dylan moments are here, the incredibly audacious speech (read by most un–Dylan like voice of Scorsese) at the Tom Paine Award dinner, the booing at Newport in 1965, his delightful Newport appearances in 1963 with Joan Baez and a shocker in 1964 where an excited Dylan, at the end of his stirring performance, flutters his arms in delight and tells his Newport audience "I love you."

Many of the major principals in Dylan's early life are interviewed, including Joan Baez, Allen Ginsberg, Pete Seeger, Dave Van Ronk, Tony Glover, Al Kooper, Suze Rotolo and others. Some of the Dylanologist cynics are disappointed that some others weren't interviewed, like his first ex-wife (Sara) or Donovan or whoever. But the most important people are there.

The story darkens a bit in Part II as Dylan decides to go the rock and roll route.

Acclaimed as a "genius" on The Steve Allen Show (the shots of Dylan grinning are priceless) he quickly moves away from the politics of the moment and, in somewhat of a revelation, admits that with everyone else using his material to hit big on the charts, he figured it was his turn.

"Like a Rolling Stone" was his vehicle and Kooper's recounting of how he got to play on the historic session is delightful. Dylan himself says that "Rolling Stone" "broke through somewhere. I'd never heard a song like that on the radio before."

As Dylan cohort and long-time character Bob Neuwirth correctly notes, the audience came to Bob Dylan, which truly is something very unusual in American music. He always made the music he wanted to make exactly when he wanted to make it.

The DVD also includes several full-length Dylan performances not included in the film, some performances by people who were interviewed and some oddball stuff, like Dylan's screen test for Andy Warhol, the unused promotional film for "Positively Fourth Street," an alternate take of the "Subterranean Homesick Blues" video that opens D.A. Pennebaker's film *Don't Look Back.*

The only thing more Dylan fans could have asked for would be a complete concert from the 1966 tour, one that shows the entire acoustic first half and the second half backed by the Hawks. Perhaps the fabled Royal Albert Hall concert?

It would be humorously appropriate since Dylan fans thought that's what they were hearing for many years, finally discovering the great Dylan bootleg actually came from the Manchester concert shown at the end of "No Direction Home."

Pennebaker has the footage. "Eventually, it'll come out," he told the *San Antonio Express-News* in 2007. "It's wondrous. Just wondrous."

The Other Side of the Mirror: Bob Dylan Live at the Newport Folk Festival 1963–1965

Released by Columbia Performance Series, October 30, 2007
Recorded at the Newport Folk Festival, Newport, R.I., 1963, 1964, 1965

Details   Sharp-eyed viewers may have already noticed that through the years, highlights from Bob Dylan's performances at the Newport Folk Festival have leaked out — some in Murray Werner's *Festival* in 1967, some in other documentaries, most notably Martin Scorsese's *No Direction Home* in 2005.

The footage, in glorious black and white, looked crisp, sharp and compelling. But since we never saw any more of it, you had to wonder if those were the only clips that survived. How wrong we were.

The Other Side of the Mirror, which hit the stores in 2007 just as Todd Haynes' extraordinary Bob Dylan film *I'm Not There* was playing in theaters across America, is the perfect companion piece — no doubt, the way this was all intended. This does, of course, smack of media manipulation, marketing ploys and all that. But so what?

Lerner and, more importantly, his camera were there to witness the extraordinary changes in Bob Dylan, singer, songwriter, national conscience and literally, a true folk hero over a monumental, mind-spinning three-year span that saw him climb from a whiny-voiced, Woody Guthrie-wannabe to an absolute folk institution (at 23!) to a icy, ruthless, untouchable pop icon a year later. Finally, we can see for ourselves as Dylan's frayed cotton gives way to black leather and how, in his own marvelously liberating, singularly courageous way, he found a way to tell his audience "no."

True, the "Dylan goes electric" moment at Newport has become almost a cliché because it has been written and talked about so often. It's as if the first time Dylan's guitar pick slammed down across the electric guitar's strings, the musical world changed.

Seeing the complete actual footage — not just a 30-second clip — hearing the boos and feeling the anger, the audience's violent reaction to what time has shown to be Dylan's greatest work, is revelatory. Go ahead and say it — "Forgive them, Lord, they know not what they do."

Consequently, just as any real Dylan fan will have to go see *I'm Not There*, so will he or she have to see *The Other Side of the Mirror*.

The DVD opens by jumping ahead — in shocking fashion, to see the tousle-haired Dylan, his thick brown curly hair a-blowin' in the wind, on stage at Newport, opening with the goofily defiant "All I Really Want to Do" from 1965. The footage is so clean and clear and the shots of Dylan up close and from behind the stage, hair blowing all over the place, make him look so approachable, friendly, even. From there, the movie goes into chronological mode, flashing first to a sit-down workshop with Bob singing the rarely performed "North Country Blues" (a "Wreck of the Edmund Fitzgerald" soundalike) and then "With God on Our Side" with the overpowering voice of Joan Baez. Hearing this particular version of this number, you wonder how in the world anyone would have thought to put those two voices together.

Next, it's Dylan alone at the microphone on stage, singing a marvelous "Talkin' World War III Blues," (Woody would be proud), a somewhat sloppy "Who Killed Davey Moore" (sounds as if it had been a request), a sincere "Only a Pawn in Their Game" and then the show-closer, an everybody's in "Blowin' in the Wind" grand finale. This is the "our Bobby" everybody wanted to love.

Then we go to 1964 and get "Mr. Tambourine Man" from one of those sit-down workshops (this footage was used in *No Direction Home.*) There's a very nice clip of Baez calling "Bobby" out of the audience to duet with her on "It Ain't Me, Babe" and "With God on Our Side" on the evening stage and then finally, Dylan alone at the microphone on the Newport stage at night, debuting his new composition "Chimes of Freedom," one of the key songs on *Another Side of Bob Dylan,* which wasn't to come out until just after the festival. It remains one of his most ambitious numbers, one where you sense the artist standing on his tippy-toes, reaching as far and as high as he can.

It remains a fascinating performance. Dylan blows the first line, has to pause once or twice to remember verses and doesn't really sing it as much as recite it at the top of his register. Yet, his obvious pride in the words, his delight in performing this populist song of freedom, a song where he was absolutely reaching out to every single person in the world — "unharmful, gentle souls placed (inside) jails," criminals, freaks, losers, loners — "every hung-up person in the whole wide universe." Dylan's loving laundry list touched the Newport audience deeply — remember, this song had not been released yet — and he sensed it, too.

He walked off stage jauntily to a wild, untamed ovation, half-raising his arms in triumph as he left. Moments later, amidst a storm of "We want Bobby" chants from the audience, Peter Yarrow (of Peter, Paul and Mary) came on and tried to persuade them that it was time to move on to Odetta. Uh, unh.

Finally, midway into the next introduction — which nobody is listening to — Yarrow turns towards the side of the stage and shrugs, as if to say, "I surrender." He gestures a delighted Dylan back on stage, the lights came up and the raucous noise stops instantly the minute Dylan jumps over to the microphone. "Hey, time, it's all a matter of time," he says, gesturing as wildly as we've ever seen him. "It's time, they say.... I can't ... I wanna say thank you [goes on tip-toe], I wanna say thank you, I love you."

In just a year, this singer will be booed off the same stage.

The footage of the 1965 songs is brilliant, too. We get a fun "If You've Gotta Go, Go Now" and a sweet "Love Minus Zero/No Limit" in the same breezy setting as the film's opening sequence. After some teasing shots of the rehearsal (and Dylan in wild polka dot shirt) we cut to the nighttime show and history. There's Dylan, at center stage underneath a giant spotlight — interrogation time — dressed in a sexy leather jacket with the idea of an onstage smile as far away from his face as it will ever be. The band, all in darkness, swings into a roaring "Maggie's Farm" and Dylan sings it with ferocity.

Then, as the boos pelt the stage, Mike Bloomfield's sweetly played intro is turned up and Dylan leads the band through "Like a Rolling Stone" — his biggest hit (and some say greatest song.) The audience response is angry and you sense Dylan tensing up as they resist this new, exciting and yes, electric sound that pours over them. This, you can see now, is quite different than the British tour that will follow, when Dylan and the Hawks fully expected resistance — got it — and came on stage ready for a full-out assault. At the song's end, Dylan quickly unplugs his electric guitar and is barely out of the camera's view (it is stage left) when a shaken Yarrow is already at the microphone, as if to apologize for the awful things they just heard.

Though it is clear he has not spoken to Dylan — Yarrow entered from stage right — he says "Bobby was ... yes, he will do another tune, I'm sure. Will you call him back? Would you like Bobby to sing another song? [Crowd roars.]

"Listen, it's the fault of ... he was told he could only do a certain period of time. Bobby," Yarrow desperately turns to Dylan for help, "can you do another song?"

Offstage and out of sight, Dylan agrees, and in the meantime, Yarrow tells the audience "He's coming, he's gotta get an acoustic guitar."

Then Dylan emerges, shoots an icy look at Yarrow, and begins to strum "Mr. Tambourine Man," then realizes he doesn't have a harmonica. He keeps strumming and asks the audience for an "E harmonica." Several are thrown, he plucks one, and goes immediately into the song, drawing a sweet breaking wave of applause from those who had treated him so angrily just moments before. It's only as the camera moves in closer, we see, on Dylan's left cheek, what looks to be a lonely tear. He was listening, after all.

On the next number, "It's All Over Now, Baby Blue," the song that appropriately closed the festival itself, notice how he almost chokes on the words "yonder" and "crying" in the first verse. Dylan bravely finishes the song, then walks away from the microphone without another word, free, free forever.

I'm Not There: Suppositions on a Film Concerning Dylan

Directed by Todd Haynes
Written by Todd Haynes and Oren Moverman
Starring Cate Blanchett, Richard Gere, Heath Ledger, Christian Bale,
   Michelle Williams, Julianne Moore, Charlotte Gainsbourg, Ben
   Whishaw, Marcus Carl Franklin.
Released: November 21, 2007

Throughout his long, enduring and unpredictable career, Bob Dylan has always been one to dabble in many mediums of creative expression. We may think of him solely as a singer/songwriter, but he's already done — and continues to do — many other things.

He's always written prose and poetry with scads of liner notes. He's officially written two books, one a unreadable bomb (*Tarantula*) the other, a stunning, extraordinarily well-done best-seller (*Chronicles, Vol. 1*).

His skill at drawing and painting has landed his art on many album covers. Many of the works in his somewhat obscure book of drawings (*Drawn Blank*) released in 1994 were redone and reconfigured in recent years and, in the winter of 2007, were exhibited a prestigious art museum in Germany.

At 65, he not only manages to stay on tour, he also had a No. 1-selling album (*Modern Times*) and is into the second season of his critically acclaimed FM radio show on XM ("Themes, Dreams and Schemes"). That's a multimedia artist for you.

When it comes to film, though, Bob Dylan's resume is only slightly more impressive than that of Pauly Shore. Somehow, film is one medium he's never been able to master, despite many extremely forgettable tries. Dylan fans know his struggles began with the anti-documentary *Eat the Document*, a wild recounting of his tumultuous British Isles' tour with The Band in 1966. Next came the wildly excessive (and almost criminally unfocused) *Renaldo and Clara*. After he sank beyond the pale with the awful *Hearts of Fire*, he tried once more with the utterly strange — even for him — *Masked and Anonymous*. Excepting, of course, D.A.

Pennebaker's *Don't Look Back*, which magnificently captured Dylan in action on- and off-stage and some brilliant guest appearances (*The Concert for Bangladesh, The Last Waltz*), Dylan's film career has been a flop.

Perhaps that explains why Todd Haynes' extraordinary *I'm Not There* — his Dylan bio that isn't exactly a bio — hit the screen in the fall of 2007 with such force, as if channeling all these years of filmic frustration into each and every frame. Nobody could have ever guessed that such a challenging, innovative film would be such a smash. Especially considering that its topic was the many lives of Bob Dylan.

It may be years until we really understand everything in this dense, delightful film. But we can say this right now. No rock and roll performer has ever had as imaginative a portrait presented on film.

Haynes never tries to dumb-down Dylan the way most rock pictures do with their subjects, trying to make things simpler for a mass audience. On the contrary, Haynes assumes his viewers know about Bob and though he gives us many instances of people attempting to classify, demystify or categorize, he never does.

Like the finest Dylan songs, *I'm Not There* both gives his audience credit for their perceptions and challenges their understanding and appreciation for the man's work, taking them on a wild 140-minute ride through the finest moments of 40 years of Dylania.

Yes, all that with room — not that it will ever happen — for a sequel, should Haynes really feel daring.

After working with Bob Dylan on his Grammy-winning *Time Out of Mind* release in 1997, producer Daniel Lanois suggested "Bob is someone who's lived a lot of lives." Whether that is where Haynes got the idea for *I'm Not There*, we don't know. But he took Lanois' concept and not only ran with it, he did somersaults.

Haynes envisioned a most unusual way to tell Bob Dylan's story, with six different characters — actually, there was a seventh, a Charlie Chaplin-like figure in his early New York days that didn't make the final cut — playing Dylan at these distinct and varied intervals in his ever-shifting career. That's odd enough.

What none of us imagined was that included among these characters would be a young black kid, a sultry woman, two Hollywood movie star-types or that the name "Bob Dylan" would never actually be uttered during the movie. Or that such a radical idea wouldn't matter one bit.

The film opens with a wide-frame, long angle, black and white shot of Dylan riding a motorcycle in upstate New York. We know Dylan will crash that motorcycle later, and in real life, many saw that moment as the beginning of the career-long series of transformations that Haynes expertly scatters throughout the next two hours or so.

Haynes leads the viewer through re-inventions or re-interpretations of the Dylan myth, skipping forward or back, offering interviews or action clips or re-enactments. It's a little like the cinematic effect of a novel like *Catch-22* or *The Sound and the Fury* where a storyline only goes so far, a different voice picks up the tale, takes it a while, then you go back to another character, this time, with a fresh perspective on what you thought you already knew.

First, we get Marcus Carl Franklin, an effervescent African-American youngster, supposedly 11 years old and full of invention, personality and confidence, determined to do something special. He gets the wild idea of maybe even meeting his hero and "namesake" in the film, Woody Guthrie. What crazy kid would ever think of such a thing?

Indeed, one of the film's truly riveting moments captures the young "Woody" seated in the Brooklyn State Hospital, where the great Guthrie, all snarls and Adam's apple, is withering away from the nerve disease Huntington's Chorea. As the young Dylan must have, young Woody sits in silent worship, tears streaming down his cheeks.

Next, we skip ahead to see Christian Bale become Dylan, now a progressive left-wing folkie, honored with the Thomas Paine Award at some hundred-dollar-a-plate dinner. Dylan steps right into the middle of all the self-congratulating, telling his audience that he identifies with Lee Harvey Oswald, who has just been charged with killing President Kennedy — a detail that Scorsese tellingly left out of the "more suitable for family viewing" *No Direction Home.* He will not be anybody's poster child, thank you very much.

Bale also returns later in the film as the born-again Bob, surfacing as Dylan in his religious period, the *Slow Train Coming* era, with a fine version of "Pressing on."

As the film continues, we also get a chain-smoking, incredibly confused Heath Ledger as stardom Dylan — actually an actor in this film, not a musician, who is theoretically a contented family man in Woodstock, hiding from his fans, his family and his muse. It's here Haynes delivers his thunderbolt. In what may be the revelatory moment in the film — something no Dylanologist ever proposed — Dylan's wife hears the startling news of the end of the Vietnam War and freezes in front of the black and white set. Right away, she says, this will be the end of their marriage. She's right. And we get it.

Earlier, the film's Joan Baez figure (Alice Fabian) made it clear that Dylan had given up on his protest-style songs, telling her "songs won't change the world." Baez, an activist, of course, disagreed. Haynes' point here is clear. Since Dylan realized the public would never stop trying to encourage him to write protest songs until the war was over, he made a tactical retreat into life as a family man/country singer.

It was a survival move, essentially taking himself — and his songs — out of the equation until it was safe to return. His wife seemed to understand he was marking time and Haynes' film makes that startlingly clear.

The concept has some merit. Dylan clearly seemed lost at that time, and it does seem odd that someone who seemed able to pick songs "out of the air" and capture the spirit of the land would make such a retreat. The civil rights movement stirred the apolitical Dylan to play at the Lincoln Memorial, just before the Rev. Martin Luther King Jr.'s momentous speech. But the antiwar movement didn't seem to inspire Dylan at all. Was it fear of assassination? Disinterest in politics? Or was he simply afraid of being seen as his generation's spokesperson, simply wishing to get away from the notoriety, of people demanding answer, responses, more protest songs?

As he says in *Chronicles, Vol. 1*, "I wanted to set fire to these people. These gate crashers, spooks, trespassers, demagogues were all disrupting my home life and the fact that I was not to piss them off or they could press charges really didn't appeal to me. Each and every day was fraught with difficulties. Everything was wrong, the world was absurd."

Or did it go deeper? Even then, did he see past the futility of trying to convince a war-like world to change its tune? It must be disappointing to write a song like "Masters of War" as a kid and recognize that, all these years later, you not only CAN still sing it, you need to, because nothing's changed.

This is why, when in the oft-misunderstood concluding portion of the film where Richard Gere takes over as a befuddled, how-did-I-get-here Bob Dylan, it's thrilling to see him unable to remain silent as he's rushed into town and hears the townspeople challenging this Moses-like authority who want to change their town and life.

The town is Riddle, a spot right out of *The Basement Tapes*, where lines from songs pass for dialogue and strange characters (and a giraffe) supply a *Basement Tapes*–like atmosphere, a wild, Halloween/Carnival ride where nothing sounds or looks normal.

This is, metaphorically speaking, probably how Bob Dylan saw the world after the triumph and turmoil of 1966, looking back at a world that he had seemed to step past. One of the wonderful things about *The Basement Tapes* is the joy, the delight in the everyday that seeps through and in the film, seeing Gere, unable to stop himself from speaking out, from letting his voice (and by implication, his songs) be heard, is thrilling. It's as if he's coming back to life, which, really, he is.

The more obvious — and, in some ways, the most remarkable aspect of the film is the shocking performance of Cate Blanchett as the snarling, drug-fueled, ahead-of-the-curve-and-the-rest-of-the-world Bob Dylan. Her death-wish Dylan is every bit as good as advertised. This is where Haynes does his wildest stuff, depicting a literally higher-than-a-kite Dylan, flying over London, ultimately having the film's Dylan character (Jude Quinn) die of a drug overdose as the film opens.

As we know, that Dylan was soon dead (in a manner of speaking) and by opening "I'm Not There" with the death of the 1966 and most famous Dylan, it somehow prepares us for all the new lives we'll see unfold over the next two hours.

So much has been written — and deservedly so — of Blanchett's performance that the importance of her lines or what her Dylan actually has to say about all these things may be overlooked. They shouldn't be. Though a couple of times, using actual song lyrics ("She's Your Lover Now") to script an on-screen conversation seems clever, if a bit strained.

Note, too that Haynes takes some not-so-subtle digs at Dylan's money-hungry manager Albert Grossman and the physically brutal 1965–66 tour schedule he subjected the frail, frayed Dylan to.

In one wildly delightful cocktail party, Grossman tells Dylan "you're a millionaire" at a time when you can tell that financial rewards seem to be the very last thing on his wild and turbulent mind. Dylan's wounded, feared reply arrests you. You can't help but wish someone was genuinely looking out for Dylan then and Haynes must sense that, too.

So when, a little while later, the film cuts to a stark black and white shot of a wrecked motorcycle in the Woodstock woods — the near-fatal crash, the instant we hear the tumbling organ chords of "Sad-Eyed Lady of the Lowlands," you feel the emotion rush to your throat and think how close we came to losing him. It is the perfect song for that spot.

As the film concludes, Blanchett's closing scene in the taxi cab, similar to the riveting closing scene of *Don't Look Back*, is crucial. It's amazing to see an artist as articulate as Dylan truly struggle to find the words to exactly express what he was trying to say, to do, what his art was all about. You see right there how and why language, sometimes, fails, as the title song, "I'm Not There," shows so very well. And why the nonsense syllables of *The Basement Tapes*— which is where Dylan headed next — seem all that much more appealing.

In a way, *I'm Not There* is to Bob Dylan devotees what Haynes himself suggested Dylan did with *Chronicles, Vol. 1.*

"There's no greater gift," Haynes said, "that any pop culture singer has given to his fans in recent memories than that book."

In rediscovering and re-examining all these nooks and crannies of our consciousness filled in by some 40 years of Dylania, Todd Haynes' *I'm Not There* gives us a chance to live it all again. It's a film that illuminates the life and art and significance of Bob Dylan in a generous, loving way. It's a welcome mat thrown at the foot of the movie screen.

TELEVISION

Bob Dylan has appeared on many television shows, too many to list them all. These include *The Tonight Show, The Steve Allen Show, The Johnny Cash Show,* and *The Les Crane Show.* With the emergence of YouTube, many of the rarest Dylan moments, such as on *The Johnny Cash Show* or the rehearsals of one of his *David Letterman* appearances, all of these and more are readily available. Same goes for his TV interview with Ed Bradley of *60 Minutes* and you also find his NPR interview with "Morning Edition" on the NPR website.

Some of these TV appearances were even used in Martin Scorsese's documentary *No Direction Home.* The best is *Dylan Speaks,* a DVD covering Dylan's 1965 San Francisco televised press conference that is now available. And a scream.

Take a wander through the YouTube directory — if you have a few hours one day — and you'll be surprised at all there is.

FIVE

Radio

Until very recently, it was very difficult — if not impossible — to find Bob Dylan on the radio. Throughout his long career, there have been only two nationwide radio broadcasts of interviews with Bob Dylan and they're both recounted here.

Then in 2006, he decided to do his own radio show called Theme Time Radio Hour on Satellite Radio. More on that in a moment.

The first Dylan interview was a Westwood One program called "Dylan on Dylan." It aired in November 1984 and is very entertaining, although interviewer Bert Kleinman clearly sounds awestruck to be able to chat with Dylan.

The second interview was in 1991, when Dylan was promoting *The Bootleg Series* and he bravely decided that publicist Paul Wasserman would be as good a foil as any.

Though no interviewer, Wasserman gives it the old college try, but Dylan sounds disheartened and disagrees with even the most simple statements. Talk about contrary.

By the end, you wish that someone would tell Bob he shouldn't feel so down about his career and his songwriting. Maybe Hank Williams did write better songs. But that doesn't mean that Dylan's songs are worthless, which is how Bob makes it sound.

Wasserman had so little success eliciting interesting answers from Dylan in this interview that Westwood One producers even spliced in some of Dylan's answers from the 1984 interview to keep things moving along.

"Westwood Radio One Special: Dylan on Dylan"

Bob Dylan, Artie Mogul, Bert Kleinman
Aired November 1984

The interview took place in a New York hotel room overlooking Central Park, where Dylan, old friend Artie Mogul, and a somewhat star-struck Bert Kleinman shared a few drinks (you can hear the wine being poured) and chatted into the wee hours.

Dylan was in a talkative mood and showed his wry sense of humor. "My shows, I'm usually in no frame of mind whatsoever," he said. "And I have to kick in some place along the line. It usually takes me one or two songs. Sometimes it takes much longer than that. Sometimes it takes me until the encore. If they get an encore."

Dylan's sense of humor seemed to surprise Kleinman, who noted that Dylan had been smiling and laughing a lot during the interview but seemed "so serious" on stage.

"Well, the songs take you through different trips," Dylan said. "I mean, you know, what's there to smile about — how are you going to sing 'A Hard Rain's a-Gonna Fall' or 'Tangled Up in Blue,' or 'With God on Our Side,' or uh, 'Mr. Tambourine Man' or 'Like a Rolling Stone' or 'License to Kill' or 'Shot of Love' or 'Poisoned Love,' how can you sing them with a smile on your face? It'd be kind of hypocritical."

What about singing on those off-nights?

"I've done things, I might have had a temperature of 104 or I might have been kicked in the side that day and couldn't hardly stand up," Dylan said. "Where it's been painful to stand there. And that's kind of humiliating in a way because you know there's no way you can be as good as you could be."

Asked about his recording future, Dylan said he'd like to see someone come along so he could pass the torch:

> I've already taken it as far as I can take it. Maybe I won't see that person, I don't know. I haven't seen any person whose taken what I've done a step further. And I don't say that in a bragging sort of way, it just hasn't gone any further.

I wanted just to sing a song to sing. And I had to write what I wanted to sing because nobody else was writing it. What I felt, what I felt was going on, nobody was writing. If I had found that person I probably would never have started writing.

"Westwood Radio One: The Bootleg Series"

Bob Dylan with Paul Wasserman
Aired Fall 1991

Interviewed by his publicist about some of the tracks on *The Bootleg Series, Vols. 1–3* in the summer of 1991, Dylan seemed in a sad state of mind. He demeaned his work and his abilities and seemed beaten down, as if he didn't want to have anything to do with music.

About the only spark of life in him came when Wasserman tried to make pronouncements about some of Dylan's songs. Then Bob's contrary streak came to the fore in a big way. For example, Wasserman talked to Dylan about the protest song "Who Killed Davey Moore?" and its similarity to "The Lonesome Death of Hattie Carroll."

> WASSERMAN: Here are two songs where the question was always one of blame.
> DYLAN: BLAME?
> WASSERMAN: Yeah, blame. Hattie Carroll was just a maid in the kitchen —
> DYLAN: Well, well but to me those songs to me were never about blame, they're more about justice than anything else.

The streak continued as they discussed "Subterranean Homesick Blues":

> WASSERMAN: I'm sure it must be very, very boring to you to hear your lines quoted back to you. By the way, that's an assumption of mine. Does it bore you to hear your own lines quoted back to you?
> DYLAN: Not really.

Or later when Wasserman tried to empathize with Dylan, Bob didn't let him.

231

WASSERMAN: What about all the stuff that Bob Dylan has to subject himself to?

DYLAN: Well, Bob Dylan doesn't have to subject himself to anything more than me.

WASSERMAN: Yes, he does.

DYLAN: You mean like this interview?

WASSERMAN: Yes. That would be one example.

DYLAN: Uh ... Yeah, it's important to encourage me to do things, if that's the question, yeah. Everyone needs some encouragement to do something. It's hard for me to start my own motor, you know. But outside of that there's not really that much of a problem.

But the best example of Dylan's contrariness came when Wasserman tried to pursue Dylan's quote about the *Blonde on Blonde* sound to Ron Rosenbaum for the *Playboy* magazine interview in 1978. Dylan, of course, denied he ever said it:

That doesn't sound like anything that would have come out of my mouth. They could have.... Look, with me they do all kinds of things. If people don't get an interview, if they can't have an interview — God knows why they would want one — but if they can't have one and they must have one, they'll write their own. They've done it in the past. That's not, you know, that's not a crime to do that. So when you say this was attributed to me, it may, it may not be true.

Wasserman logically tried to follow up Dylan's outright denial of the comment: "You're saying it's not true?" Dylan answered, "No, no. You repeat it, you say this to me but just because it has my name on it doesn't mean it was said by me. It could have been a misquote, it could have been pieced together. Let me take another tack here. Let's say it is exactly what came out of my mouth ... uh, uh, well, there's really no reason to elaborate on it."

So did he say it or didn't he? It sounds like he did, but didn't want to have to explain it.

Neither did he want to elaborate on how he sees himself.

"Well, my role as an artist would be to stay true to my art.... Who says it's art though? Not me."

"You don't consider it art?" Wasserman asked.

"No. My stuff?" Dylan asked, his voice rising. "No. Why should it be? My stuff don't hang in museums.... It's performance. It's like dance, it's like anything else you see, you see movement on the stage it's like a play, it's stuff that happens on the stage. That's what make the records. See it's not the other way around."

But when Dylan started talking about his own work, there was an air of failure around him:

> None of my songs are that good. It's the way they're performed. Hoagy Carmichael's songs are much better than mine. So are George Gershwin's. And Irving Berlin, too.
>
> Hank Williams' songs are all better than mine. It's the performing of that song. You're not going to go nowhere with just a good song, you have to be able to perform it.
>
> To the outside world, they might look at my life and see it as a great success but my point of view that might not necessarily be true.... My work fulfills me but that's all it has to do. That's not saying a lot.

Sounding discouraged by the way Dylan put himself and his songwriting down, Wasserman tried to get some acknowledgment of success. "But you do feel that you're living up to your creative potential?" he asked. Dylan responded: "Well, not ... uh ... sometimes."

Theme Time Radio Hour

On May 3, 2006, XM Satellite Radio came up with a programming thunderbolt the likes of which nobody could have anticipated.

Bob Dylan, the reclusive, exclusive genius of rock and roll music, had agreed to do 50 radio shows. The guy renowned for on-stage mumbling and a lifelong reticence around unsuspecting microphones was actually going to sit down in a studio (or create his own) and spend an hour each week playing records? Who is kidding who? That sounded like a recipe for as big a flop as, say, "Hearts of Fire."

Yet like with so much of Dylan's career, just when you think he's gone off the deep end, he'll come roaring back with a huge, overwhelming success. Sparked by a quirky sense of humor, his impeccable and unpredictable taste in music, Dylan and producer Eddie Gorodetsky wind up producing a show that is full of surprises and lots of chuckles.

Each week's show is built around a theme. And Dylan has found a wide assortment of topics, ranging from Baseball to Father's Day, from Trains to Dogs, from Friends and Neighbors to the Bible.

Though it's fun hearing the songs, it's Dylan's between-songs commentaries that make the show roll. You get a little bit of everything.

Jokes: "I was talking to this one guy from Texas, he was bragging about his ranch. He said, 'Bob, I get up in the morning, I get in my car, and I drive for eight hours when I reach the other end of my ranch.'

I said to him, 'I used to have a car like that, too.'"

Commentary: "You know, Elvis (Presley) wore a cross, a Star of David and the Hebrew letter 'Chai.' He explained his jewelry habit by saying 'I don't want to miss out on Heaven due to a technicality.'"

There is even, from time to time, confession.

"Prince, just like Judy Garland, he's from Minnesota. 'Little Red Corvette' is one of Prince's most well-known songs, his biggest hit at the time and his first to reach Top 10 status in the USA. Prince is from the same sorta area of the country I'm from, so we have plenty in common. The first Corvette was made by Chevrolet in 1953. I bet that was before Prince was even born. It was an instant success and cost three grand. I know because I tried to buy one with no money down."

Surprisingly (though not really; if you listen to the show, Bob sounds like he's having a blast) Dylan has signed on to do another year with XM Satellite Radio, beginning in September of 2007.

And as XM's Lee Abrams notes in his blog, he senses a change in the weather around ol' Bob.

"I don't REALLY know him, but I have a strong sense of what he can deliver on the radio with all of the stars lining up. Speaking of Stars lining up, they have. Whether it's by design or pure chance, Bob seems to be opening up. ... a bit. I sense he'll go to the grave as a mysterious genius and musicologists two centuries from now will be waxing on about his vision. But for now, he did 60 Minutes ... the book ... the Scorsese documentary. This window may never open again. It is now a personal mission to see that this thing happens. It's not about the deal. It's about the extraordinary opportunity to hear Bob in his own words. To peek inside the soul of a master. To subtly observe the inside his soul without disturbing the mystique."

Amen.

SIX

Selected Books

Tarantula

By Bob Dylan
Published by Macmillan Company (May 1971)

Bob Dylan's one and only novel almost never came to be, which wouldn't have necessarily been a bad thing. Curiously, the book has neither added to nor detracted from his achievements. Which makes it quite unfathomable.

It started innocently enough. In the fall of 1965, when Dylan's star was on the rise, he signed a book contract with Macmillan. According to the book's Foreword, by Macmillan editor Bob Markel, Dylan submitted the manuscript and later visited the office in June of that year. The two discussed plans for the book, which was to come out later that year.

"We brought a set of galleys to him so he could take one last good look at it before we printed it and bound it and started to fill all the orders that had come in," Markel wrote.

"It was June. Bob took a break from some film editing he was doing *[Eat the Document]*. We talked a little about the book and about Rameau and Rimbaud and Bob promised to finish 'making a few changes' in two weeks. A few days after that Bob stopped working. A motorcycle accident forced him into a layoff."

Of course, nothing Bob Dylan does can ever go the way it is supposed to. So the long-awaited novel was on hold. Indefinitely.

In 1968, Dylan slammed the book in an interview with Happy Traum and John Cohen — the same John Cohen mentioned in the liner notes to *Highway 61 Revisited* (which, incidentally, are remarkably similar to the style Dylan used in *Tarantula*).

"I just put down all these words and send them off to my publishers and they'd send back the galleys," Dylan said. "I'd be so embarrassed at the nonsense I'd written I'd change the whole thing. And all the time they had a hundred thousand orders."

Dylan showed signs of becoming a budding literary critic when he analyzed the novel for his old friends. "The trouble with it, it had no story," he said. "I'd been reading all these trash books, works suffering from sex, excitement and foolish things."

In the meantime, preview copies of the galleys had been sent to critics, so the novel was out. Widely bootlegged, some of it was even printed in newspapers and magazines. After all that fuss, Dylan finally decided it was all right to let Macmillan publish what he'd written five years earlier — probably for mainly financial reasons.

The book was not well received, which is not surprising, since Dylan's critique of the book — that it doesn't have a story — is true. A novel probably ought to have a story.

The book is not wholly without merit; there is some interesting writing. Essentially, it seems that the book is a collage of everything Dylan was writing back then (ca. 1965). There is a somewhat confusing narrative or general stream of thought, which occasionally is interrupted by vignettes or some quite humorous letters. None of it is coherent, really. But it is quite funny in spots.

For example, the first vignette in the book: "the censor in a twelve wheel drive semi stopping in for donuts & pinching the waitress/he likes his women raw & with syrup/he has his mind set on becoming a famous soldier."

Then it's back to the "narrative," which reads like this:

> manuscript nitemare of cut throat high & low & behold the prophesying blind allegiance to law fox, monthly cupid & the intoxicating ghosts of dogma ... nay & may the boatmen in bathrobes be banished forever & anointed into the shelves of aloive hell, the unimaginative

sleep, repetition without change & fat sheriffs who watch for doom
in the mattress.

It is difficult to read, and more difficult to fathom. But if you take
your time and try to imagine Dylan's voice saying these lines, then it
can be enjoyable in small doses.

Village Voice music critic Robert Christgau wrote an interesting
review of the book in the *New York Times* Book Review in June 1971:

"The only literary precedent that comes to mind is 'The Naked
Lunch,' but in a more general way 'Tarantula' is reminiscent of a lot
of literature because it takes an effort to read it. Unless you happen to
believe in Dylan, I question whether it's worth the effort, and don't
call me a philistine — it was Bob Dylan who got me asking such questions in the first place."

Though there really is no plot and most of it is just plain weird,
the humor, and there's a lot of it, is quite refreshing.

(Book Grade: C+)

Invisible Republic:
Bob Dylan's Basement Tapes

By Greil Marcus
Published by Henry Holt and Company, 1997

The shadow of Bob Dylan is all over Greil Marcus' first book, the
classic *Mystery Train*. Though Dylan is not the topic of any single chapter — Randy Newman, The Band, Sly Stone among others make the
cut, Bob does not — there is no mistaking his influence on all of the
modern-day artists as well as on Marcus himself. For example: would
you have thought to examine the lyrical content of a Sly Stone song if
there hadn't been a Bob Dylan who preceeded him?

In some early interviews, where Marcus' writings on Dylan and
his work drew some fire (the opening line of his review of "Self-Portrait" is oft-quoted — "What is this shit?") and in Alex Ross' fine *New
Yorker* piece in 1999, Marcus declared his independence. "The funny

thing is, I'm not a Dylan person," he told Ross. "Many years went by when I didn't care about him at all."

Those words may seem like shocking to Dylanologists like Clinton Heylin, Stephen Pickering, Paul Williams, Stephen Scobie and others who continue to chronicle Bob's every utterance.

However, with this book and the one that would follow it, *Like a Rolling Stone: Bob Dylan at the Crossroads*, Marcus can no longer make that claim.

He may not have the comprehensive Dylanology credentials of the late John Bauldie or as complete a grasp of the Dylan arcana that many of these others do, but Marcus' thoughtful — sometimes too thoughtful — writing on Dylan's work is always worth a read and well worth consideration. Many modern novelists would do well to have such dedicated, introspective examinations of their work.

Frankly, as someone who entered the world of Dylania as a teen-ager, it was fascinating to learn all about Harry Smith's *The Anthology of American Folk Music* and its very likely influence on Dylan and on the Tapes themselves. Unless you came out of folk music or worked for Folkways Records, who had ever heard of it?

Many of the other characters who populate the book, Dock Boggs, Frank Hutchinson, Clarence Ashley, are delightful and Marcus isn't stretching himself all that much in linking those extraordinarily unique individuals with our Bob, who, let's face it, fans, does often seem as if he came from another planet.

Yet while any Dylan fan ought to be grateful for *Invisible Republic* and its ambitious attempt to sort out — via taste — the highly complicated musical ingredients (and legacy) that went into Dylan's Basement Tapes, there are more than a few moments where the reader goes, "Now wait a minute here."

Remembering that Dylan was a 25-year-old star on the mend, recuperating from the wild and woolly days of the 1966 tour, heavy amphetamine use (we suspect) plugging in on a daily basis with some equally young Canadian musicians in a pink rented house in upstate New York, there are times that Marcus finds way more importance in a song that to most of the rest of the civilized world sounds dashed off, perhaps inspired by the afternoon beer or post-lunch reefer or who knows what else.

By the way, there is an interesting radio program that aired on KPFA in Berkeley, CA. on May 5, 1997, where Greil Marcus and interviewer Jon Carroll play some unreleased Dylan cuts, discuss *Invisible Republic* and Bobbie Gentry's song. It's a fun show but not completely convincing. When you hear the cuts Marcus raves about, it's a little more difficult to see where he is taking this whole argument.

It is entirely believable that Dylan and the guys who came to be known as The Band were indeed looking for a new sound, where to go next, how to find a way to make their kind of music in the midst of a turbulent musical scene that was raging out of control. And more than anything else, the Basement Tapes sound like fun, Dylan winging it at the microphone with sympathetic backing from guys who probably got a kick out of seeing what he'd come up with next.

It's a little more difficult to take the imaginative leaps that Marcus does on a song like "Lo and Behold" or "Apple Suckling Tree," tunes that sound spontaneous, on-the-spot, delightfully unplanned. It's as if Dylan was experimenting with superb musicians who could help him express — musically — what he'd wanted to say lyrically (and vocally.) There is a richness to this music, almost a tapestry of new sound, woven together from all sorts of influences, influences that Marcus does try to track down like a bounty hunter.

While it's entirely possible that he's dead-on in his suggestion that "Clothes-Line Saga" was written as a response song to the popular hit "Ode to Billy Joe," that is what it sounds like. But his suggestion that Dylan was making a political comment on then–vice president Hubert Humphrey's mental status — the line "Have you heard the news, the vice president's gone mad..." seems extremely far-fetched from apolitical Bob.

The other concern some might have with *Invisible Republic* is Marcus' insistence on writing about songs that are unavailable (i.e., largely unheard by much of his reading public).

While we recognize that writers need to follow their muse, there is also a sense of the author being in on a secret that the reader is not; sort of a "Well, it's too bad, you didn't get to hear this, like I did."

239

So when you finally do hear a long-rumored, remarkably praised bootlegged song called "I'm Not There" — and it's an interesting wisp of a song, it's disappointing to see that you can't find much of what Marcus does when you hear it.

As you read on, you find yourself wondering if perhaps this guy is working himself into a bit of lather over a one-take version (and only one take — ever) of a song that is not only unreleased, it's pretty much incomprehensible?

If Dylan or his management or Columbia Records thought it was such an incredible song, chances are they would have released it on any one of the eight or nine retrospectives they already have out. But they did not.

You can believe that, as with "Blind Willie McTell" or "Series of Dreams," the decision to hold it back is just Bob being willfully difficult. He's done that before.

Or you can believe that for an imaginative writer like Marcus, it's also possible that a vague and generally imperceptible musical canvas is a perfect place for his Shroud of Turin.

If you do not ever hear this song, Dylan Nation, you will live. It's not like the live "Like a Rolling Stone" at Manchester, say. Not close.

Which, for some, does brings up the nasty issue of exclusivity. To a writer of privilege like Marcus ("Sure, Greil, you want to hear the entire session tapes of 'Like a Rolling Stone'?" "Sure, Mr. Pennebaker, I'd love to watch your version of the "Eat the Document" material of the 1966 tour, the one you called "Something is Happening"") devoting nearly an entire key chapter of a book on the Basement Tapes to a song that so very few have heard seems almost unfair.

And while this certainly isn't Marcus' intention, it does seem that he's way more likely to write about material that's extraordinarily difficult to find than the standard releases. That may be for the best of reasons, certainly. Give him his due. But I'd also like to think that Marcus did that regretfully, because he had to have that information in there to make his point.

But I also wonder how much of it is him saying, in so many words, "Well, I got to hear this and you didn't and if you did, you'd understand why I think about Dylan like I do."

You hate to be critical of someone who truly is trying to get to the bottom of the swirling pool of Dylania. It's very brave of him to make the effort. Ultimately, *Invisible Republic* is a book that you're glad was written. But you'll find yourself returning to *Mystery Train* much more often.

Chronicles, Vol. 1

By Bob Dylan
Simon and Schuster 2004

After the 137-page typo called *Tarantula,* Bob Dylan's 293-page memoir *Chronicles, Vol. 1* is a welcome, refreshing portrait of the artist in three guises: as a young man on the move; an established — if disgruntled — rock star trapped by fame and a disillusioned mature artist, trying, once again, to find the thread of creativity.

Vividly remembered, skillfully drawn, *Chronicles, Vol. 1* shows that if Bob Dylan had never picked up a guitar, blown through a harmonica or written a single song, he would still have something to say to this world. It is both surprisingly good and unexpectedly readable.

Nominated for a National Book Award, *Chronicles, Vol. 1* offers four different glimpses into the life and creation of Bob Dylan. And at the finish, if you don't look back and say, 'Wow, what a life,' you're way more cynical than you need to be.

There are those who will insist that Dylan has a convenient memory, that he always colors things to make himself look better and so on. Critics always have something to say. Sometimes, they're correct.

But with any author — and with this one in particular — you always have to give them a little bit of the benefit of the doubt to buy into their story, the improbability of the plot, etc. No writer's reality exactly matches our own individual reality. What we think we know about Bob Dylan has been so manipulated by so many people for so long, it's difficult to know what to think or believe.

The amazing thing with Dylan's book is how skillfully and how colorfully he is able to flesh out his early days in New York City, recalling something from 40-plus years ago with what seems to be extraordinary accuracy. If you talked to the other person involved, it's likely they might remember it differently. But isn't that life?

Dylan's ability to describe a room, a glimpse of the city in wintertime, a friend's library, is amazing, particularly for a guy who generally has to boil his ideas down into song lyrics.

> *I sat up in bed and looked around. The bed was a sofa in the living room and steam heat was rising out of the iron radiator. Above the fireplace, a framed portrait of a wigged colonial was staring back at me — near the sofa, a wooden cabinet supported by fluted columns, near that, an oval table with rounded drawers, a chair like a wheelbarrow, small desk of violet wood veneer with flip-down drawers — a couch that was a padded back car seat with spring upholstery, a low chair with rounded back and scroll armrests — a thick French rug on the floor, silver light gleaming through the blinds, painted planks accenting the rooflines.*

Dylan is lively on the page — some fine writers are not — and you find yourself whizzing through the book faster than you should. You can't help it. It's very readable and evocative.

His comments on his musical contemporaries as well as those who influenced him are astute, fascinating and at times, profound. And geez, look what happens when you let him near a library.

> *I cut the radio off, crisscrossed the room, pausing for a moment to turn on the black-and-white TV. Wagon Train was on. It seemed to be beaming in from some foreign country. I shut that off, too, and went into another room, a windowless one with a painted door — a dark cavern with a floor-to-ceiling library. I switched on the lamps. The place had an overwhelming presence of literature and you couldn't help but lose your passion for dumbness...*
>
> *I liked the French writer Balzac a lot, read* Luck and Leather, *and* Le Cousin Pons. *Balzac was pretty funny. His philosophy is plain and simple, says basically that pure materialism is a recipe for madness. The only true knowledge for Balzac seems to be in superstition. Everything is subject to analysis. Horde your energy. That's the secret of life. You can learn a lot from Mr. B. It's funny to have him as a companion. He wears a monk's robe and drinks endless cups of coffee. Too much sleep clogs up his mind. One of his teeth falls out, and he says, "What does this mean?" He questions everything. His clothes catch fire on a candle. He wonders if fire is a good sign. Balzac is hilarious.*

Naturally, some critics complained that Dylan didn't talk enough about his glory years or the writing of "Like a Rolling Stone" and "Highway 61 Revisited" or deal with the controversy at Newport or even the famed "Judas" moment on the 1966 tour. And there's nothing about his *Blood on the Tracks* confessional, his conversion to "born-again" Christianity or the later tours.

Every Dylan fan would love to read Bob's thoughts on those moments in his music. And maybe he'll get to that in *Chronicles, Vol. II*. Or maybe not.

When writer Greil Marcus attempted to set up an interview with Bob for his most recent book — a book which claims that "Like a Rolling Stone" is the greatest rock song of all time — Dylan's associates told Marcus that Bob doesn't remember much from that time and that Marcus writes better about that era than Dylan can remember it. Or something like that.

That may well be true. So, you ask, how can Dylan write so colorfully with such extraordinary detail about his early days in New York City, an era which preceded "Like a Rolling Stone" by four or five years?

Who knows? Maybe it was easier to embroider his early life? Or maybe, because of his young age, he remembered it more clearly.

And as for the writer's choice of topics, how can you truly criticize that? We can't tell our writers what to write. Gee, Mr. Twain, *Huck Finn* is a great book, but it doesn't have enough Hispanics in it. Or say Mr. Melville, would *Moby Dick* have been better with a love interest? Now this is not to equate Dylan's work with two American classics. It's not quite at that level. But you get the point.

Critic Alfred Kazin said in his memorable essay on William Faulkner, "Let the writer have his say." Period. That is: let the writer give full voice to whatever comes to his/her pen. Which, happily, is exactly what Dylan did in *Chronicles, Vol. 1.*

Just as with his albums, there are — and always will be — songs that are left off, perhaps someday we'll see the outtakes from *Chronicles, Vol. 1.* If they are as well-written as the book, it sure would be fun to see what he left out.

But if you look at it from his perspective, why would Bob Dylan write a book to begin with? Well, maybe because people nowadays are seeing such a different world, perhaps Dylan wanted to recapture the New York City and the hungry young artist who came sailing in, ready to change the world of popular song.

Or perhaps he wanted to explain, as he does in the chapter called "New Morning" what it was like to be Bob Dylan at the time of Woodstock. He couldn't do that in an interview — not really. But you truly get a sense of the isolation of stardom and the frustrations that go along with it.

In the "Oh Mercy" chapter, you get a real sense of what it's like to work with the guy, the unique twists and turns of his mind, what a remarkable sensibility he truly has. Our greatest writers — and at this point, I don't think it's wholly off-base to suggest that Bob Dylan is one of America's finest writers — have always had their own, unmistakable way of writing about the world. How unusual that Dylan's writing voice is as distinctive as his singing voice.

If you closely examine *Chronicles, Vol. 1*, the underlying theme, of course, is young kid wants to make good. There are extraordinarily bold statements, there are howlers, stunning one-line descriptions and a genuine sense of sharing. Which is why the book is so disarming.

For all these years, we've known how private Bob Dylan is, how mysterious, how cautious and how willfully disruptive.

Now, all of a sudden, he's telling us how he learned from Jon Pankake or met Jack Dempsey or recorded for John Hammond and it's like he's saying to us, "Hey, this was really something. This happened to me. Can you believe it? Come along with me on this magic carpet ride."

The lone hint that Dylan's dropped about Vol. II (to Jonathan Lethem in his excellent *Rolling Stone* interview) is that he said he can remember as far back as *Blonde on Blonde*—his majestic 1966 album (not mentioned in this book) and that that was about as far as he could recall. He also mentioned recording the Traveling Wilburys record and "Under the Red Sky" at the same time, how unusual that was. So maybe we can look forward to that, too.

We probably won't hear much about "Like a Rolling Stone" or the boos at Newport or the tour that led to "Don't Look Back" or that famous taxi ride with John Lennon in the wee hours of a London morning, a snippet of which was included in "Eat the Document." Or "Renaldo and Clara" or what kind of lover Joan Baez was.

That's OK. The main thing is, Dylan found that in writing *Chronicles, Vol. 1,* he had to work at it. And he was willing to. Why now?

"Well, it probably was because enough things have resolved themselves," Dylan told *Rolling Stone*'s Jann Wenner, "and I had an editor who was a good ally. I could have probably done it earlier, but I just didn't have the encouragement."

Bob Dylan. Working with an editor. Amazing.

"What I didn't like about (writing *Chronicles, Vol. 1*) was the constant rereading and revising, because I'm not used to that," Dylan told Wenner.

"If I wasn't inspired to do it, I wouldn't do it. So great flashes would come to me. These waves would come, and I would have to either go back to where I could write things and keep typewriters here and there and do that. But it was enjoyable in that I only did it when I was inspired to do it and never touched it when I wasn't. I never tried to manufacture the inspiration."

Which is probably just as well. It'd be more enjoyable to hear about Dylan touring today, what he's reading and writing and maybe even what he thinks of the whole Dylan Renaissance of the last five years. Come to think of it, that'd make a great book. (Hey, Bob ... take a hint.)

Like a Rolling Stone:
Bob Dylan at the Crossroads

By Greil Marcus
Published by Public Affairs Books, 2005

Not many writers would be ambitious enough to decide to write a book about a single song. Even if the song is a killer and nearly six minutes long.

Yet that's exactly what Greil Marcus decided to do with *Like a Rolling Stone: Bob Dylan at the Crossroads*, taking his readers back to that magical mid-sixties time when Dylan traded off the denim-shirted trappings of folk-star supremacy for shiny polka dots and dark sunglasses and rock stardom.

After conquering the world of folk, winning the love and respect of sixties do-gooders all over America, Dylan decided to make a bid to rule the charts — something that Martin Scorsese's superb *No Direction Home* reveals in its own elliptical Dylanesque way. "A lot of other people were having hits with my songs," Dylan said. So, the implication was, why not me?

Marcus, in attempting to recapture that moment in our history and Bob's, lets it all hang out here, giving us the sociopolitical temperature of the nation, various and sundry digressions into Vietnam, the Pet Shop Boys, the Watts riots, Sam Cooke and many others.

The power of the song remains unmistakable. Why it retains that power, after all these years, is not — and probably cannot — be explained here.

What many will find most interesting about the book is tracing the actual process of recording a song. Dylan apparently cleared the way for Marcus to actually listen to every single bit of recorded tape from the sessions that produced "Like a Rolling Stone," that is, every single take.

Marcus pulls out all the stops here to describe how this long, almost inexplicably powerful song nearly refuses to be recorded, almost like some wild bucking bronco that refuses any attempt to corral it.

Dylan, the musicians, everyone involved with the process seems to sense that they're on to something — nobody knows what. Fortunately, they kept after the song that was in there as did Dylan, even if he wasn't quite sure where he was headed or what he would find when he got there.

As Marcus explains in what may well be the most memorable part of the book,"Like a Rolling Stone," the song that would become Bob Dylan's biggest single hit, perhaps his most famous song ever was played — in its entirety — exactly one time.

That somebody was able to actually record it for posterity is amazing. And Marcus is able to capture the elusiveness of that song. As he explained in a subsequent interview, "Listening to the whole session was not like sitting in a recording studio," he said. "There are few things more boring than listening in on somebody else's recording session. But this is a tape of people trying to get at something that resists them. That's one of the interesting things about 'Like a Rolling Stone,' it resists whoever tries to play it. It almost is a thing in itself.

"It's almost as if it has its own body and its own mind. I think in this case, it as so big, Bob Dylan was trying to say so much, with so much vehemence, so much was riding on this song, this absolutely had to be it. This had to be something that would not only leave the Beatles and the Rolling Stones in the dust, it would leave his previous career in the dust. It would make it irrelevant. It would allow him now to go forward and do things he'd never done before. All that goes into the way that he sings it."

Albums and Their
Weeks on the Chart

Appendix A: Albums and Their Weeks on the Charts

The Basement Tapes 9
The Bootleg Series, Vol. 5 Live 1975 The Rolling Thunder Review 9
Street Legal 8
Under the Red Sky 8
Good as I Been to You 8
Dylan 7
Bob Dylan at Budokan 7
Empire Burlesque 6
Oh Mercy 6
The Bootleg Series, Vol. 4 "The Royal Albert Hall Concert" Live 1966 .. 5
Another Side of Bob Dylan 5
Times They Are A-Changin' 5
Hard Rain 5
Saved 5
The Bootleg Series, Vol. 6 "Concert at Philharmonic Hall 1964" 4
World Gone Wrong 4
Shot of Love 3
Biograph 2
The Bootleg Series, Vol. 1–3 2

Four albums — *Bob Dylan, Real Live, Knocked Out Loaded* and
Down in the Groove — did not make the charts.

APPENDIX B

Chart Positions

Appendix B: Chart Positions

Songs Ranked A+

1. "Don't Think Twice, It's All Right"
2. "The Times They Are A-Changing'"
3. "It Ain't Me, Babe"
4. "Subterranean Homesick Blues"
5. "Mr. Tambourine Man"
6. "It's All Right, Ma (I'm Only Bleeding)"
7. "Like a Rolling Stone"
8. "Ballad of a Thin Man"
9. "Desolation Row"
10. "Visions of Johanna"
11. "Stuck Inside of Mobile with the Memphis Blues Again"
12. "All Along the Watchtower"
13. "Knockin' on Heaven's Door"
14. "It's All Right, Ma" (Live)
15. "Tangled Up in Blue"
16. "Shelter from the Storm"
17. "Shelter from the Storm" (Live)
18. "Every Grain of Sand"
19. "I and I"
20. "Up to Me"
21. "What Good Am I?"
22. "She's Your Lover Now"
23. "Foot of Pride"
24. "Blind Willie McTell"

25. "Series of Dreams"
26. "Tryin' to Get to Heaven"
27. "Not Dark Yet"
28. "Desolation Row" (Live)
29. "Mr. Tambourine Man" (Live)
30. "Just Like Tom Thumb's Blues" (Live)
31. "Like a Rolling Stone" (Live)
32. "Things Have Changed"

Annotated Bibliography

In writing *Bob Dylan: A Descriptive, Critical Discography and Filmography* in 1995 and in updating it 13 years later, the author used an array of resources, from newspapers and books and magazines to the Internet to bootleg records and tapes. It takes a while for the whole story to emerge, as with many creative artists, and the intervening years have done a lot to flesh out the life story and artistic progress of Bob Dylan. Here's one man's look at what's out there:

DYLAN'S DOZEN

If you want to know about Bob Dylan, these are the books to start with, in order of importance.

1. Scaduto, Anthony. *Bob Dylan: An Intimate Biography*. New York: Grosset and Dunlap, 1971.
   Though it may seem a bit outdated now, Scaduto does a compelling job and actually gets Dylan to cooperate with him in some sections. Revelatory.
2. Dylan, Bob. *Chronicles*, Vol. 1. New York: Simon and Schuster, 2004.
   A stunning bit of writing, one that's unmistakably Dylan, and yet still a big surprise. It's hard to imagine how he could remember everything so vividly but his writing is convincing, entertaining and as fresh as spring water. That is a neat trick when you're writing about events that happened 40 years ago.
3. Shelton, Robert. *No Direction Home*. New York: Beech Tree/William Morrow, 1986.
   A rambling, wild, untamed text, with a lot of interesting information about Bob's early days from a guy who was close to him at that time.

Some of it is very believable, some of it seems wildly imagined. But Dylan's life has always been full of wonderful speculation, right?

4. Heylin, Clinton. *Bob Dylan: Behind the Shades Revisited*. New York: William Morrow, 2001.

   Heylin doesn't know as much as he thinks he does (only God could), but his passion for Dylan is remarkable, and this book, which updates the first version of *Behind the Shades*, is very readable and informative.

5. Marcus, Greil. *Invisible Republic: Bob Dylan's Basement Tapes*. New York: Henry Holt, 1997.

   Revelatory in that it lifts a curtain over a whole world of Bob Dylan influences. That said, some of the ideas in here are really whacked, but you have to read it to really understand Dylan's progression through *John Wesley Harding* and *Nashville Skyline*.

6. Rolling Stone. *Bob Dylan: The Essential Interviews*. New York: Wenner, 2007.

   Though a real Dylanologist would have had all these interviews collected from their original sources (I know I did), it's a great way to keep everything in one spot.

7. Griffin, Sid. *Million Dollar Bash: Bob Dylan, the Band and the Basement Tapes*. London: Jawbone, 2007.

   You never know who the writers are. Sid Griffin, lead singer and songwriter for the late, lamented alt-country group The Long Ryders ("Lookin' for Lewis and Clark"), turns his considerable talents to a popular topic among musicians, the Basement Tapes. And his work is definitive. While Greil Marcus' *Invisible Republic* certainly broached the subject first, Griffin discusses every single cut, paying particularly close details to the recordings themselves, where and when they may have been cut as well as the circumstances in the musicians' lives at the time, things that weren't noted elsewhere.

   Did you know, for example, that Woody Guthrie died right in the middle of that fruitful summer? Did you note that in Dylan's version of "You Ain't Goin' Nowhere," released a few years after the Basement Tapes had made the rounds, he name-drops (Roger) McGuinn? Why? Turns out that in the Byrds' version of that song, released before Bob put his version out, McGuinn gets a verse out of order. So Dylan gets his revenge.

   No other book or story pays such particular attention to the tapes and their backgrounds and which songs were chosen for the official release. Why there's even a map of Woodstock, where Dylan's home was, where Big Pink was, where Dylan had his motorcycle accident, in short, everything you can think of.

It simply is a marvelous work and Griffin's status as a musician no doubt helped open some doors. What remains fascinating, though, is how the Basement Tapes, such a revelation to others, seem like no big deal to those who participated in them. Get it!

8. McGregor, Craig. *Bob Dylan: A Retrospective.* New York: William Morrow, 1972.

Hard to find but a wonderful compilation of rarely seen or quoted articles on Dylan that, taken together, give you a complex, fascinating look at the emerging artist.

9. Dylan, Bob. *Lyrics: 1961–1985.* New York: Alfred A. Knopf, 1990.

An updated version of the 1973 *Writings and Drawings*, it includes the lyrics to all Dylan's albums since the first book, as well as those to "Dusty Old Fairgrounds," an outtake that was included in *The Bootleg Series,* and several entertaining bits of prose, such as "Alternatives to College," "11 Outlined Epitaphs," and "Off the Top of My Head," all of which are written in the curious, elliptical style Dylan used for *Tarantula.* The lyrics, of course, are nice, though Dylan doesn't always get the recorded and the printed lyrics to agree. You don't know which came first. But if you're interested in Dylan's work as a writer, this book is essential. Simon and Schuster also issued *Lyrics: 1962–2001,* and there are several songbooks available on the Dylan website as are just about all of Dylan's lyrics (many of which don't agree with the recorded versions!).

10. Dylan, Bob. *Writings and Drawings by Bob Dylan.* New York: Alfred A. Knopf, 1973.

Dylan's first official collection of his lyrics is fun reading, especially since the recorded lyrics and the ones published in this book aren't always the same. But there are revealing tidbits here: a typing sheet Dylan used to start "Subterranean Homesick Blues," some strange drawings, and a few lyrical passages. This came out during Bob's big dry spell, so it was welcome. In addition, this was Dylan's first acknowledgment of bootleg material, in that he included the lyrics to songs like "Rambling, Gambling Willie" and "She's Your Lover Now" even though those songs weren't released by Columbia Records for nearly 20 years. The book also includes Dylan's brilliant "Last Thoughts on Woody Guthrie," which also wasn't released until *The Bootleg Series* in 1991. His drawing skills are, uh, unusual.

11. Bauldie, John. *Wanted Man: In Search of Bob Dylan.* New York: Citadel, 1990.

If there is anything about Bob Dylan that needs to be known and Clinton Heylin doesn't know it, John Bauldie did. A first-rate Dylanologist, Bauldie collected brief interviews with an assortment of Dylan's cronies and succeeded in offering a taste of what it's like to deal with such a curious figure. The small paperback book isn't intended to be *The Sound and the Fury*, and it isn't. But it's fun and informative, like Dylan fan magazines *The Telegraph* and *Wanted Man*.

12. Marcus, Greil. *Like a Rolling Stone: Bob Dylan at the Crossroads*. New York: Public Affairs, 2005.

Not many writers would be ambitious enough to decide to write a book about a single song. Even if the song is a killer and nearly six minutes long. That's exactly what Greil Marcus decided to do, taking his readers back to that magical mid-sixties time when Dylan traded off the denim shirted trappings of folk-star supremacy for shiny polka dots and dark sunglasses and rock stardom. The fascinating documentation of the recording of "Like a Rolling Stone" is worth the price of the book. Turns out the famed recording was the only complete run-through Bob and the band ever managed to get.

OTHER WORKS ON DYLAN

Benson, Carl, ed. *The Bob Dylan Companion*. New York: Schirmer, 1998.

An entertaining assortment of Dylan-related materials that leans a little heavier on the more positive articles written about Bob.

Blake, Mark, ed. *Dylan: Visions, Portraits and Back Pages*. London: DK Adult/ *Mojo* magazine, 2006.

It might take a little work to find this one but the search is worth it. *Mojo* magazine is easily the most informative, best-written and most interesting magazine on rock and roll. And one reason is the writers take it seriously. Dylan's story is mapped out with all sorts of interesting tidbits. And while you're at the magazine rack, be sure to keep an eye out for *Mojo* or *Uncut* magazine covers with Dylan. You can bet they will have fine reading material, impeccably researched and beautifully delivered.

Cable, Paul. *Bob Dylan: His Unreleased Recordings*. New York: Schirmer, 1978.

This is a handy book for collectors of bootleg recordings of Dylan's songs, particularly those people who are wondering about bygone days. Cable exhausts every known (and unknown) rumor surrounding Dylan's recording dates and pins down much of the bootleg material. However, he seems overwrought about some of the unreleased material, making it seem as though the world is a worse place because these few songs were never released. But overall, his book serves a useful purpose.

Corcoran, Neil, ed. *Do You, Mr. Jones?* London: Pimlico/Random House, 2003. Here is a hard-to-find but unusually interesting collection of essays/interpretations/navel gazing by a wide-ranging assortment of Dylan fans, critics, experts and obsessives. Great reading.

Cott, Jonathan. *Dylan.* New York: Doubleday, 1984. This book is a major disappointment. The photographs are beautiful, but Cott's brief text, unfortunately, doesn't come up to snuff. Of all Dylan's interviewers, Cott was the one whom Dylan seemed most comfortable with. Yet when it came to writing the definitive book on Dylan, Cott couldn't bring himself to criticize Dylan or even explicate some of his complicated lyrics, and the result is a piece of fluff from a writer who was certainly capable of an in-depth insightful work. Scaduto's biography is much more penetrating than this coffee-table book.

Dylan, Bob. *Tarantula.* New York: Macmillan, 1971. Weird, even by Bob Dylan standards, it's difficult to imagine anybody sitting down with this over a coffee break. Definitely for the hardcore fan.

Dylan, Bob. *The Bob Dylan Scrapbook 1956–66.* New York: Simon and Schuster, 2005. While it's probably not actually written by Bob, it's filled with backstage passes, ticket stubs, handwritten lyrics and other oddities, so it's sort of a Golden Book of Bob Dylan Memorabilia. (Notice it only goes through 1966, so there may be more on the way!) I looked at it on the shelf and thumbed through it. Didn't buy it.

Gray, Michael. *Song and Dance Man: The Art of Bob Dylan.* London: Hart Davis, MacGibbon, 1972. Gray, an English scholar, looks at Dylan as the latest in a long line of lyric poets and writes about his music that way. At times, he gets a little carried away, but as the first author to consider seriously Dylan's work as poetry, he deserves praise for his courageous stance.

Gross, Michael. *Bob Dylan: An Illustrated History.* New York: Grossett & Dunlap, 1980. Heavy on the photos, light on the insight, it's a nice-enough retrospective of Dylan's career. If you like photos of the man from the early days through the seventies, you'll enjoy this book.

Heylin, Clinton. *Bob Dylan: The Recording Sessions (1960–1994).* New York: St. Martin's Griffin, 1995.

Some interesting information about Dylan's recording methods, what was recorded when, what made the record and what didn't.

Humphries, Patrick, and Bauldie, John. *Absolutely Dylan: An Illustrated Biography*. New York: Viking, 1991.

With numerous pictures you've never seen before and all kinds of interesting information in the back, thanks to that wizard Bauldie, this book is a welcome addition to the Dylan archives, listing outtakes, concert dates, and other notable moments. Patrick Humphries's opening essay, a quasi-chronology of Dylan's career as it affected Humphries, is perhaps more personal than it should be — the book is called an illustrated biography of Bob Dylan, after all — but it's not bad.

Kramer, Daniel. *Bob Dylan*. New York, Citadel, 1968.

This collection of photographs by Daniel Kramer is interesting, and the essay that accompanies it gives you a good sense of the wildness of Dylan's life at that time. If you're really into photos of Dylan, you'll love this book.

Lee, C.P. *Like the Night: Bob Dylan and the Road to the Manchester Free Trade Hall*. London: Helter Skelter, 1998.

If Greil Marcus can do a whole book on a single song — even if it is a great song — C.P. Lee can do a book on a whole concert, can't he? Particularly if he happened to attend that show. And the show turns out to be the epic Dylan "Judas" moment at the Manchester Free Trade Hall in 1966. There is probably way more information here than you need, but it was such a pivotal moment for Dylan that the book is an interesting read.

Mellers, Wilfred. *A Darker Shade of Pale*. London: Faber & Faber, 1984.

Comparable to Stephen Pickering's convoluted study of Dylan as a Jewish mystic, this book by Mellers, a musicologist, goes to great lengths to portray Dylan as "Jewish Amerindian and White Negro." The problem is that it's not until page 111 of this 236-page book does the author really gets around to talking about Dylan's music.

Miles. *Bob Dylan in His Own Words*. London: Omnibus, 1978.

This is a collection of excerpts from interviews with Dylan from 1963 to 1978. Much of what Dylan said has been quoted in other works, naturally, but there are a few surprises.

Pickering, Stephen. *Bob Dylan Approximately: A Portrait of the Jewish Poet in Search of God — A Midrash*. New York: David MacKay, 1975.

The photographs are wonderful, but the text, well, let's just say unless you read Hebrew texts for fun, you'll find Pickering's stilted style hard to take. And the killer is that Dylan told Pickering that "he liked the clarity of his views."

Ribakove, Sy, and Barbara Ribakove. *Folk Rock: The Bob Dylan Story*. New York: Dell, 1966.

Reminiscent of the old *My Weekly Reader* style of writing, this little fan biography is humorous and quaint. While Bob Dylan was putting rock and roll music through some mind-bending changes, this biography would have you believe he was just a regular guy.

Ricks, Christopher. *Dylan's Visions of Sin*. New York: Ecco, 2004.

If, back in 1965, Christopher Ricks, Boston University's Warren Professor of the Humanities, had written a book, offered a course or maybe even uttered out loud that he considered Bob Dylan a poet, there would have been an insurrection at least on a par with Boston's famous Tea Party. Bob Dylan? That whiny voiced, chain-smoking, college dropout? A poet? Yes, America, that's what Ricks says about Dylan's work, treating many of his songs to the kind of up-close and personal scrutiny that would shrivel virtually every other rock and roll lyricist on the face of the Earth.

What Ricks does is break down the song, not just line by line, sometimes word by word. On the one hand, it's wonderful that someone with such a rich and immediately accessible literary background was willing to take a shot at analyzing Dylan's work. On the other, somebody has to read it. And though much of what Ricks has to say is illuminating, particularly so for someone not as well-versed in modern poetry (yes, which means you, the rest of the world), it is a challenge to try to breeze through a page or two at a time. Then again, what's the rush? What some readers have done is look for their particular favorite song — and many of them will likely be here — and try and follow Ricks' references and running commentary.

Anyone who's followed Bob's career recognizes his ability to turn a phrase, so it is not all that surprising to find someone who recognizes Dylan's great ability to communicate with words and images. However, it will occur to you — as it did me — that on some of these songs, Dylan did not give anywhere near the amount of thought to these particular lines that Ricks does. In a way, it's similar to Greil Marcus finding all he did in "Lo and Behold" on *The Basement Tapes*. You read it, think about it, and find yourself saying, "I don't know about that one."

Since there are few musical writers/critics who have as commanding a knowledge of modern poetry, it's difficult to be able to truly critique Ricks' work on its own lofty terms. For someone interested in

Bob Dylan, it's a rare opportunity to read what a real literary expert thinks of rock and roll's greatest poet. Quite a lot, as it turns out.

Riley, Tim. *Hard Rain: A Dylan Commentary*. New York: Alfred A. Knopf, 1992. The author of an acclaimed book on the Beatles, Riley turns his eyes to the career of Bob Dylan. He is more specific than most in describing the varied twists and turns of Dylan's career, and there are some inspired bits of descriptive writing, but Riley doesn't always get the lyrics right. For example, he describes "Please Mrs. Henry" from *The Basement Tapes* as a song in which "a drunk who can't hold his jism begs for sexual mercy." In fact, the song is about a drunk who has to go to the bathroom and doesn't have any money for a pay toilet.

There are several other instances where Riley is just a bit off, either in quoting the lyrics or in comprehending the songs. For example, regarding "As I Went Out One Morning" from *John Wesley Harding*, Riley says it has "more to do with the temptations of a fair damsel who walks in chains than with America's first outlaw journalist, Tom Paine." This interpretation is wrong. Every Dylan buff knows that when Dylan received the Tom Paine Award from the Emergency Civil Liberties Union in 1963, he gave a speech in which he said he identified with Lee Harvey Oswald and was promptly booed. The message of the song seems clear. Tom Paine appears at the end of this song about a man (Dylan) who is tempted to try to rescue a woman in chains — a symbol of oppressed people everywhere. Dylan offers a helping hand, but the oppressed woman takes his arm, and the rescuer immediately sees that he may be the one being exploited. Then in comes Tom Paine, who apologizes for her behavior. It seems more like a protest song about the people who protested when Dylan stopped writing that kind of song.

Certainly, this book is readable and interesting, but Riley doesn't quite have the feel for Dylan that he did for the Beatles.

Rinzler, Alan. *Bob Dylan: The Illustrated Record*. New York: Harmony, 1978. This is a kind of Bob Dylan primer, with color portraits of the album covers and a brief essay about each one. It's a good-enough look at Dylan's recording career to 1978. The essay is pretty strange, though. Rinzler says that *Desire* can be seen as "a reply" to Carole King's *Tapestry*. Either he's never heard Carole King or he doesn't know Bob Dylan, who's about as likely to record a response to Carole as to Neil Sedaka or Bobby Rydell. There are a lot of great photos, however, and if you don't mind Rinzler, you'll enjoy the book.

Rolling Stone. *Knocking on Dylan's Door: On the Road*. New York: Pocket, 1974. This collection of articles that appeared in *Rolling Stone* about Dylan's tour with The Band is an interesting book that most Dylan fans probably already have.

Scobie, Stephen. *Alias Bob Dylan.* Calgary, Alberta: Red Deer College Press, 1991.

Scobie is an English scholar who teaches courses on Bob Dylan and a Dylan fanatic. His great theme is Dylan as "Alias," just like his hometown of Hibbing, Minnesota, his many guises, and so forth. Some of Scobie's analysis of Dylan's lyrics is quite good, but some of it is really reaching. However, Scobie definitely treats Dylan's work with a great deal of respect, probably more respect than Dylan himself gives it. But, of course, the final question is this: Can an artist who has explored so many areas (novels, films, and all types of music) be reduced to fitting a single theme? Scobie thinks so. You may not.

Sloman, Larry. *On the Road with Bob Dylan: Rolling with the Thunder.* New York: Bantam, 1978.

As you might expect, this "On the Road" book is too long, and for much of it, the author is struggling just to get credentials to cover the tour. He finally does gain access, but not to Dylan, who is rarely quoted in the 413 pages. Some of the writing is funny, some of it is silly, and unless you're a diehard Dylan fan, you'll be bored by most of it. But if you really want to know what life on the Rolling Thunder Revue was like, you'll find out here.

Sounes, Howard. *Down the Highway: The Life of Bob Dylan.* Berkeley, CA.: Grove, 2001.

Howard Sounes certainly did a lot of legwork on this one, tracking down Dylan divorce papers here, marriage certificates there and getting all sorts of dirt on the guy, including the "secret marriage" and all that stuff. Give him credit for that if you wish. If you're into that sort of thing, you'll enjoy this book. There's more way dirt there than in Bob Spitz's biography or Anthony Scaduto's, that's for sure.

Spitz, Bob. *Dylan: A Biography.* New York: McGraw-Hill, 1988.

In the foreword, Spitz announces that he intends to demystify Bob Dylan. He then spends 550 pages trying to do so, and fails. Spitz certainly did his homework and reportedly drew some inquiring phone calls from Dylan once Dylan found out who Spitz had spoken to. But Dylan had nothing to worry about. There's nothing Kitty Kelleyish about this book, which is unfortunate, since that tone might have livened up the book. It is professionally done, and there are some interesting bits of gossip, but you never get the sense that Spitz understands Dylan or his work. By the end of the book, you wonder why someone who apparently had so little feel for Dylan spent so much time and effort writing a biography. Spitz gets an A for effort and a B+ for comprehensive research. But for his grasp of the subject and the artist's material, a lower grade is in order. One expects more from a biographer of Spitz's reputation.

Thompson, Elizabeth, and Gutman, David, eds. *A Dylan Companion*. New York: Da Capo, 1990.

This crackerjack collection of articles and reviews of Dylan's work contains many tasty samples from every phase of his career, including some from England that American Dylan fans probably never read. It also includes Andrew Sarris's review of *Don't Look Back* (he sort of liked it but admires Dylan), Pauline Kael's scathing review of *Renaldo and Clara*, the speech Bruce Springsteen gave when he introduced Dylan at the Rock and Roll Hall of Fame ceremony, and all sorts of fun things. Oddly, the book makes no attempts to register Dylan's impact on the rock-critic community. There are no album reviews, per se, save for Richard Williams's essay on *Oh Mercy* in the *London Times*. But it is an excellent and worthwhile compilation.

Thompson, Toby. *Positively Main Street: An Unorthodox View of Bob Dylan*. New York: Coward-McCann, 1970.

As the first author to go poking around in Dylan's past, Thompson deserves credit. There are some interesting little tidbits about Bob's early days, and you get the sense that Thompson sees Dylan as someone important but doesn't ever get around to explaining why.

Williams, Paul. *Performing Artist: The Music of Bob Dylan*. Novato, CA: Underwood Miller, 1990.

Paul Williams has long been one of the most entertaining and enthusiastic rock critics. He is also a major Dylan fan, as shown by this book, which takes you through Dylan's work to 1973. At times, Williams seems overzealous in describing a vocal performance or recording, and his attempt to tie the title — Dylan as a performing artist — into every facet of Dylan's work is labored.

With regard to some of the unreleased material he goes on and on about, you may wonder if the real reason that it got such treatment was that Williams heard it and you didn't, not that it was anything extraordinary. A good example is the song "Sign on the Cross," which was discussed at some length in the section on bootleg material. Williams thinks the song is a masterpiece, whereas others think it's a grand joke that doesn't quite work. But Dylan is that kind of artist. He wants a response, and he gets one from Williams here — quite a positive one, in fact.

Williams, Paul. *Watching the River Flow: Observations on his Art-in-progress.* London: Omnibus, 1996.

> Some more entertaining — if just a tad ejaculatory — prose on happenings in Dylanland. This also includes the famed Williams chronicle of Dylan's religious transformation, "Dylan: What Happened," of which purportedly Bob bought several copies to distribute to friends.

RECOMMENDED ARTICLES

Ross, Alex. "The Wanderer." *The New Yorker*, May 10, 1999. A wonderfully entertaining piece as Ross follows Dylan on tour and writes about what he sees and hears in Dylan's music. Excellent work.

Wyman, Bill. "Bob Dylan" *Salon.com*, May 21, 2001. A fine summation of Dylan's career, the highs and lows and unpredictable moments.

Gilmore, Mikal. "Dylan's Self-Portrait." *Rolling Stone*, October 6, 2004. An illuminating review of *Chronicles, Vol. 1.*

Jacobson, Mark. "Tangled Up in Bob." *Rolling Stone*, March 26, 2001. A fine look at the weird world of Dylanologists worldwide.

Menand, Louis. "Bob on Bob." *The New Yorker*, September 4, 2006. Insightful, playful look at Dylan and interviews, as revealed in *The Essential Interviews.*

Draper, Jason. "Dylan's Jukebox." *Record Collector*, March and April 2007. Bob Dylan fans the world over owe Jason Draper and *Record Collector* magazine a debt of thanks for these two issues, which compile many of Dylan's introductions and quips from his XM Satellite Radio show. Wonderful stuff.

Cohen, Scott. "Bob Dylan: Not Like a Rolling Stone Interview." *Spin Magazine,* Vol. 1, No. 8, December 1985. Hard to find the original article around these days, though it is available online. But it remains an absolute classic and must-read. Simply delightful stuff. Dylan and Cohen really hit it off and their conversation is far-reaching. Too bad it isn't included in *The Essential Interviews.* It's a dandy.

RECOMMENDED WEBSITES

www.bobdylan.com: Considering it's a corporate site from the record company, it's not bad and offers an unpredictable assortment of things.

www.boblinks.com: For the hard-core Dylanite (is there any other kind?) you can find out the set list for every show Bob has done for years and years and also check out some of the reviews.

www.bobsboots.com: Of course, bootleg albums are against the law and I can't imagine any law-abiding citizen ever lowering his standards and pur-chasing something that wasn't an official Columbia-approved release. But there sure are a bunch of 'em out there.

www.dylandaily.com: Usually way more information than you ever need to know about Bob — all in one very convenient, easily accessible place.

www.expectingrain.com: The site, compiled by Karl-Erik Andersen in Nor-way, has a terrific and an eclectic look at everyday happenings in the world of Bob Dylan and related artists.

Index

Index

Index

272

Index

Index